#MeToo –
counsellors and psychotherapists speak about sexual violence and abuse

EDITED BY
**DEBORAH A. LEE AND
EMMA PALMER**

First published 2020

PCCS Books Ltd
Wyastone Business Park
Wyastone Leys
Monmouth
NP25 3SR
United Kingdom
contact@pccs-books.co.uk
www.pccs-books.co.uk

This collection © Deborah A. Lee and Emma Palmer, 2020
The individual chapters © the contributors, 2020

All rights reserved.
No part of this publication may be reproduced, stored in a retrieval system, transmitted or utilised in any form by any means, electronic, mechanical, photocopying or recording or otherwise, without permission in writing from the publishers.

The authors have asserted their right to be identified as the authors
of this work in accordance with the Copyright, Designs and Patents Act 1988.

#MeToo – counsellors and psychotherapists speak about sexual violence and abuse

British Library Cataloguing in Publication data: a catalogue record for this book is available from the British Library.

ISBN 978 1 910919 53 8

Cover design by Jason Anscomb
Typeset in-house by PCCS Books using Minion Pro and Myriad Pro
Printed in the UK by TJ International, Padstow

Praise for *#MeToo – counsellors and psychotherapists speak about sexual violence and abuse*

'This innovative and ground-breaking book is an exceptional and much-needed contribution to understanding sexual violence and sexual abuse. It provides invaluable insight to the experience of those who work with and support survivors of sexual violence who are also survivors themselves. It allows us to bear witness to how survivor practitioners engage in their work with survivors and demonstrates how powerful and transformative it is to give voice to and share lived experiences. It is an indispensable addition to our understanding of sexual violence and deserves a place on every practitioner's bookshelf.'
Christiane Sanderson, senior lecturer in psychology, University of Roehampton, and consultant in sexual violence and childhood sexual abuse

'The capacity to work with experiences of sexual violence and abuse is an essential competence for all counsellors and psychotherapists. *#MeToo* presents a diverse, accessible, and deeply moving collection of chapters on this issue, from both personal and professional perspectives. As such, it is a vital resource for our field.'
Mick Cooper, Professor of Counselling Psychology, University of Roehampton

'This book is truly transformational. It not only documents the #MeToo movement by bringing together therapists in dialogues about the impacts of their personal experiences of sexual abuse in a powerful and moving way, it also deconstructs and disrupts the ways we talk about these experiences and reconstructs the phenomenon entirely. Throughout it challenges notions of 'us' and 'them' and shows us how to hold ambivalence, as de Beauvoir taught us in her 'ethics of ambiguity'. Either/or becomes both/and, such as in the desire to be seen and to be hidden, to feel agency and to experience dependence, to feel special and to be shame-ridden, and wanting to hurt and feeling empathy for abusers. 'No, we will not be silenced!' shout the authors, united. It is a convincing plea for #WeToo and the power of standing together in solidarity against shame and victim-blaming. This book is a powerful testament of how abuse is a relational experience – a counter-story to the individualisation and pathologisation so rife in our society.'
Dr Gillian Proctor, lecturer, University of Leeds

'If you don't find yourself reading this book with your whole mind–body self, then you are missing a unique opportunity for being moved, kinaesthetically touched by the personal stories and learning what it means to work therapeutically towards a soul–soma integration. The different theoretical perspectives, writing styles and conversation structures made me read the book in a 3-D way: as a (socio-political) witness, but then also hearing the different voices that were previously silenced and also feeling in my own body and movement the emergence of deeply hidden memories. Spirituality, politics and intersectionality are at the heart of this utterly inspiring book that sensitively stimulates reflections, inner processes and questioning of conventional therapy practices. It is essential reading for therapists and non-therapists alike.'

Sissy Lykou, UKCP registered psychotherapist, embodied movement psychotherapist and supervisor; programme leader, MSc in Contemporary Person-Centred Psychotherapy, Metanoia Institute

'Intensely powerful – a book about pain and remembering, but also about testimony and hope.'

Nicole Westmarland, Professor of Criminology, Durham University

CONTENTS

	Foreword Kim Etherington	*vii*
	Preface	*x*
	Introduction	*1*
1	Retribution Seb Randall, with Celia Urbach	*15*
2	'Survivors are everywhere': our #MeToo, #WeToo journey Kaur, with Deborah A. Lee	*26*
3	Lighthouses, rocky shores and safe harbours Concetta Perôt, with Clarinda Cuppage	*38*
4	How we talk to girls about 'sex' Taylor Broughton, with Sarah J. Wilson	*53*
5	Sexual abuse and surviving with(in) psychology Jemma Tosh, with Fionnuala Dempsey	*64*
6	Therapists' lived experience in counselling and psychotherapy training Liz Smith and Sara Teresa Mollis	*83*
7	Survivors of sexual violence training as psychotherapists in the UK Deborah A. Lee, with Peggy, Sam and Phoenix	*100*
8	#MeToo on the internet Tara Shennan, with Haley Clifford	*126*
9	Reconnection through dance movement psychotherapy Amanda Light, with Tina Johnson	*141*
10	Shattering the sounds of silence Reena Shah, with Clarinda Cuppage	*157*

11	While I was sleeping *Andrew Pari, with Katy Woodger*	*173*
12	#WeToo: groupwork as an act of solidarity and resistance *Leah Salter, with Emily Jacob*	*188*
13	Pushing, pulling and parts coming together *Joy Farrimond, with Emma Palmer*	*204*
14	Dirty secrets, ecocide and the specialness of the world all around *Emma Palmer, with Charleen Agostini*	*214*
	Poem – #MeToo *Clare Shaw*	*227*
	Contributors	*231*
	Name index	*239*
	Subject index	*245*

Dedication
In memory of Dr Graham Edward Fowler and Polly Higgins

Acknowledgements

We would like to thank all of the chapter authors and conversation partners for their care and courage in writing for and giving shape to this book. Thank you to all at PCCS Books. Our heartfelt thanks to everyone who has supported us on our journeys – not just as we co-edited this book, but before and since.

For Deborah, most of the book happened after her partner, Dr Graham Edward Fowler, was diagnosed with a serious illness. He died in August 2019. Many people were very caring, and Deborah would like to particularly thank Claire Cohen, Sharon Hutchings, Jatinder Sandhu, Rachel Harding, Ambika Erin Connelly and Eric Baumgartner for their friendship.

Deborah would like to thank Graham for his love, care, kindness, compassion, integrity, intelligence and wit; for everything; for saying how she'd found her meaning and purpose, and for keeping her going when times were tough. You are always in my heart.

Emma would like to dedicate this book to Polly Higgins, who, after a very short illness, died on Easter Sunday 2019. Polly was a huge inspiration to a lot of people. Sometimes dubbed 'the earth's lawyer', Polly campaigned for ecocide to be included as one of the United Nation's crimes against peace. They shared a love of the earth and getting things done, and ecocide is one of the themes of Emma's chapter at the end of this collection. Polly's life and death spurred her on in the final stages of finishing this book. She was the sort of person who dared friends and colleagues to 'be great' – a phrase taken from the title of one of her books (Higgins, 2014). Long may this spirit continue in honour of her life and work in our world, however that manifests.

Emma is also very appreciative of Paul Crummay, Joy Farrimond, Beth Livingston and Vicky Preece for their helpful, supportive and reparative conversations in the course of editing this book. Thanks to Tone Horwood for excellent supervision at key moments. Above all, she would like to thank Justin Roughley for his steadfastness, big-heartedness and sense of humour. Finally, a deep bow to her allotment and all the other-than-human beings there, for helping to keep it real and reminding her to slow down, to plod and to tend.

Reference

Higgins P (2014). *I Dare You to be Great*. New York, NY: Clink Street Publishing.

Foreword

Back in the early 1990s, I ran courses at the University of Bristol for therapists and others working with people who had experienced sexual abuse. This was in response to my realisation that several therapists I came across seemed anxious about doing this work and concerned about making things worse for their clients. Having stumbled across my own partly formed memories of abuse a few years earlier, during my first experience of being a client while training as a counsellor, I wanted to tell them what I had learned about how to help people like me, what I had found helpful and unhelpful and what I then, and still, needed in my healing.

Before this I had been training social workers about working with sexual abuse, alongside a woman I knew who provided therapy for abused children, and I was both shocked and impressed when she opened the course by stating that she had herself been abused during childhood. What I noticed as the day progressed was that participants began to say 'me too': the atmosphere felt safer, conversations became more intimate and opportunities for learning from each other expanded. Later, when I ran similar courses for therapists and took my first tentative steps to disclose, I found myself afterwards experiencing extreme stress and sleepless nights, as though I had done something terribly wrong. I had broken all the rules of silence, of family loyalty, and taken the risk of presenting myself as vulnerable, even though I had said nothing explicit.

As time went by, these after-effects reduced in intensity, and later, when I began to write my own stories as part of my reflexive engagement in research, I looked back in some amazement at the degree of disturbance I had experienced at that time. However, there were a couple of later occasions when I was somewhat shaken again by two male colleagues' responses to my writings. The first was a participant in one of my research projects, who told me:

Well, I thought 'extremely self-exposing and risky' because you were in effect or indirectly… I can't remember precisely how you put it… but referring to your own experience of abuse. And that was the striking thing. It's what I remember most of all about your paper… but that's all I remember about you, at least with the distance of time. But even as we were sitting at lunch today, somehow that came into my mind, I just remembered that, and… And I'm just very aware whilst speaking… the sense I have is like being on a pontoon… we're right there, and it's an exciting place to be, it's tremendously exciting. And the sort of rapport I feel in talking to you about this. It's so relevant to the work that we're doing… And that's also very exciting… it's like breaking new ground – frightening – it's frightening…

The other colleague had published an article on the use of self in research in which he had questioned the wisdom of me being 'seen' in my own writing. During a subsequent conversation I asked him what it was about this that concerned him. He replied:

What's kind of coming up for me is a sort of ambivalence about my own exposure and my own hiding. That, yes, I want to be in print and no, I don't, you know? It's like I want to be seen and I don't want to be seen and, yes… I want to be on the stage, and I want to be hidden under the chair at the same time.

Those conversations took place in 2003, and now, 16 years later, I have been shaken once again, but this time by a different kind of experience. The stories in this book have shaken, disturbed and exhilarated me. This book is very timely in the aftermath of the viral spread of the #MeToo phenomenon in 2017. Deborah A. Lee had already been researching and thinking about therapy and sexual violence by then. She approached PCCS Books with #MeToo in the field. So for Deborah it wasn't so much a response to #MeToo as part of her ongoing work. Once she had the book contract in hand, she invited Emma Palmer to co-edit with her. Together they have invited people involved in the field of therapy to create a community of voices that tell a collective story that can transform the readers as well as the writers. The inclusion of responses from the readers that follow the individual stories is a stroke of genius, allowing the wider readership to resonate with both aspects, and those resonances will go on and on as this work goes on living in minds and hearts.

As the #MeToo movement has grown, and as I've read the chapters for this book, I have been reminded of conversations I have had with clients, students, supervisees and my own therapists over the years, wondering how long the sexual abuse of children and assault of women and men will go on, usually ending with something like, 'We won't see it in our lifetime though.' But, as I approach my eighth decade, the silence is being broken, in some cultures, in some environments and yes, not everywhere, but now I have hope for the future, knowing that the healing has begun and will continue.

Stories of lived experience have meaning beyond the local and personal context. They resonate with others and outlast their telling or reading. Sometimes they have profound consequences. They can change us in ways we may not always anticipate because they can move us emotionally, inform and challenge us intellectually, change public and political attitudes and opinions, and influence future actions.

Each of the stories in this book bears witness to the lived experience of being sexually abused. Deborah and Emma have provided a platform from which these voices can be heard, thereby giving testimony. When we give testimony to experience through writing and publishing our trauma stories, we bear witness to the past and challenge the idea that terrible experiences are too awful to be told. We also create a possibility for change and a better future.

I will leave the last word to Laurel Richardson, who tells us:

> ... the collective story overcomes some of the isolation and alienation of contemporary life. It provides a sociological community, the linking of separate individuals into a shared consciousness. Once linked, the possibility for social action on behalf of the collective is present, and, therewith, the possibility of social transformation. (1997: 33)

Kim Etherington
May 2019

Reference

Richardson L (1997). *Fields of Play: constructing an academic life*. New Brunswick, NJ: Rutgers University Press.

Preface

The seeds for this book were sown well before #MeToo, as well as developing alongside the #MeToo movement, as it too developed.

The seeds were sown by Deborah, while training in person-centred and experiential psychotherapy. Nowhere (before or since) had she felt so defined by a herstory of sexual violence, caught in a tangled web of others' responses, trying to find her own ways forwards. It was impossible not to write about it and, eventually, to see if others wished to write about it.

This book grows from and has been inspired by the PCCS Books *Our Encounters with…* series. This series has been ground-breaking in appreciating and exploring lived experiences and complex themes: *Our Encounters with Madness* (Grant et al, 2011); *Our Encounters with Suicide* (Grant et al, 2013); *Our Encounters with Self-Harm* (Baker et al, 2013), and *Our Encounters with Stalking* (Taylor et al, 2017).

Deborah pitched the idea of an *Our Encounters with Sexual Violence* to PCCS Books. Although the series had come to an end, PCCS Books enthusiastically welcomed a proposal for an edited collection of writings on sexual violence and abuse.

Looking for possible co-editors, Deborah thought back to when her first articles on lived experiences of sexual violence were published in *Psychotherapy and Politics International* (2017a, 2017b) – the first written in 2016, before the 2017 iteration of #MeToo 'went viral'. She remembered receiving an appreciative email from Emma (whom she had met through Psychotherapists and Counsellors for Social Responsibility (PCSR)), in which Emma acknowledged her lived experiences.

Emma too is no stranger to taking risks in writing about taboo and personal subjects: for example, about the decision to remain childfree in her second book, *Other than Mother: choosing childlessness with life in mind* (Kamalamani, 2016). Emma had been taken aback by the phenomenon of #MeToo on social media, which was also the first time she had spoken more publicly about having experienced sexual abuse. As soon as Deborah asked her to co-edit, she knew she would agree, sensing the importance of the book both for the therapy field and in taking action at a time when lasting changes felt more possible. She agreed, partly in the spirit of acting in service for those with less or no voice – and also felt terrified. The desire to do something useful, hopefully adding depth, nuance and action in saying '#MeToo', has (mainly) overtaken the terror. Deborah and Emma's co-editing partnership took off in January 2018.

The shoots of the book were tended by both Deborah and Emma as co-editors. We were originally working with a third editor who, unfortunately, was unable to continue. We are grateful to her for her early input. The book's contributors – chapter authors and conversation partners – have obviously played a vital part, as have those who have gone before us, to whom we refer in the introduction.

This book takes as one of its starting points how isolated and 'othered' therapists with lived experience of anything that can be perceived as 'shameful' can feel. Adams (2013) describes 'the myth of the untroubled therapist' in her book of that title. We say, 'What if we challenge that? What if we use #MeToo to help us do that – to change things?'

This book is part of the change.

#MeToo – counsellors and psychotherapists speak about sexual violence and abuse is not just a book. Over the past 18 months of its gestation, it has become a community of people: therapists, clients, supervisees – some of them all three – who have experienced sexual violence and abuse. It has become a community of people exploring aspects of the history, philosophy, theory, ethics and practice of counselling and psychotherapy in relation to lived experiences of sexual abuse and violence; a community reflecting and acting politically in response.

We invite you to join us, in whatever way calls you.

Deborah A. Lee and Emma Palmer
May 2019

References

Adams M (2013). *The Myth of the Untroubled Therapist*. London: Routledge.

Baker C, Shaw C, Biley F (eds) (2013). *Our Encounters with Self-harm*. Ross-on-Wye: PCCS Books.

Grant A, Biley F, Walker H (eds) (2011). *Our Encounters with Madness*. Ross-on-Wye: PCCS Books.

Grant A, Haire J, Biley F, Stone B (eds) (2013). *Our Encounters with Suicide*. Ross-on-Wye: PCCS Books.

Kamalamani (2016). *Other than Mother: choosing childlessness with life in mind*. Alresford: Earth Books.

Lee D (2017a). Shocking revelation! There are women survivors of sexual violence training as person-centred psychotherapists. *Psychotherapy and Politics International* 15(1): e1396.

Lee D (2017b). On 'coming out' as a rape survivor. *Psychotherapy and Politics International* 15(2): e1415.

Taylor S, Grant A, Leigh-Phippard H (2017). *Our Encounters with Stalking*. Ross-on-Wye: PCCS Books.

Introduction

The term #MeToo was first coined by New York-based civil rights activist Tarana Burke in 2006. It emerged from her work with young women of colour who had experienced sexual abuse. #MeToo 'went viral' on social media in 2017, starting with rape accusations against the Hollywood film producer Harvey Weinstein. It swiftly encompassed the testimonies of millions of people across the globe: women, men and those identifying as non-binary. They cautiously and courageously – given the potential for victim blaming and victim shaming – wrote '#MeToo' by sharing their lived experiences of sexual violence and abuse, many for the first time. Perhaps it was the first time there seemed to be a decent chance of it mattering, on a wider stage (or anywhere, in fact).

The #MeToo movement has joined with existing sexual violence and abuse activism to contribute to opening up moving, meaningful opportunities for community, solidarity and action. We've been moved as we've witnessed this, time and time again, in preparing this book, and we hope that you'll *sense* that community and solidarity, that call for action, as you read. Some amazing things happen when people say '#Me Too' together. We don't even have to agree with each other – as we and some of our contributors discovered – for creativity to emerge.

In seeking to hear the voices of people who have experienced sexual violence and abuse, *#MeToo – counsellors and psychotherapists speak about sexual violence and abuse* stands alongside individual personal memoirs of sexual violence and abuse, such as Saward's (1990) *Raped*, Weaver Francisco's (2000) *Telling*, Venable Raine's (2000) *After Silence*, Brison's (2002) *Aftermath*, Sebold's (2003) *Lucky*, Freedman's (2014) *One Hour in Paris*, Douglas's (2016) *On Being Raped*, Gay's (2018) *Hunger*, and psychotherapist Black's (2017) *Unbroken*.

In bringing together in one place a range of voices of people who have experienced sexual violence and abuse, our book makes a contribution to edited collections of first-person writings about the subject, such as Clark and Pino's (2016) *We Believe You*, Moulton's (2017) *Things We Haven't Said*, and Gay's (2019) *Not That Bad*.

In welcoming a variety of writing styles, including the creative, the book also connects with contributions such as the *#MeToo* poetry collection edited by Alma (2018), Li's (2017) *Dark Chapter*, Louis's (2018) *History of Violence* and Novey's (2018) *Those Who Knew*.

In the therapy field, our work joins very many books and articles, written over many years, that have explored clinical perspectives on sexual violence and abuse – some pathologising, some not. We connect, as we will explain, with non-pathologising approaches (see Watson, 2019).

When we sought contributions for this book, asking far and wide, we purposefully left broad parameters around who the contributors were and what and how they wrote, to honour the variety and spontaneity of #MeToo testimonies. Our wish was for this book to be shaped by experience and a community of voices, speaking how they chose, rather than attempting a pre-determined shape. While you *will* find a variety of modalities of therapy represented, and a range – sometimes intersection – of personal identities, we always realised we wouldn't be able to 'cover' all or most modalities or personal identities. Our aim is simply to open up spaces for more #MeToo writing to emerge.

In choosing, editing and curating the chapters, we have particularly sought to showcase ways in which #MeToo is emerging, unfolding, deepening, connecting, challenging, changing, surprising and persisting in a world where perpetrators of sexual violence and abuse abound, frequently untroubled. The book represents a variety both of lived experiences and writing styles. The chapters and conversations in some way weave together what we take to be the personal and the universal.

In its evolution since 2017, the #MeToo movement has brought to light much more about the nature of sexual violence and abuse in a variety of settings, professional and personal: for example, #ChurchToo and #MeTooPhD. This book, using a term suggested by chapter contributors Liz Smith and Sara Teresa Mollis, offers #TherapistsToo.

A #MeToo by psychotherapists and counsellors and their conversation partners is of huge significance for the profession and its practitioners because counselling and psychotherapy, like everything else, are located in structures of power, status, control, oppression and privilege. Too often – especially pre-#MeToo – the lived experience of people who have experienced sexual violence and abuse has been invisible in our everyday discourse. This invisibility has also happened in counselling and psychotherapy; we frequently see/hear divisions between 'us' (therapists) and 'them' (clients) when clients have experienced sexual violence and abuse. And, as is explored in these pages, sexual abuse and violence is often regarded on therapy training courses as something that happens to clients but not to us, as trainees/trainers, so maintaining 'othering' and the 'them' and 'us' divide. These divides, we contend, fail to capture how the perpetration of sexual violence and abuse is pandemic, rather than a minority experience, and how there is nothing 'pathological' about people with lived experiences of sexual abuse and violence.

The ubiquity of sexual violence and abuse has been made even more ubiquitous by #MeToo. Living in #MeToo times has sometimes felt relentless; everybody has seemed to have an opinion – not always helpful or constructively offered. From the beginning we have, as co-editors, been acutely aware of the potential impact of this book on those contributing. The book has changed us – for better and/or worse; it has been hugely creative and reparative some days, and on others we have seen contributors revisiting despair. As fellow travellers, we have often felt the impact too, from painful through to liberating. We wish to express our immense, heartfelt gratitude to all involved, including those whose contributions we didn't have space to accept and those who were not – for whatever reasons – able to complete the journey with us.

In this introduction, we will give a small flavour of each of the chapters. We seek to capture some of the swirling and layering we perceive in #MeToo and in this book. We use these sorts of words because we see #MeToo as complex – new yet existing, exciting yet distressing; something taking shape, being shaped, shaping, shifting, helpfully and unhelpfully. For us, #MeToo isn't and wasn't a historic/historical moment from which we can now look back and reflect, post-#MeToo. It's then, now and next. Just as we think we might fully understand some of #MeToo's manifestations, more depth emerges, offering different ways of seeing, challenging what we already thought we knew. Most importantly, it informs what we do next with what we know now. The swirling and layering is evident in the individual chapters, all remarkably creative responses, without exception. There is richness of experience and creativity in these pages, which we feel is both enriching to read and informative in how to respond, to ourselves, others and the wider world.

In our editing and curating of the chapters, we hope to have captured, in and through our choices, a lack of complete linearity and neat resolutions. Instead, we have aimed to offer the weaving of an abundance of important and meaningful threads that reflects the complexity of life and relationship both in and beyond therapy. While we can offer a taste of what the chapters contain, reading a book like this will be a very personal journey and evoke very personal responses. Every time we've read each chapter, we've found new aspects to appreciate, and observations, words and responses we didn't see on the previous read. This includes ideas that speak to us differently as they unravel and concepts we still haven't quite grasped or can't quite yet fully take in. Our hope, in offering this book to you, is that it will be a starting point; let's see what will happen next. Some chapter authors, inspired and spurred on by this experience, are already talking of future writing projects, so watch this space.

We thought about making this introductory chapter work, in part, as content notes and/or trigger warnings, and it may perhaps function like that at times. We're also aware that whatever we write here cannot be taken as an exhaustive guide to what will be in any of the chapters and, more importantly, cannot encapsulate what each individual reader may find difficult in some way, perhaps because it touches on personal experiences. Ultimately, seeking to write with content notes and/or trigger warnings in mind felt like trying to offer too much fixity about individual contributors' experiences and positions, in a field where rigidity can already be problematic. So, instead – feeling care for everyone involved – we say simply, take care; take the book at your own pace and read what you're drawn to reading when you're drawn to reading it.

A note about terminology: we originally used the term 'survivor' when we sought writers and conversation participants for this book. We did this because we wanted to be clear that we were not simply seeking therapists who had 'worked with' or 'treated' people who have been abused; rather, we sought therapists who were prepared to place themselves as fellow travellers in writing with us – whether they chose to use their own names or remain anonymous. We recognise that the term 'survivor' is contested, along with other terms for people who have experienced abuse and violence and who are still alive afterwards, such as 'thriver', or 'overcomer' (a term used by Tina Johnson in Chapter 9) or 'victim'. We realise that all such terms come with meanings, some which may be unwelcome to some and welcome to others, and that this may change.

Contributors have chosen the words that work for them at the moment. Katy Woodger, to whom the term 'survivor' does not speak, has written about the term in conversation with chapter author Andrew Pari. So too have co-editor Emma, with her conversation partner Charleen Agostini, and Tina Johnson, in conversation with Amanda Light. Neither of us co-editors feel particularly comfortable owning any of the words that are currently on offer to people who have experienced sexual violence and abuse, even though we may use some of them some of the time. We think it's an area in which much more work is needed, with the emergence, perhaps, of new language and new meanings.

And finally, a short note about the structure of the book and the 'conversation partnerships', where each author has been paired with another person with something to bring to the topic. The personal meanings of #WeToo are a key theme of this book and come up repeatedly, explicitly and implicitly. Indeed, it is built into the fabric of the book in terms of the relationships formed and the experiences shared. No chapter author worked entirely alone. Everyone was either paired up with a conversation partner or paired themselves up with a conversation partner. The latter happened when chapter authors and conversation partners already knew one other and wanted to be together for this project. People chose how they wished to work together, some conversing as they wrote, some responding to almost-finished work, some deciding to write together. We can't say that all pairings ran smoothly; human beings were involved, after all. Having said that, it was amazing how well much of the writing and pairing went. A few people's pairings changed, some at the very early stages and others very late in the process. We feel that each completed (and uncompleted) partnership brought something new. As co-editors, we were also alongside contributors when we were needed.

The book opens with the chapter by psychotherapist Seb Randall, entitled 'Retribution'. Seb writes vividly and with great immediacy, taking us beyond what might be expected of a #MeToo book right from the start. He moves from his origins in 'an expatriate world within the implicit violence and rituals of colonial legacy', around the world, to a kidnap and rape in London on a cold and wet April night. He says: '... the knowledge that I had the choice to kill my attacker but showed pragmatic mercy leaves me unperturbed.' The chapter then turns to conversations between Seb and Celia Urbach, an integrative transpersonal counsellor, whose father was a Kindertransportee. Tensions emerge between the two conversation partners, who each grew up in differently traumatic circumstances, with apparently very different ways of making sense of their experiences. Accompanying them – almost holding our breath – we can read the beauty of what may happen when we take the risk to remain present, and engage deeply with each other, eventually finding resonance.

Chapter 2 is by Kaur, a Sikh woman, who uses a pseudonym for cultural and family reasons, and is also a therapy client, and Deborah A. Lee, a person-centred psychotherapist and co-editor of the book. This is the moving story of two women who have known each other for years, but only recently as fellow survivors. '"Survivors are everywhere": our #MeToo, #WeToo journey' (echoing Leah Salter and Emily Jacob's chapter title later on in the book) begins with some of Kaur's childhood experiences: 'Who were all these men? Why were they hurting me? Why could I hear heavy breathing?' Touching conversations between Kaur and Deborah – ranging from the importance to both of them of physical intimacy in therapy, to the meanings they draw from personal presentation – bring out some of the nuances of living on, every day, after sexual violence and abuse. Maybe fellow travellers will find some resonances and/or things to think about here – including that they probably already know people who know things they know.

Chapter 3, 'Lighthouses, rocky shores and safe harbours?' begins with Concetta Perôt, integrative counsellor, psychotherapist and director of Survivors' Voices, questioning #MeToo from the perspective of one who has spent time responding to calls to the National Association for People Abused in Childhood (NAPAC) helpline: 'It seemed to me that the impact of the media attention became a growing public health issue, triggering buried traumas and bringing people forward to seek help.' She points out how #MeToo's celebrity focus can feel silencing if you do not have 'media-sexy' experiences, something both she and her clients have felt.

Concetta goes on to discuss Sicilian culture from personal experience, having grown up in the Sicilian immigrant community in 1970s and 1980s London. Like Kaur in Chapter 2, she identifies the need for more culture-specific exploration in #MeToo discourses. She says, very powerfully, that: 'Sicilian culture is glued together with the practice of "omertá", the honour code inculcated in us that you never, ever, speak to anyone outside of the family, especially to any authorities, about what goes on within the family. By writing this, I am breaking that very code.' Sharing writing from earlier in her life, Concetta describes a young woman who visits her family home: a 'blank page', silent and subjected, someone she could not bear to become.

Recognising that 'professionals', including therapists, can be harmful, Concetta offers examples of how clients have felt harmed and practical ways forward. Fellow integrative counsellor Clarinda Cuppage makes a response to the chapter, sharing Concetta's concerns and encouraging her proposals. There's strength in the support that we can offer to each other as therapists venturing into territory that can be uncertain, dangerous, even deathly, where there's a dearth of 'safe harbours'.

In Chapter 4, Taylor Broughton, a US psychotherapist-in-training living in Scotland, writes about 'How we talk to girls about "sex"' – specifically, how we have sex-positive conversations with young women in the context of 'the realities of sexual assault stories'. We are pleased to have two authors from the US – Taylor and Andrew Pari (Chapter 11) – in our collection, given #MeToo's emergence and prominence in the US and the contemporary context of US President Donald Trump's administration. Taylor argues that sex-positivity insufficiently recognises sexual assault. She posits the era of #MeToo as an important opportunity for creating nuance and sophistication in how we talk about 'sex' to girls. Taylor says of her own sexual education: 'It taught me to be scared and it taught me that my decisions around sexuality didn't matter.' She argues: 'There needs to be a safe place to be curious, to ask questions, and to feel secure.' In a different context, we can see some threads linking with Concetta's chapter about silencing and not being silenced.

Fellow counsellor and psychotherapist Sarah J. Wilson responds to Taylor. Coincidentally, as Sarah started responding to Taylor's piece, she was asked by a friend for her advice about how to raise conversations with her daughter about sexual assault. As Sarah engaged with Taylor's work, she felt her original response to her friend had been insufficient and realised the huge complexity of the subject area. Here, Sarah reflects on the inadequacy of her own Catholic sex education, the complexity of consent and how bodies are transgressed and infringed upon. She underlines the very different attitudes towards touch and calls for the recognition of the complexity of sexuality in our society and all the issues to which it relates: for example, power, self-esteem and misogyny, among others. Sarah raises a point that appears a few times in this book: touch can feel enjoyable while still being unwanted, uncomfortable and abusive. Finally, Sarah argues strongly for the need for men to be involved in these conversations, in the hope that they can support boys in their rites of passage to manhood.

In Chapter 5, 'Sexual abuse and surviving with(in) psychology,' Jemma Tosh, a chartered psychologist and prolific writer, reflects on growing up queer and genderfluid in Northern Ireland, and sees herself as both a survivor and a victim. It's a powerful narrative that follows on from Taylor's concern to change the discourse around 'sex'. The chapter details 'complex intersections of gender, sexuality, race, place, and historical context.'

As a child, when Jemma sought to disclose abuse, she was told: 'Don't worry about it, dear, God will punish him.' Later on, Jemma was encouraged to believe that she 'deserved' abuse. When she began training as a psychologist, she was appalled by the 'gendered tropes and rape apologism' she encountered, but – as she began to 'become her own therapist' – she learned to navigate away from victim-blaming texts and explanations, starting a journey that is not yet finished.

A conversation between Jemma and her longstanding friend, community worker Fionnuala Dempsey – who identifies as queer, genderfluid and autistic – deepens the exploration of 'being your own therapist', pointing out that the 'helping' professions can, at times, be anything but, and highlighting the importance of recognising intersectionality.

Liz Smith and Sara Teresa Mollis wrote Chapter 6 while both were training in person-centred psychotherapy. An important thread throughout their reflective chapter is the potential risks and dangers of writing it while trainees. They fear being perceived as 'them' before they've fully become 'us' – ie. qualified therapists. In their words:

> Those who have the power to assess us could find us too challenging of their orthodoxy and as such find us lacking. If we fall too much out of line, we might not get our seat at the table.

Inventively using Carl Rogers' seven-stage process as their framework, they offer an experiential exploration of 'the conspicuous absence of #MeToo and therapists' lived experience in counselling and psychotherapy training'. In a field where we are encouraged to 'show our working', Liz and Sara do just that, offering extracts from their deepening conversations and growing connection as they worked on their chapter. This 'might give our readers insight into our discussions and emotions, as well as a sense of the time and place in which we were writing – a sense of authenticity, perhaps, that cannot always be conveyed through analytical prose alone.'

In a variety of ways, all the book's contributors work with and write very powerfully with this desire for authenticity. As we said earlier, we invited contributors to write how they wished, and they took us up on that. Some wrote autobiographically; some drew on fiction; some produced academic pieces interwoven with lived experience, and all engaged in and wrote rich conversations. We hope the book will contribute to influencing how the profession writes; it can sometimes be quite detached and sterile – are we fearful, perhaps, of being visible and fully seen?

In Chapter 7, 'Survivors of sexual violence training as psychotherapists in the UK', Deborah A. Lee (at the time of writing also in person-centred training) draws on her own research in which Peggy, Sam and Phoenix (all pseudonyms) were co-researchers. This work suggests what might happen when experiences of sexual violence and abuse *are* spoken of while the psychotherapist is still training. Phoenix, for instance, talks of how some fellow psychotherapists-in-training found sexual violence and abuse (which they knew she had experienced) 'uncomfortable' to hear about, and their response was like 'a bus crash' and, the next minute '[a] fucking train coming from the other angle'. She says this was down to 'people not owning their own shit'. Deborah imagines science-fiction scenarios, drawing on work by Carl Rogers and Marge Piercy, to ask if the future might bring change.

Training is sometimes discussed uncritically, neutrally, as something that is provided for the good of all participants. Likewise, many trainings are presented as apolitical and fail to address, let alone embrace, diversity in the work and how staff and students relate. It is time that training providers became more politically aware, for a number of reasons, some of which are highlighted in Chapters 6 and 7. Perhaps #MeToo can continue the tradition started by others, such as Pink Therapy, which emerged in response to the failure by most therapy training organisations in the UK to address issues of sexual diversity in their curricula, or the Black, African and Asian Therapy Network (BAATN), which initiated the 'Each One Teach One' mentoring programme for trainee therapists from black, Asian and minority ethnic (BAME) communities, or the Aashna Centre's 'Let's All Get Uncomfortable' series of workshops that challenge training organisations to put cultural diversity at the heart of their courses.

In Chapter 8, '#MeToo on the internet', integrative therapist Tara Shennan explains what she feels therapists need to know about internet sexual abuse. Tara highlights the importance of language, arguing that if we refer to 'unwanted sexual contact', we have applied an 'adult filter'; far better to ask young people if they've 'had any sexual contact online'. Based on her own experiences of the misuse of the word 'trust', Tara never asks clients to trust her: 'a valuable lesson for clients to learn is that trustworthy people don't spend a lot of time telling them how trustworthy they are or constantly asking to be trusted. They simply *are* trustworthy.' Tara explores many of the myths around internet sexual abuse, including the oft-heard and important-to-challenge victim-blaming notion that children need to learn how to make 'better choices.' The chapter offers interventions for therapists working in the field. Tara advises: 'Where possible, avoid vague terminology; using euphemisms often compounds shame.' A conversation with fellow counsellor Haley Clifford draws out more of the meanings of the location of internet sexual abuse.

In Chapter 9, 'Reconnection through dance movement therapy', dance movement psychotherapist Amanda Light draws on feminist new materialism and posthumanism, autoethnography (journals written while she was training), and conversations with Tina Johnson, a friend and fellow practitioner with whom Amanda trained. Amanda points to 'growing recognition that sensory studies and embodied therapies such as dance movement psychotherapy might help bring people who have experienced child sexual abuse to a place of integration.' As such, she writes, 'it is surprising that somatic interventions are not being more readily used alongside standard therapeutic practices.'

Following Tara's call for a fuller exploration of the nuances of language, Amanda issues a plea for greater recognition of mind-body connections and relationship with other-than-human and more-than-human life. In common with all contributors, Amanda takes us beyond simplistic neoliberal conceptualisations that 'the answer' to 'the problem' of people's distress is six sessions of cognitive behavioural therapy, within which what and who caused that distress is largely irrelevant. Amanda says of her own experiences of talking therapy: 'Although it was a relief to finally reveal what had happened, talking through my past experiences led me into a spiral of depression within which I became stuck, and from which I didn't so much emerge as just grew bored.' For Amanda, 'it wasn't enough to just talk about it, I needed to cry, scream, hit cushions, stamp my feet and outwardly express the horrors that had been held, secretly, in my body for many years'. Poetry and nature, the other-than-human, are explored, and we see Amanda and Tina, her conversation partner, 'dancing barefoot in the garden' as their friendship deepens.

In Chapter 10, 'Shattering the sounds of silence', integrative psychotherapist Reena Shah also uses autoethnography, including the evocative use of photographs, alongside narrative enquiry with two women, Anna and Molly, both therapists and survivors, to explore the intertwining of therapist and client stories of childhood sexual abuse and its role in 'shattering the silences'. As in Jemma Tosh's chapter, there is intersectionality here – something that needs more attention in the therapy world. Reena's chapter returns us to language; what does it mean when a night-time abuser uses a different language (Guajarati) to the language loved by young Reena, who reads Enid Blyton by day? What is happening when Molly's male client, who has been sexually abused, smokes, eats a banana and overtly looks at his watch as if to check he's had his money's-worth? A clinical vignette reveals how 'words are not always enough in finding a shared understanding'. This piece explicitly invites our responses, prompting many thoughts, feelings and questions for us as co-editors.

In conversation with Reena, integrative counsellor Clarinda Cuppage picks up the themes of silence. She too was silenced and voiceless as a child growing up in the Roman Catholic faith. Clarinda explores how she has subsequently used her voice to develop the Survivors' Voices project on behalf of the charity One in Four, to enable those who have experienced sexual abuse and violence to find their voice through writing their own story.

In Chapter 11, 'While I was sleeping', Andrew Pari, psychotherapist and founder and director of Sexual Assault Awareness (our second US contributor, alongside Taylor Broughton) makes immediately clear his aim not to shy away from anything. The time has come for Andrew to write his truth, and write it he does. Like Reena Shah, Andrew notes the confusion that sexual abuse creates for a child: his abuser was his 'daytime friend and [...] night-time horror'. At the beginning of the book, Seb Randall wrote of retribution. Andrew's chapter takes us somewhere else, to a place that he acknowledges is unusual, where the person who abused him writes: 'I wish to undo what I did because of the damage I have done to your life.' Katy Woodger, a fellow therapist and Andrew's conversation partner, took her abuser to court and featured in a powerful BBC One documentary, *Abused: the untold story*, which presented the accounts of several people who had survived sexual abuse in childhood. She says: 'I have to live with the fact that if he [my abuser] had been sent to prison for those offences that pre-date what happened to me, rather than receiving the suspended sentence he did – presumably in pursuit of rehabilitation – then he wouldn't have been able to do what he did to me.' Tough issues are explored here, demanding that the reader decide where they stand.

Chapter 12, #WeToo: groupwork as an act of solidarity and resistance', by Leah Salter, a family and systemic psychotherapist, celebrates groupwork. Written with Emily Jacob, a coach and neurolinguistic programme master practitioner, the chapter takes us beyond therapy dyads (some of the positives and negatives of which have been critiqued in previous chapters) to discuss group work in a statutory setting. Leah and her colleagues work with the politics of child sexual abuse, with #MeToo, and with #WeToo, rather than privileging discourses of diagnosis and deficit. Leah reports that being in the groups helps participants escape 'patienthood' and being pathologised as 'disordered' by finding solidarity with others.

Leah and Emily 'bring into focus... a wider social narrative based on solidarity, from which new stories can emerge – stories that speak to collective resistance – and challenge the idea that having experiences such as sexual abuse might preclude women from becoming therapists.' Emily Jacob reports that, despite being initially sceptical about being a conversation partner, her own work has been enriched by the collaboration and she is now considering creating 'story circles'. She has explicitly realised the power of #WeToo to 'bounce forward' in her own Facebook community. This book, they point out, has done the same by creating a community of contributors.

In Chapter 13, 'Pushing, pulling and parts coming together', we have a chapter that nearly wasn't here. Joy Farrimond, an experienced therapy client, was originally the conversation partner for a writer who decided not to continue with her chapter. So we asked Joy to become the chapter writer and to write with co-editor Emma Palmer, a body psychotherapist and her friend of many years. Joy describes vividly a familiar sense of push and pull when deciding whether to do so: 'Sharing my experiences was serving an important function in relation to the silencing that had happened in childhood. That part of me that had been silenced wanted to be heard and there was hope that sharing my experience of survival and growth might help someone else in some small way.' However, it ran against her instinct, developed in childhood, to hide. We feel it's important to note this 'push and pull' as a theme in #MeToo writing more generally. Almost three years down the line from the social media sensation of #MeToo, it still has not become easy to say '#MeToo'; there's much more work to do. A second theme to emerge is this desire to help someone else who has experienced sexual violence or abuse. Joy also flags up a theme that emerges in many places in the book – the generosity of authors and conversation partners in giving their time to this book.

Co-editor Emma Palmer, with Charleen Agostini, a recently retired process-oriented psychotherapist, closes the book with Chapter 14: 'Dirty secrets, ecocide and the specialness of the world all around'. This chapter began with Emma spontaneously writing her original #MeToo testimony. Through embodied reflection and part-poetry prose, Emma moves her focus between sexual abuse and war (associated with the war trauma in her paternal ancestral line), and draws parallels between sexual abuse and ecocide, and the sixth extinction crisis. All of these stem from oppression, 'power over' and disconnection from other-than-human and more-than-human life. She discusses with Charleen how and why she (Emma) doesn't relate to the label 'survivor'. Together, they explore the responsible-ness of the healing work of therapy, and in particular how, through somatic experiencing, imagining causing harm to her abusers means Emma doesn't enact harm in real life. They name how this work helped her to *feel*, echoing Joy's exploration of feeling and not feeling in the previous chapter. Emma's chapter ends with a plea for the planet: 'that healing be healing for all that lives, not just the human ones, in this age of intersectionality and in this head-spinning vast web of interconnection.'

Clare Shaw's poem, which she wrote after reading all the chapters, is only 'concluding' because it comes at the end. As we have stated, there is no neat linearity to this book, and nor is there to lived experiences of sexual violence and abuse. There are no neat 'conclusions' to be made and no 'recoveries' to be scored on a chart. The poem is about unlocking voices and finding words, and is based on the story of Helen Keller, who could neither hear nor see, yet was able to find her voice by touch. Beautiful, moving, haunting, it will stay with us all, long after reading.

References

Alma D (ed) (2018). *#MeToo. Rallying Against Sexual Assault and Harassment: a women's poetry anthology.* Oswestry: Fair Acre Press.

Black M (2017). *Unbroken.* London: John Blake Books.

Brison S (2002). *Aftermath.* Princeton, MA: Princeton University Press.

Clark A E and Pino, A L (eds) (2016). *We Believe You: survivors of campus sexual assault speak out.* New York, NY: Holt Press.

Douglas RM (2016). *On Being Raped.* London: Beacon Press.

Freedman KL (2014). *One Hour in Paris: a true story of rape and recovery.* Chicago, IL: University of Chicago Press.

Gay R (ed) (2019). *Not That Bad: dispatches from rape culture.* London: Allen & Unwin.

Gay R (2018). *Hunger: a memoir of (my) body.* London: Corsair.

Li WM (2017). *Dark Chapter.* London: Legend Press.

Louis E (2018). *History of Violence* (L Stein, trans). London: Harvill Secker.

Moulton E (ed) (2017). *Things We Haven't Said: sexual assault survivors speak out.* Minneapolis, MN: Zest Books.

Novey I (2018). *Those Who Knew.* London: Viking.

Saward J with Green W (1990). *Raped.* London: Bloomsbury Publishing.

Sebold A (2003). *Lucky.* London: Picador.

Venable Raine N (2000). *After Silence: rape and my journey back.* London: Virago.

Watson J (ed) (2019). *Drop the disorder! Challenging the culture of psychiatric diagnosis.* Monmouth: PCCS Books.

Weaver Francisco P (2000). *Telling: a memoir of rape and recovery.* New York, NY: Harper Perennial.

Chapter 1

Retribution

Seb Randall, with Celia Urbach

A blustery North Sea carried me roughly overnight to Denmark. A toddler with his own passport signified a premeditated detachment from a mother who wanted me gone while she gave birth to my sister. This was not a spontaneous act. My father's sister told me that she tried, but failed, to console me. Following three weeks' banishment at the British Embassy in Copenhagen, where my grandfather was the ambassador, my return to our Chelsea flat overlooking the murky Thames in Cheney Walk brought me back to my friend the milkman and our daily rounds with crates, clattering up and down the rickety lift. As a toddler, trust in strangers was growing.

A year later I sailed to Beirut with my mother and sister, taking a detour to see Vesuvius from the sea, and into the care of a Lebanese foster mother, Yvette, while my birth mother took on the role of a glamorous diplomat's wife from behind permanent sunglasses and a headscarf. I saw very little of my father, who was away much of the time working undercover for MI6, fighting the Cold War. Some years passed and, at sea again, the three of us followed my father to Mexico City: first on the Queen Mary, then by train, out of New York, down through deep Southern states and along the Mississippi for a while, over the border and up the winding Sierra Madre. My father and Yvette met us at the station in a long white Chevrolet. Three years passed, then Yvette returned to Lebanon and I moved to Düsseldorf.

British Army school in Germany was a hard place where I fought myself into a new existence. I badly missed Yvette and the sedate colonial seclusion of expatriate life, in which I had lived as an observer more than participant. When I was 11, my parents consigned me to a state boarding school. I was rationed to two return flights home a year, in the summer and at Christmas. I experienced school as chaotic, vicious, miserable and frightening. Bullying and violent pranks were normal and normalised in a setting where the teachers had little idea of, or control over, what was going on. As in internment camps, some of the older inmates were given authority to administer justice, which some did according to their own sadistic impulses. Others were kind and tolerant; friendships grew in febrile solidarity. Most of the boys were army kids or Londoners with difficult family circumstances, for whom the elegant buildings and countryside were an escape from city strife. Rumours circulated in a nearby village that the school housed juvenile delinquents, that it was a Borstal. I was desperate to leave. My father made one visit to hear me out. He took me to lunch, but it was clear straight away I had no chance of leaving. We walked through the rain back to the station and he got me a platform ticket from a machine. I watched the train disappear down the track and drowned. I was 12, on my own, returned to prison.

During the Easter breaks, I slept some nights on friends' sofas in dilapidated council estates in South London but didn't want to push my luck, so I'd walk the streets selling cigarettes one at a time for a small profit to buy food and asked passers-by for spare change. The days passed easily. I could disappear and nobody would notice. I talked with street dwellers, shared cigarettes and drinks, learned vicariously from their stories. I told them about the places I had lived in. I grew fond of strangers.

One cold and wet Sunday night in April, at around three in the morning in Leicester Square, I was dodging the rain under dark plane trees when a black cab drew up and the window slid down. A balding, smiling man with a round face leaned out of the dark interior, blew out some smoke and asked me if I would like to come to his flat to dry out. He said it would be nice and warm. He had a spare bed that I could sleep on as long as I needed. I believed him – my rescuer! The door swung open and I climbed into the fuggy cab. He gave me a cigarette. We exchanged friendly banter as the cab hissed wetly west through London towards Ladbroke Grove. What a stroke of luck!

We arrived at a four-storey cream stucco house with sharp black railings like teeth by the front steps. The rain was coming down like stair rods. Smile washed off, the man led me up to a black door opening onto a landing at the bottom of a steep, narrow, linoleum-covered staircase with sharp aluminium edges. A clutch of fear turned my guts as the heavy door thudded shut. A nod towards the top. Another door at the upper landing opened into a tiny room, not a home – a dingy cube with two single beds and a washbasin. I looked into a crash-pad. The window led out onto metal fire escapes… escape? I was shoved in. The door closed behind us and I heard the scrape of a key. I looked up to see it disappear into a pocket. A clenched fist was offered to my face, crushed to clean sheets, small mercy. This is interesting… worse has happened… soles slapping wet sand… racing beach… chip waft… sea foam… white clouds… blurry dog… child shriek.

He slept and I tried to leave. First find the key, but he woke and threatened me with a punch. The man was strong and I was a child. So I waited. Later he calmed down and pretended to be my friend. Making less of it. He told me he worked as a door manager at a night club in the West End. I did not understand what that was. He asked me if I would like to meet some girls who would have sex with me. Maybe he wanted to broaden my experience. Quite thoughtful, almost kind – sort of compensation. He told me where he worked and that I could meet him there. (I'll save that for later.) Perhaps we could have a drink? I said I would have to think about that, but I thought to myself that it was probably unrealistic. He reckoned I was Spanish. (Did this make it OK? Foreigners are fair game?) Maybe a suntan was unusual at that time of year in London, all those years ago? Maybe he liked Spanish boys? Thoughts to keep going with for the time being.

Long hours passed, then he gestured to an open door. I stumbled, bruised, back down the stairs and blinking into bright sunshine and puddled streets. An open space, a park behind railings, unseen in the early darkness. I clocked the house – I know where you hang out, mate – then marched to the tube and headed east, far away, to the other end of town. I jumped the tube to Forest Gate where, near the station, I found a stable block next to a scrapyard. I pulled open the unlocked door. Inside was straw-strewn and dungy over black cobbles, a horsey smell. Through the gloom, I saw a ladder at the back that led me up through a hatch into an attic stacked with straw and hay bales. A dirty window overlooked wasteland littered with old furniture and a burnt-out car. Sunday quiet. The watery sun made streaks through dusty, musty air. Safe, I slept long on straw laid over floorboards.

I woke in the late afternoon, filled with angry sadness and relief. Alive and wiser. Soft rain teared down the mucky window. I felt an idiot. What was I thinking? Oh well, need to get out of the stable, find food and walk about. I kept the attack to myself; telling someone would make it real, more true. Who would believe me? Who could I tell? Not my parents, 2,000 miles away, who would have made it worse with all their worry about keeping up appearances. They would have struggled, and I wanted to protect them from their failings. They had not protected me but I did not blame them; they had their lives to lead and I had mine. Not my friends, who would have laughed and taken the piss, which is how we used to mess with anything serious. Fair enough, I thought. Anyway, it was over, nothing could change that, and I had survived. The passing years have held that night in the cracked pages of my clasped book.

A few weeks after the kidnap, I decided to ask a school friend who lived in Battersea if he could get a gun from his older brother, who I knew had an ex-service Webley .38 revolver he had used during an armed robbery. The brother had not been caught, he was only 17 and had since decided to go to college. He had stashed some cash and got a chance to change his career prospects while he was still ahead. I already knew he wanted to get rid of the gun, but not into the wrong hands. On the other hand, I had a justifiable mission. I thought I might take up the man's offer of West End girls, then shoot him in front of his mates. I sampled the thought and played it back to myself as a kind of film. This would have led to a period in youth detention, arguably an improvement on my school, but embarrassing and possibly complicated. A better, more nuanced plan was to go back to the black door with fangs at the bottom of the stairs near Ladbroke Grove and wait for the man, hoping I could catch him at his tricks. I knew roughly when his shift as door manager ended in the early hours.

I planned to lurk at the side of the front steps, out of direct view of the road. The taxi stopping would give me a chance to aim. Having handled guns at rifle club, I knew how to hit a target; I had time and patience. The thought of revenge made me feel good and powerful. I imagined him pleading and sobbing, and then I knew his terrified face would kill my rage. I would feel sorry for him, undermining the purpose of my plan; I would become crippled by compassion. A part of me regrets that I didn't kill him, or at least shoot him up a bit – perhaps both knees, damaging him so he would be reminded every time he stood up or tried to walk. I could have done either. I would certainly have got away with it – him on the steps, crying in pain or dead in the dark; me running across the park, hiding the gun for safe retrieval later and jumping the tube – but I chose not to.

During holidays in my early teens, I would show up at the occasional boisterous police poolside barbecue in Amman, to which I was invited by my father's spy colleagues in the Jordanian General Intelligence Directorate. Guns were all over the place. The guests would not have had my qualms. Revenge, honour and death were different in that world. My friend Salma told me a story about sitting in a car beside her brother Mahdi, looking over the rosy evening glow from Jabal Amman, when a man she did not know started to chat to her through the open window. Her brother got out, walked around the back of the car and shot him. No action was taken; it was reported as an honour killing, and her brother had friends in the police force. I thought I could have done with a brother like that when I needed my honour restored.

The marines on the roof of my home in Bahrain ate cereal in the kitchen while I dismantled and reassembled their Bren light machine guns. With a bit of practice, I could do it without looking. Mornings, my summer holiday job was to check the underneath of the car for bombs, taking care not to trigger the tripwire across the drive attached to a warning flare. These arrangements followed the blowing-up of one of my father's colleagues. One night, I listened at the door to my parents having one of their frequent alcohol-sodden fights. This one was different in moral purpose. My mother was upset because my father had been ordered to poison a suspected terrorist leader from Oman. The argument seemed paradoxical, because my mum supported the death penalty, while my father was passionately opposed. Later that summer, my father started to have fits. As he shuddered on the bedroom floor, I cycled furiously for help up the dusty track, feeling sorry for him; he looked so frightened.

My boarding schooling ended, and I visited my parents for the last time in Manama, Bahrain. I was 17 when my father gave me a parting gift of £20 and 200 cigarettes while I waited for the London flight after a last summer with my family. As the plane climbed, banking steeply, I could see the dark-green palm trees below, fringed by white sand and azure sea. I was afraid of what lay ahead and already wanted to return to the life I was leaving. I recognised then how irretrievable this point was, even as I traversed it and the VC10 delivered me to an uncertain future.

Back to London's streets and sofas, gardening, making leather goods, selling door-to-door until I steadied, made a home and started on adult life. I worked on building sites by day and studied sociology and psychology by night at Holloway College. Weekends I got into activism, working on projects in Camden for kids and old people.

When my life had become more settled, I started my own psychotherapy, then trained as a therapist, initially person-centred and later in psychoanalytic psychotherapy. From what I have heard from others' stories, acts of sadism and torture can often evoke feelings of revenge towards the attackers, as well as guilt and the seduction of forgiveness. Some clients have told me they felt that their previous therapists tried to nudge them away from revenge, towards acceptance, to find resolution. Perhaps those therapists struggled to tolerate vengeful rage?

Many people subjected to sexual violence have been strongly drawn towards revenge fantasies. For my own part, the knowledge that I had the choice to kill my attacker but showed pragmatic mercy leaves me unperturbed. Mercy is not equivalent to forgiveness in my court; the rapist will remain unforgiven, forever a non-person, a pariah stripped of his citizenship-of-the-world status. I wonder how he fared, how he justified his actions. Had he attacked other people before me? The crash-pad looked like forward planning to me. Had his attack on me emboldened him to attack others? Or kill them? Or perhaps some victims couldn't live with the experience and killed themselves? Maybe I should have killed him? I might have been a life-saver. It never occurred to me to leave it to the police – zero chance of a prosecution, I thought, and anyway I would not have liked the exposure, having to explain what happened – too much detail. Far better to keep it in-house, tidy. Had I killed him, I would have had no regrets. Maybe his parents would have been sad, but that's death for you. Anyway, they could have done a better job raising him. I had just cause. It would have been his choice, not mine. Kidnap and rape could be made more of a risk for perpetrators. There are quite a few who have got away with it, as far as I can tell. An old Islamic parable describes death as a grain of sand in the desert. This is not to say I support capital punishment – ever. Or maybe he felt guilt and reformed himself, became an ex-rapist, worked in a crisis centre as reparation for his misdeeds, became a model citizen.

I was a child with distant parents, living in an expatriate world within the implicit violence and rituals of colonial legacy. In my own country, I was an immigrant, belonging neither to my parents' culture nor to the cultures of my various host countries. I emerged unscathed from a disrupted and truncated childhood and an adolescence inscribed with secrets and violence.

Conversation with Celia Urbach

Before I wrote this account about selected aspects of my childhood, predicated on my recollection of a kidnap and rape, I met Celia, my designated 'conversation person', in a north London park and we discussed our lives for a while. We got on well enough; it seemed that we had much in common. We met again a few months later, after Celia had read my story, and talked for a couple of hours. After our conversation, we exchanged a couple of emails, but I was left with the sense that we had missed each other, somehow. We arranged to meet again and agreed that Celia would, in the intervening period, write a response to my story and our subsequent meetings.

Celia's response to Seb

It was unusual for me to participate in a project like this. I have not had much experience of 'coming out' in the world. I wasn't sure what to expect. I was to be paired with another therapist/#MeToo 'survivor' who would write their story.

We would have a conversation. The story and the subsequent conversation would form a chapter in a book.

The first surprise for me was that I had been paired with a man. I agreed to the pairing without hesitation, but with hindsight I wonder if the gender difference was more challenging than I admitted to myself. We had our first meeting before you, Seb, wrote your story.

It quickly became apparent to me how different we were. You struck me as a maverick rebel, self-assured and independent in your thinking. Next to you, I felt conservative and imagined you would see me as straight and conventional.

We talked quite openly – intimately – about our lives and our relationships. You seemed confident about your choices; you questioned some of mine, stirring doubt and insecurity in me. I felt my own fearfulness next to your sense of freedom and adventure – my own uncertainty alongside your confidence.

I now see that we were entering into a dynamic whereby, in the face of someone who expresses themselves with certainty and confidence, I become increasingly uncertain and vulnerable.

We talked about our #MeToo experiences: yours a one-off, brutal attack, in the context of a childhood characterised by abandonment, neglect and the threat of violence. Mine, a largely forgotten early-childhood experience of being used – probably repeatedly – as a masturbatory object, within the context of an apparently happy (although idealised) childhood.

To me your story was deeply shocking and very sad. Not only the brutal kidnap and rape you suffered, but also the harsh circumstances, the abuse, the neglect and the loneliness of your upbringing.

However, in spite of the brutality and cruelty you endured and your revenge fantasies, you gave me the impression that you suffered no lingering effects from the assault. Did I misunderstand you here? By contrast, I felt that the exploitation of my body for sexual purposes at such a young age had robbed me of parts of my sexuality.

We went on to talk about revenge fantasies, which was what you particularly wanted to focus on. I got confused, because you seemed to be talking about actual acts of revenge, rather than fantasies. You said to me that you had to believe in your fantasies for them to work, which I could understand. But it seemed to me that you wanted to affirm violence itself as a legitimate form of redress.

I didn't want to dismiss your experience. The fact that your violent assailant would have – almost certainly – gone on to abuse others was meaningful. But, while I could understand the impulse towards retribution, I was not convinced that you would necessarily have slept easy in your bed had you acted on your fantasy. I tend to think that violence – quite apart from the destruction it causes to others – risks leaving the perpetrator with a further untold psychic burden.

When we tried to talk about this, it felt awkward. It's hard for me to know what happened for you, but I think you flinched. I wonder what it was like for you?

From the subjective position I had adopted inside our dynamic, I imagined that you saw me as one of those therapists you mentioned in your story, who couldn't tolerate vengeful rage. I thought again that you perhaps perceived me as conservative or overprotected, unable to cope with the harsh reality of some people's lives. Looking back, I know I explored none of this with you and I may merely have been reacting to my own projection.

We had a third meeting, which you asked for in order to clarify what had happened between us, but I'm not sure that we did clarify much. Talking about these things felt difficult. You told me how your childhood had familiarised you with violence and the trappings of violence. I got the impression that you feel more comfortable in the presence of people who are at ease with violence than with people like me who are shocked by the brutality of your story. If I understood you right, you said you preferred people not to make a fuss but to just give your experience a nod and move on, as if you didn't want the trauma and pain to be mirrored back to you.

We talked further about our personal lives, and once more I became a bit tearful and vulnerable when talking about mine. Thinking about the dynamic between us, I was beginning to wonder about the confidence you seemed to hold in our conversations and the vulnerability and doubt that I carried.

I reflected more about our apparent differences, turning to friends and colleagues to try to make sense of it all. This led me to think about the hidden similarities between us. Although my upbringing might have been relatively protected in comparison with yours, my father came to the UK at the age of 14 – a Kindertransportee, a refugee of the Holocaust. He was the only survivor of his family; the others were killed. He was, in fact, the victim of one of the greatest acts of state-sanctioned violence ever.

How does a person cope with an experience like that?

I have learned that there is a pattern among Holocaust survivors of having 'idealised' images of family. The next generation feels compelled to be perfect in order to compensate for the inconceivable losses of the previous one. Unlike your upbringing, where conflict and the threat of violence seem to have been an everyday reality, in mine, conflict didn't seem to be acceptable. To please my father, I had to be a good girl.

I wonder whether part of my dad's solution to his violent history was to repress his rage and that this was the background to my upbringing, leaving me with no healthy access to my own anger. I certainly feel no anger in relation to the man who took away my innocence, used me for his own pleasure and left me with the shame that rightfully belongs with him. I think that it would be a step towards my own recovery to feel that anger.

Your experience and upbringing feel in some ways like the mirror image of mine. I wonder if dissociation from your vulnerability and powerlessness was the solution you found to the attacks you had to endure?

Perhaps each of us has found a strategy to manage the violence in our histories, but in doing so we have sacrificed parts of ourselves. Perhaps, when we meet, we encounter those lost parts in the synergetic field between us and we get to feel and hold the other's shadow in that encounter. Perhaps, in fact, we are two sides of a coin – each of us holding the key to the other's wholeness.

Seb's response to Celia

As our conversation progressed, I had a growing sense that my story had not resonated with you. There were aspects with which you appeared not to connect, although you were consistently attentive.

It felt as if our discussion had evolved into a quest to uncover the impact that my rape had on the rest of my life and on my subjectivity. Perhaps this is more relevant when a person seeks help to address the pain and distress that sexual violence has caused them. I felt the conversation began to drift towards a search for explanations for hypothesised problems. It seemed as if my desire for retribution troubled you – that it was not a fantasy, it was a plan. A threat without the means and will to enact it is an empty threat with no weight and no restitutive potential. I was not seeking the conferral of legitimacy for my morally indefensible plans, made while a child, but the sense of relief you expressed that I had not killed him deflated me – I felt my decision to show mercy had been devalued.

What you do or do not believe in is not relevant to me now, when it is directed at something that happened decades ago. I did not expect you to affirm or judge the truthfulness in my rendition. You offered your moral position: you were pleased I did not kill him. When I admitted to you that I would have slept like a baby had I carried out my plan, I hoped you would have understood that, because I meant it; at the time and in the aftermath of the attack, I felt powerless and that I had little control of the situation. My revenge plan restored some sense of control to me and brought out something precious, dignified and lasting. Had I reported the crime, I would have ceded that control to the vicissitudes of the criminal justice system, in which I had no reason to have confidence, and it would therefore have deepened my sense of disempowerment and anguish.

I found your story very moving. I don't think I have ever met someone so close to the Kindertransport rescue. Your existence following the survival of your father is testament to the possibility of good in the face of unimaginable evil, which helped me comprehend your moral stance towards my story. You were much younger than me when your abuse occurred, and it robbed you of innocence and left you with a lingering sense of shame. You say you don't feel angry towards your abuser, but I do.

I'm not sure about dissociation. As time has passed, these diagnostic psy-words have become clichés. I find it difficult to make meaningful sense of them; they do not help me to articulate subjective experience; nor do they explain much. Along with some of the jargon used by our profession, they have the power to obfuscate as well as to explicate – or, worse, their use constitutes a discourse of authoritarian expertise.

For me, the attack did not have a lasting effect. I had the opportunity and means to deliver justice in my own adolescent way, and I chose not to. This helped release me from the chains of victimhood. It is an observation of the human condition that vengeance is sweet – most likely, an evolved reward response to the elimination of life-threatening predators. Without these innate and other destructive imperatives, we humans would probably not have survived this far from our biological beginnings.

Violence is capricious. In contrast to you, I feel I got away lightly. I am sure my attack would not have happened without the precursors of parental neglect, but it had faded into a distant memory and I was initially ambivalent about revisiting it. However, once the idea of writing about it was mooted, I became increasingly drawn to cross the bridge over the gulf of time that separates me from those abandoned days.

On the whole, my life since childhood has gone well – much better than expected. In a way, my experience of being attacked has exposed my own capacity for violence and directly taught me something of the human condition. I am neither survivor nor victim – the attack, now unearthed and exposed to light, seems like just one of many bad things that have happened to me and I have to live with.

So thank you for exploring this with me, and for sharing some of your own experiences. In the end we found some resonance.

Celia's postscript

Having read your further words, it's hard not to come back one more time.

Inevitably, in an exercise of this kind, one is bound to be selective. In retrospect, I'm sorry to have skipped over our initial meeting in the park, which was spirited and vital and which I enjoyed very much. There was much we seemed to share in the two hours or more that we spent together. Even after the difficulties I encountered in our subsequent meetings, I felt an affection and an affinity with you, which I failed to mention above.

I'm sorry that some of my responses left you feeling misunderstood. It takes courage to 'come out', and even more to subject a written piece to the scrutiny of others. I should also add that, regardless of the dynamic that emerged between us, I fully recognise the importance of embracing the shadow side of the human psyche and acknowledge the value you gained from processing your experience in the way you did.

I now wonder if, during the course of this exchange, I was overly focused on my feelings of vulnerability, and insufficiently aware of the power I held, as the one who was given the task of reading and responding to your piece.

So thank you, too, for giving me the opportunity to explore this with you.

Chapter 2

'Survivors are everywhere': our #MeToo, #WeToo journey

Kaur, with Deborah A. Lee

Kaur's #MeToo

Sitting in a room waiting to see a counsellor at the age of 16... I knew why I was there – well, I thought I did. I was at breaking point – tired of hiding the bruises and wounds inflicted by a family member, which I'd endured out of a sense of duty to try to keep the peace in a chaotic household. Little did I know – or maybe I did – what my body and mind would start remembering.

Sitting in a GP treatment room at the age of 21, after the death of my father, being examined by the GP – my body seizing up when she examined my stomach. 'Have you ever self-harmed?' I was asked, rather bluntly. What did that have to do with the physical pains I could feel in my stomach, my chest, around my neck? She sent me packing with a prescription for antidepressants, unaware her roughness and bluntness had triggered a plethora of sensations and pains in my body for which neither she nor I had any explanation.

Sitting in a waiting room again, at the age of 22, waiting for the counsellor to call me in. Again, I thought I knew why I was there. I wanted to process the grief of my beloved father dying. I was a mess. My life felt chaotic yet empty. The unexplained pains and strange body sensations were still there, sometimes constantly. I was working nights while studying for my postgraduate qualification. I was exhausted, yet I couldn't sleep.

A year later, seeing the same counsellor, I was in a different place: I had said it – #MeToo – although my body had been saying #MeToo for some time. The pain and the body sensations were the result of my body remembering. Now my mind was remembering too... my hour-long sessions with the counsellor would start with some small talk and then it would begin; my head would be sucked back in time, to the heart-breaking, soul-destroying memories. Who were all these men? Why were they hurting me? Why could I hear heavy breathing? Why couldn't I see? Why couldn't I move my hands? Why was the floor so cold? My body would seize up from the sheer terror and fear. My head would say it wasn't happening to *my* body. It wasn't happening to *me*. It couldn't have, could it?

Could I possibly have forgotten that this had happened over and over again, year after year, for much of my childhood? My body would be telling me a different story. Session after session, I would come round to find myself curled into a ball, shaking, crying, unable to breathe, terror seizing every inch of my body, feeling sore, like I had been dragged naked though broken glass. Yet there was no blood, no bruises, no cuts.

The body remembering is a strange thing, especially when the mind does not remember. However, the body remembering while the mind remembers destroys your sense of being, your sense of worth, and the desire to exist in a body that does not feel yours.

My counsellor, who saw me for the best part of a decade and was a huge part of my journey, has been, until now, the only other person who knows the reality of my #MeToo story. I feel guilty knowing that my #MeToo experiences must have consumed so much of her life. She taught me that I deserved to be held and comforted through my flashbacks and memories. Because I believed it only happened to me because I was a bad, horrible person. It had happened to me because I desperately wanted love and affection from those around me. She gave so much of her time to me. She adapted her techniques, she learned, she read, she taught me. She held me through each and every new memory. She was kind, she helped me to cope, she is probably the reason why I am still alive today.

Kaur and Deborah A. Lee's #WeToo

We've known each other for years and years, and for most of that time we had absolutely no idea we were both survivors of sexual violence. We started to connect when Deborah 'came out' in an academic journal (Lee, 2017), and Kaur wrote a personal note of congratulations. Later, when one of the original contributors for this book was unable to proceed, we agreed to write together and exchanged a series of richly intimate emails. The content of these ranged from religion and culture to bodily presentations to perceived implications of anonymity (and absence of).

A key message we'd like to convey in our chapter is how our #MeToo/#WeToo journey together (we are inspired to write '#WeToo' by Leah and Emily's use of this term in Chapter 12) in these pages, and beyond, is one of growing community, solidarity and even self-acceptance. We don't argue that all survivors will feel like us, but we do find our story deeply heartening – an instance of what #MeToo seeks to achieve.

Deborah: Thank you so much for sending your writing. I felt anger, distress, then went in and out of the room without purpose a couple of times. I thought, wrote some notes, then went back to feeling anger and distress.

Kaur: I wondered, after I had sent it, if it was along the lines of what you were expecting. I suspect not. I'm sorry for the distress it caused you. I hope you're OK.

Deborah: I was glad I had those responses to it; it deserves it. When I've shared my own writing with people who didn't know, they'd sometimes say it was 'shocking,' whereas I look at my experiences and don't find they have any particular impact on me. I wonder if you might be thinking the same sort of thing? You know what happened to you, and you don't see it quite as someone who didn't know already would see it?

Kaur: When I first read your writing, I was shocked, upset and angry that you had been subjected to these experiences. I go in and out of two extremes: acknowledging what happened as being wrong and being shocked, and then feeling like what happened is normal – well, normal for me.

I think this is for several reasons: the shame that it happened being so deep within me; the self-blame that was so ingrained in my being, although to a lesser degree now. And the secrecy surrounding my experiences – not being able to share my experiences solidifies that shame and self-blame. So, in a sense, why would I be shocked by my own experiences?

Therapy has played a really important part in allowing me to assign some of that blame back to my abusers. It's allowed me to recognise that what happened was wrong and it wasn't my fault and, consequently, has allowed me to feel shock at the abuse I was subjected to. The very first memory I have of stuff happening, I must have been about seven. I know I was confused about why it was happening, but I didn't know any different; I didn't know it was wrong. I remember my therapist crying on more than a few occasions, when hearing what my abusers had subjected me to. I couldn't understand why she was sad, why hearing my experiences had made her cry. To me, it was just something that happened. I was scared and confused, but I wasn't shocked. So I didn't understand why she was. Feeling her emotions and picking up on her sense of injustice has helped me to acknowledge the shocking reality of what happened to me. For me, I think that is the power of therapy and sharing experiences – the acknowledgement that it was wrong, it shouldn't have happened, brings the realisation that what happened *is* shocking.

Deborah: When I read your writing, I thought back to when you wrote to me when my first piece came out (Lee, 2017). I thought, of course! Once I knew you knew similar things, I realised I should have already known it; perhaps I did know it but I was looking inwards, not outwards. Your bearing and seriousness. Of course. One never knows how one looks to other people. Someone who didn't know anything of my experiences until I told her recently said she'd always thought I 'knew about' trauma; she said she could 'see it in me'. I have no idea what that might mean as I can't see myself. But if I think of you, I get a sense of you as not entirely in your own body.

Kaur: It's really interesting to hear how you saw me, because you are right – we don't have a sense of how we look to others. I remember all those years ago when I first met you, I was of the view that you were incredibly good at being an academic, which was inspiring in itself! I admired that you were a female academic and did it so well. Even though we were colleagues, I don't think our work lives crossed much. But I sensed that there was a lot more to your story, and that your quietness, your reserved nature, were not just due to your personality traits (I relate to these traits!).

Deborah: I received your email a couple of days ago and have had to work through the whole idea of being 'inspiring' and 'incredibly good' before I could bear to come back to this and say anything. The idea of that, rather than of writing anything about trauma, was what was holding me back.

Kaur: I can understand that. I also find it quite hard to take praise and compliments.

Deborah: I told a friend last night that I was suffering because someone found me 'inspiring', and it does sound absurd. She was worried about me! But I think it's something around the self-hatred that comes with a lot of what I've experienced in life. I struggle to see myself kindly.

Kaur: I see your Twitter activity in my news feed and pick up from that how much people value you, particularly for your work as an academic. I don't know you personally, but I am sure that people also value the personal side of you. But I get why your confidence is so low. I think that is the nature of what we have both experienced – our self-confidence being battered. I switch between feeling quite proud of myself on my good days and just feeling like a shitty person – wife, mother, employee, sister – on my bad days. The bad brings out the really bad stuff.

I still have a card that my therapist wrote for me. On the front there is an artist's image of a dark blue sky at night with a shining star. In the card she wrote all the things she loved about me, my character and my personality. I don't think anyone has ever said or done anything like that to make me feel valued and appreciated. On the bad days, I read that card to help remind me that I am not the bad, horrible person I feel I am. My therapist told me on a regular basis that she was amazed by my resilience, my strength to carry on, to do a PhD, to continue working, and that I have been able to 'hold my shit together'. On the good days, I can recognise that she is absolutely right.

I think knowing that you could relate to my experiences prompted me to contact you and made me more comfortable in disclosing my experiences. A high level of empathy is another trait I believe I have, and that you have it too. Reading your response to my piece of writing touched me, although it made my heart heavy knowing that you felt angry and distressed. Are high levels of empathy another one of those traits we are more attuned to as survivors? I am certainly highly empathic and recognise that this can sometimes be to the detriment of my mental health. I believe this is due to my experiences – I can identify with others' pain and distress, knowing how it feels, how isolating and soul-destroying such experiences are. Being highly empathic is part of the reason why I want to preserve my anonymity, which I will explain a little later.

Not being entirely present in one's body is something I identify with strongly and is related to the shame of living with what happened to my body– it's about not wanting to be in a body that doesn't feel mine; feeling sick to the core when I think about what has been done to my body. Who would want to exist in such a body? Does that impact on the way I carry myself? Can others see it? I hadn't thought about it and related the two before, but now I can see it – yes, why wouldn't it? If such experiences can impact on mental health so detrimentally, then why not on the way one carries oneself?

Appearance is important to me. The clothes I wear allow me to hide the physical scars. Concealer helps me to hide the huge dark circles under my eyes from the lack of sleep; a bit of blusher puts some colour in me and wipes away that pale death-look from my face. It presents a 'persona' that hides the physical signs and mental impact of my experiences.

Deborah: At my worst times, I take off my make-up in the dark as I can't bear to look at myself. I hadn't thought about the importance of make-up to me as well until you raised it. I have to get it on as soon as possible after waking up. I need to create a persona that appears to be in control.

Kaur: Same here, and for that exact same reason!

Deborah: Someone recently – wrongly, in my view – referred to me as having 'perfect' make-up.

Kaur: I agree with this person!

Deborah: I had blepharitis recently and had to get used to not wearing mascara – it had such an impact on how I felt about myself (even worse). When the blepharitis went away, it was a delight to go and buy mascara and get it on.

Kaur: I recently had a blocked gland in my eyelid and my eye swelled up and was sore for days. I couldn't wear concealer for about two weeks. Concealer is the one thing that helps me take on the persona of me 'being together.' Without it, I felt so exposed and very self-conscious (more than normal).

Deborah: I like your outfits, by the way. You always look so professional and polished. (I hope you can hear this?)

Kaur: Hmmm… thank you, and it was hard to hear.

Deborah: In the book, I know you want to remain anonymous. What are you planning to call yourself?

Kaur: I don't know yet, if I'm honest – although I do want to keep my Sikh identity. Largely because I think sexual abuse, exploitation, rape, ritual and faith-based abuse are areas that are not acknowledged or spoken about in the Sikh community. This is something that really does my head in. Because I know that reluctance to engage in conversations about these issues adds another layer of silence, shame and guilt to survivors' experiences.

Deborah: I often wish I'd stayed anonymous. People stare! What's it like to not be known? I almost want to take a step back and be proud of you for keeping your anonymity and vicariously enjoy it somehow. I respect the way you keep your anonymity.

Kaur: Do you really wish you'd stayed anonymous? I can't tell you how much respect I have for you, for putting yourself and your experiences out there, in front of your professional colleagues. I am seriously in awe of your immense courage. And it is phenomenal that you are using your experiences to do something (such as this book and the various articles you have written) that will shape the practice of therapists and also impact on the lives of survivors.

Deborah: Thank you!

Kaur: I only wish I could use my experiences to do something positive. Of course, being anonymous, I can't. Because technically, without saying #MeToo in my own name, I don't really have a voice. That is why I agreed to be part of this book. It is my way of trying to do something positive with these experiences.

Deborah: I think you're doing a brilliant thing. I don't feel that being anonymous compromises that one bit.

Kaur: I wonder if people stare at you because of their inability to comprehend the reasons why someone would share their experiences? Or is it due to them just simply not knowing how to relate to someone who has experienced sexual abuse? I think this says more about the society we live in and the cultural norms that serve to protect the identities of abusers. I think you are amazing for the courage you have shown. For someone like me, who has told only one other person in this world what happened to me, you have helped to shift the secrecy and shame surrounding my experiences a little more.

Deborah: Am I following this correctly? Only your therapist and I know what you've shared?

Kaur: Yeah, that's right.

Deborah: That's such an honour. I felt so warm towards you when you wrote to me. I hope how I responded was OK at the time. I think who one shares with and how they respond is incredibly important. I'm anxious now that I may have got it wrong.

Kaur: No, not at all. I don't know what made me want to share – I don't know why I did. I think I wanted to reach out to you as I was shocked – although it made sense – that you had experienced what you had been through. I was sorry and sad for you. Reflecting, I am actually quite shocked that I did disclose. Maybe some of it was to do with being inspired by your courage to disclose. Some of it was to do with wanting you to know that I understood, that I *really* did understand. Maybe some of it was to do with me feeling alone with my stuff. I don't know. Maybe a mixture of these things.

Deborah: I was so fortunate that the person I told after I told a therapist got the whole thing spot-on. After I said the word, I dissociated so badly that I didn't think I could get back. I couldn't open my eyes for what felt like hours. He just sat with me. He didn't panic, he wasn't speaking, but just knowing he was still there and absolutely present (I could feel it) was so important.

Kaur: This warmed my heart and I am glad you got the support you deserve and needed. Anonymity is important to me (for now), for the reasons I mentioned about culture and family honour. Also, my older brother was one of my abusers. I have always struggled to identify this as 'abuse' because of the feelings that are associated with it. I know that, in the context of the other abuse that was happening at the hands of my other abusers, it was different, and that is why I perhaps felt like this. However, I do now realise that it was an abuse of his power over me. Just thinking about disclosing my experiences, even just to immediate family members, makes me feel uneasy. Would I be believed? What if I wasn't? And what if I was? This would destroy any family I had, and this relates back to my point about being highly empathic – I don't think I could cope with the guilt of knowing that I had destroyed their sense of 'family'. I don't think I could cope with knowing that my experiences had caused them hurt.

Deborah: This is so awful. I really appreciate the dilemma you've been in and are still in, and how long you've been in it.

Kaur: Anonymity is a double-edged sword. At times, I wish people did know. I have next to no support. If I'm triggered, then I have to work my way through it. If I feel some of the old feelings re-surfacing, I have to remind myself of what the 'wiser side' of me knows. It is incredibly lonely at times.

Deborah: I know what that's like and I'm so sorry. I am here for you. I was triggered immensely by something recently, and you were there by email. It really matters that we're there for each other.

Kaur: Thank you, that means a lot. Being triggered is part of everyday life, especially since I read and hear about sexual exploitation in the news and all over social networking pretty much on a daily basis.

Deborah: How is it to do that?

Kaur: It's hard. As much as I don't want to engage with the stories, I still feel compelled to hear/read them. Maybe it is something to do with being able to relate to someone else's experiences. It makes me angry and upset every time I read or hear something to do with sexual violence. I suppose it confirms that there are fucked up people in this world. And some of those fucked up people are my abusers. Never is it to do with the Sikh community. Yet I know it happens, because it happened to me. Culture and religion are two mechanisms that allows the identities of abusers to be hidden and the pain and the suffering of survivors to be silenced. The notion of *izzat* (family honour) is drilled into females from a young age. Through culture, you are already teaching females from a very young age that anything to do with sexual intimacy, abuse or exploitation is a 'threat' to family and community *izzat*. Is it any wonder that survivors feel responsible – wrongly – for what happened to them and are reluctant to come forward or to seek help?

Work and study have been my coping mechanisms from a young age. I was studying for my postgraduate qualifications while I was in therapy. I also worked nights, and then full-time. I have worked since I was young. My parents owned a grocery store, so I used to help out quite a bit, especially as they were also holding down full-time jobs. Work has helped to give me some structure, organisation and goals to work towards. While I was in therapy, work and study were something to focus on, something to help distract my head from being constantly drawn back into the memories, distract from the pains. It sounds really positive that I used work and study as a distraction, right? In a way, it was; in many ways, it wasn't. I have a tendency to run myself down, take on everything, despite knowing I am at breaking point.

Deborah: I just keep going until I suddenly realise I have passed the point where I should have stopped.

Kaur: I am constantly exhausted and drained, although now it is perhaps more due to the children not sleeping. I recognise when I am at the point of exhaustion, but I will rarely take time out for myself. I wonder whether keeping busy is a coping mechanism or a form of self-harm.

My therapist often told me that she was amazed at how I managed to carry on with work and studying while experiencing the constant new memories and flashbacks and on the little sleep I was getting. She was of the view that I coped by compartmentalising my life and keeping different aspects of it separate. To me I was just doing what I needed to make it through the days and nights. But she was right – compartmentalising my life has been one of my coping mechanisms, and I still do it to cope with the daily challenges of life.

Deborah: My therapist was always telling me to put the bad stuff 'in a container' after a session. I couldn't manage it! I love the idea that compartmentalising works for you. It adds to my knowledge as a therapist – that some people are able to work with the idea of 'containers'.

Kaur: There was a time in my life when the new memories were coming back constantly and I wasn't able to put this stuff in a container. Work, study, life and dealing with the backlash of the memories were all one constant blur. It felt like a very long time. The fear, anxiety, shame and self-loathing were always there. I suppose I was (and am) fortunate that I was able to focus my head on other things, even if it was for short periods of time, to give myself the distraction that was needed.

Deborah: I'm wondering how you kept going. I don't know if self-harm was just what was asked or whether it was the case, and you don't have to say, of course.

Kaur: I wonder how I kept going too. I self-harmed in more ways than one through my teenage years and at times when things got 'too much' during my 20s. It was a release, and a form of punishment. I think there is such a focus on the disclosure that everything that happens between the happening and the disclosure is not really acknowledged. How do we cope? How do we manage the consequences of abuse and still keep our lives together? For instance, we are both academics, you are now also a therapist, and we have somehow, despite our experiences, been able to develop successful careers. Would that have been possible without coping strategies? I don't know!

Deborah: In our original email exchange, I also talked about my coping strategies, and I'm absolutely fine about sharing them with you, but I've pulled back in this chapter, aware that I'm not anonymous. I've felt guilty about that and you've reassured me that it's OK, and I thank you for that. We have to work at our own pace.

Kaur: Agreed, and it's fine. I've gone back and removed some of my disclosure too. I'm not yet comfortable with it being out in the public domain.

Deborah: You mention touch in your opening contribution. I assume you mean physical holding? Personally, I believe that touch can be healing. There are those who think that it's contra-indicated for survivors. I think it's been the most powerful part of being in therapy, and my therapist was a man.

Kaur: For sure, I agree, that has been the most powerful part of being in therapy for me too. I was very uncomfortable with any form of physical contact from my therapist for a long time...

Deborah: Yes, me too. In our first hug, I had full control. He just kept his arms out in front.

Kaur: ... and that resulted from feelings of shame, disgust and for a long time feeling 'untouchable'. I even struggled with sitting directly opposite my therapist and being in her line of vision. The shame was too consuming for me. I didn't want to be seen. So she adapted and we used to sit side by side. Allowing her to comfort me and hold me through flashbacks and new memories helped me to keep a sense of 'OK, this is a flashback, it's not happening to me now', and also gave me a sense of someone being there to 'rescue' me back from there.

Deborah: I think it's the 'No, you don't do that with survivors' that upsets me. For me, therapy is art, magic, not 'interventions' by a 'professional'. In person-centred thinking, therapy is a relationship, and touch can be very healing.

Kaur: Physical touch is important – well, it was for me, in helping me to feel safe and secure. Perhaps that is why I recalled so many memories while in therapy. And it helped lessen that constant, overwhelming feeling of shame and that I didn't deserve to be comforted, which is related to the self-blame. Knowing that my therapist knew what was going on in my head, what I was seeing, what I had experienced, and still wanted to console and comfort me took away some of that self-blame and shame. Having someone there who was gentle contradicted the roughness and pain I had experienced. She cared and was bothered about what happened to me, which made me realise that actually what happened to me was wrong and it wasn't my fault.

Deborah: You've finished therapy?

Kaur: My therapist moved away. She offered to put me in contact with other therapists, but I didn't want to start all over again. It took me a long time to develop that relationship with her, plus I had been on a constant rollercoaster of new memories re-surfacing one after the other. Processing the memories mentally and dealing with the emotions that go with it were draining. So perhaps I was ready for a break from therapy. Over those six or seven years I was in therapy, I saw, felt and witnessed things (in my mind's eye) that I never imagined could ever happen to anyone. I was broken, but perhaps not as broken as I would have been if I hadn't had the support of my therapist.

Something that was incredibly important in my journey was the opportunity to write about my feelings, flashbacks, things I'd remembered, and for my therapist to read it. I was not able to say verbally what I had remembered. The shame of trying to convey this was too much for me to cope with. Had I not had the opportunity to write down and email her when I needed to, a lot of what I remembered would have stayed in my head.

Deborah: This process of us writing together has been so powerful. We've shared so much. I would never have thought, all those years ago when we first met, that we'd reach this point. Survivors are everywhere. We aren't really encouraged to 'know' that in society. Your courage in writing to me that day has led us somewhere that I feel so honoured to be.

Kaur: I feel the same. I've learnt a lot through this process of sharing and have come to realise the power of saying #MeToo and identifying with another survivor. I never imagined that I would ever disclose to anyone except my therapist, yet here we are. I appreciate and value that you have been able to share with me and the support you have given to me during this process. It's certainly been a powerful and positive experience.

Reference

Lee DA (2017). Shocking revelation! There are women survivors of sexual violence training as person-centred psychotherapists. *Psychotherapy and Politics International* 15(1): e1396.

Chapter 3

Lighthouses, rocky shores and safe harbours

Concetta Perôt, with Clarinda Cuppage

Since 2012, when the extent of Jimmy Savile's[1] crimes began to be revealed, I, along with millions of others, have listened to wave upon wave of media reports about sexual abuse. It seemed as though a dam had burst. Every new scandal breaking in the media would spark recognition and pain, bringing silent whispers of '*Me* too' to my lips. Abuse by celebrities, by people in power and by various institutions started coming to light. Simultaneously, there has been an uncovering of some of the systemic silencing of victims and the collusion with abusers in various sections of society.

Working on the National Association for People Abused in Childhood (NAPAC) helpline in the post-Savile days was as much a privilege as it was sobering. At times it felt as though every other call was prefixed with 'I've never told anyone what happened to me, but it's in the news all the time and I just can't keep it down anymore.' It seemed to me that the impact of the media coverage was a growing public health issue, triggering buried traumas and bringing people forward to seek help.

Into the midst of these new waves of truth-telling and silence-breaking entered the current iteration of the #MeToo movement, which went viral

---

1. Jimmy Savile (1926-2011) was a British television personality and charity fundraiser who was knighted in 1990. While he was alive, he was the subject of two police investigations for abuse but was never charged. Police investigations after his death recorded allegations against him of the sexual assault of 450 victims aged between five and 75.

on social media in 2017. I see #MeToo as a metaphorical lighthouse in the darkness and confusion. In my view, it has acted and continues to act as a strong focal point and a guide to possible directions forward for society. I think the 'lighthouse effect' of #MeToo lies in its potential to help us connect with our own suppressed truths and with other whisperers of 'Me too'. This inner/outer connection brings some hope that maybe, just maybe, countless victims and survivors of abuse will be able to reach out, find connection and be supported in healing from the harm done to them.

Reflecting on my own experiences as i) a survivor of multiple forms of childhood abuse, ii) a long-standing seeker of help to recover from these experiences, and iii) a helper of other survivors, my feelings of encouragement about the 'lighthouse potential' of #MeToo are, nonetheless, tempered with concerns about the rocky shores that surround us as we seek to find safe (or safer) harbours to process our most distressing individual/societal truths.

In this chapter, I discuss three particular rocky shores and how they relate to our practice as counsellors and psychotherapists: the lack of impact by #MeToo in certain spheres and cultures; the reflex reaction of societal denial when faced with abuse and, last, the effects of inadequate, incompetent and pathologising 'help'.

The lack of #MeToo impact in certain spheres and cultures

Therapists – and others in support roles – need to be aware that the positive 'lighthouse effect' of #MeToo is not equally distributed across all social spheres and cultures. Indeed, some of our clients may be from cultures where there is a desperate lack of public voices to help them 'de-normalise' and voice their own abuse.

The oxygen of publicity provided by celebrities sharing their experiences of sexual violence resulted in the #MeToo phenomenon from 2017 onwards. However, there has been a tendency for the media spotlight to focus on abuse perpetrated by high-profile people or celebrities, leaving in the shadows the more prevalent abuses that happen in the mundane, hidden and domestic spheres of life.

Similarly, while the UK's Independent Inquiry into Child Sexual Abuse (IICSA) has struggled with its already broad remit – abuse in state and non-state institutions – the exclusion of abuse within the 'institution of the family' can inadvertently feed into this minimising dynamic – a point that IICSA readily acknowledged when I raised it.

The danger is that it conveys the message, accidental though it may be, that 'What happened to me doesn't count because I was not abused by a celebrity, footballer or priest'. This has certainly had a negative impact on me, and I have heard clients expressing similar sentiments. Excuse the crude pun, but there is nothing 'media sexy' about being abused by your husband, father, mother or brother in the privacy and mundanity of the domestic sphere. There are no movie stars, red-carpet events or award ceremonies for those of us who have witnessed and experienced abuse in the home.

Similar to these more hidden spheres of life where the #MeToo spotlight has been less visible are the silencing cultures where abuse is 'hidden in full view'. In such cultures, metaphorical lighthouse building is a very risky business, so risky that we dare not whisper 'Me too' in case we are heard and seen. These are the cultures and sub-cultures where abuse is so wound up with historical, institutional and culturally sanctioned power that daring to speak up and bring some accountability carries the risk of being ostracised, branded – or worse.

I grew up in one such culture, the Sicilian immigrant community in 1970s and 1980s London. In Sicilian culture, men have had the right to own their wives and daughters in every way, including sexually – a form of sexual abuse that is rarely written about. Being born female has been seen as a curse. I often reflect on the impact of hearing the so-called blessing, 'May you have many sons,' shouted to the bride and groom at every wedding I went to as a girl. Being a girl was obviously the opposite of a blessing. I instinctively knew this from not having the freedom to attend sport clubs or friends' houses for playdates or sleepovers, or to do normal teenage things like wear make-up – especially once I hit puberty. I had to be chaperoned everywhere by a male member of the family and was explicitly told by my mother that, as women, we had to be submissive and that the violence perpetrated against us was 'a cross we have to bear'. There was no need for the head of the household to hide the bruises he caused, because the culture accepted that he had the absolute right to rule his family and do whatever he deemed necessary to preserve the 'family honour'.

Sicilian culture is glued together with the practice of *omertá*, the honour code inculcated in us that you never, ever speak to anyone outside the family about what goes on within the family, and especially not to any authorities. By writing this, I am breaking that very code. The further south you travel in Italy, the more it becomes an honour-based culture, with practices of honour-related violence. In Italy, until 1981, it was written in statute that, if a person committed a crime such as assault or murder to 'preserve family honour,' this could be used as a mitigating factor in court, allowing perpetrators of family violence to be let off with lighter sentences (Article 587 of the then *Codice Penale*). The first time I ran away from home as a teenager, I was duly returned to my raging father, who told me, 'In Sicily, when girls do this, we kill them. I will let you off this time.'

It is important that we recognise clients in our counselling rooms who have experienced abuse in silencing cultures, like my own. Some of these sub-cultures, like my Anglo-Italian/Sicilian one, may not be immediately obvious to practitioners. Some, as we have seen in the media, may be cultures based around workplaces or professions. It is incumbent on us to be culturally sensitive therapists, in line with our ethical frameworks, taking responsibility for educating ourselves with regards to our clients' cultural contexts (BACP, 2018). In so doing, we stand a greater chance of tuning into any cultural power dynamics that may be silencing our clients. Such messages include, 'Don't speak; don't make a fuss; what happened to you is nothing; it's normal, it does not matter. It is shameful to even think about telling people outside of the family what goes on in the family.'

How do those of us who have experienced abuse within these silencing cultures find our voice if it is so risky to speak up? We may desperately seek others from our culture with similar experiences, through books, social media or groups. I have searched for writings by others from my Anglo-Italian/Sicilian culture to whom I can say 'Me too'. After 20 years, my search has led to practically nothing – a few historical accounts (mostly in the US) and certainly nothing contemporary. Perhaps it is time for me to begin contributing to the creation of a cultural narrative – a new lighthouse – so that the #MeToo lightbeams may start to penetrate the thick fog in the Italian-Sicilian immigrant community?

Societal denial when faced with abuse

The #MeToo movement has helped to carve out a space in time when abuse in all its various ugly manifestations – sexual, physical, emotional, psychological, financial, perpetrated towards children and adults – has become more visible. These abuses have always existed under our noses and are slowly coming into the light.

This moment of relative openness is full of potential for human evolution. However, our ability to sustain a society-wide conversation about abuse is delicate and fragile. At times, observing the #MeToo movement has felt like watching a heavy lorry crossing a rickety bridge – wondering if the bridge will buckle under the weight of previously untold truths. Will we see an evolution in the way we respond to disclosures and the long-term impact of abuse? Responses include those of friends, family, cultural and religious communities, social workers, police and the criminal justice system, schools, healthcare professionals and, of course, counsellors, psychotherapists and mental health practitioners. Research with the latter group has found that abuse histories are not being routinely asked about and identified among clients in mental health settings, and that, where abuse is disclosed, it is frequently not met with appropriate help (Read et al, 2017, 2018). Is this evidence of a societal reflex to avoid discussions about abuse, even among those trained to respond to mental distress?

The unholy trinity of dismissing, denying and blaming is familiar to many survivors. The pain of being met by such responses is a common thread in what survivors tell me, both while I was on the NAPAC national helpline and at the many peer events I have helped facilitate through Survivors' Voices, a UK peer-led organisation of which I am a co-founder. Many have been labelled 'mad' or 'bad', or have simply been ignored, shunned and silenced when they have sought to say what has happened, whether to a teacher, family member, priest, doctor or mental health practitioner.

Disclosure is not a one-off event. Many barriers stand in the way of speaking about what has happened along the full length of a survivor's journey: from the abuse to their present day. This might include attempts at disclosure when the abuse happened and first disclosures as part of help-seeking years later – often at crisis points in life – right through to attempts to tell the fuller details of our experiences in order to process the trauma. All these points of disclosure are fraught with the potential to be met with dismissive or harmful responses. The barriers to disclosure can be both internal to the client and external in professional cultures and individual practitioners. Often cited by professionals is their own fear of causing distress by 'opening Pandora's box' and not knowing what to do or say (Young et al, 2001). The pros and cons of professional routine enquiry into abuse experiences can be debated (Read, Hammarsley & Rudegeair, 2007; Scott et al, 2015a). Research evidence suggests that survivors have a preference to being asked routinely about abuse, in order to remove the burden of disclosure from them (Scott et al, 2015b; Smith, Dogaru & Ellis, 2015). Yet, it is not just *whether* we ask about abuse experiences in the course of our work; it is also *how* we ask and the *context and environment* in which the asking is done that help or hinder survivors in feeling safe enough to tell.

Sadly, you cannot discuss barriers to disclosure without also acknowledging attitudes of denial and victim-blaming among professionals. These have frequently come to light at Survivors' Voices peer-gatherings that I co-facilitate. Comments such as these are not uncommon:

> I had a therapist who said 'Of course, one thinks that they remember an event from childhood when actually very little of what they remember is actually true,' and when I asked her if she believed me, went on to say

that it shouldn't matter to me whether or not she believed me about the abuse.

I went to a specialist psychotherapist who, when I told him about my abuse, would not listen to me and refused to validate my experience.

A psychotherapist said to me in a harsh, stern voice, 'So, if your father was as abusive as you say he was, why were you attached to him?'

As long as there is even a hint of denial and disbelief, survivors will not feel safe enough to bring up their experiences of trauma, which are often buried deep within them and encased in fear and shame. From many years of listening to people who have experienced abuse share their journeys, as well as from my own experience of seeking therapy, I know there is a reflex to turn away from the horror of abuse, even within those professions supposedly trained in deep listening. This avoidance reflex can be seen as a 'communal dissociation' from that which is too hard to bear. Avoidance as a healthy protective movement of the psyche is familiar to all humans, survivors and non-survivors alike. However, when avoidance persists and becomes embodied in cultures, systems and professions, it can morph into the unholy trinity of dismissing, denying, and blaming.

This repetition of dismissive, denying, and blaming reactions by helping professionals, whether intentional or not, can deeply retraumatise survivors. As therapists, we need to continuously check our own internal processes in response to abuse. Am I being avoidant and fearful of what the client is sharing? Am I being dismissive? Am I blaming the client for their 'symptoms' of distress? Am I disbelieving them? Supervision is critical to help us develop in-the-moment awareness to help prevent inadvertent collusion with this societal avoidance reflex. Failure to be aware can inadvertently unleash the silencing dynamic in our counselling rooms, reinforcing the shame and secrecy expertly internalised in survivors by those who have harmed us.

A good starting point for counsellors and psychotherapists is to seek out survivor-led training, in order to gain nuanced expertise on how best to respond to survivors, hidden or otherwise, who come to therapy. At Survivors' Voices, we conducted a survivor-led research project in partnership with King's College, London and the Wellcome Foundation, which resulted in a charter for organisations on how to engage abuse survivors safely, meaningfully and effectively (Perôt & Chevous, 2018). This is being used to guide training and good practice. One of the good practice points in the Charter states:

> Instead of avoiding the subject of abuse, we will learn to ask well, work collaboratively with survivors and give choice in a safe and supportive atmosphere.

Intentionally creating a safe environment for clients to disclose and process abuse is critical, and we can use models such as polyvagal theory to guide us (Porges, 2011). We can also learn from initiatives such as Identification & Referral to Improve Safety (IRIS) in primary care, which intentionally creates environments that will facilitate disclosure of domestic violence, such as GPs using prompt questions, posters on the back of toilet doors, GP training in how to recognise and respond to signs of possible domestic abuse and creation of clear referral pathways (Feder et al, 2011).

Inadequate, incompetent and pathologising 'help'

The hope of the 'lighthouse effect' of #MeToo is that it leads to an increase in help-seeking. The fear is that those seeking help do not get it.

I spent some of my psychotherapy training at a specialist counselling service for adult survivors of all forms of child abuse. Like most other specialist third-sector abuse support services, it has seen a significant increase in referrals and a lengthening (and, in some agencies, closure) of waiting lists (Halliday, 2015). In 2019, I attended a meeting of the UK All Party Parliamentary Group (APPG) on Adult Survivors of Child Sexual Abuse. Evidence presented by third sector agencies, civil servants and parliamentarians to its survey of adult survivors about access to support (APPG, 2019) was the first official acknowledgement I have heard of the public health issue represented by the unmet needs of the large numbers of people who have come forward seeking help post-Savile/#MeToo.

Despite the UK government's pledge to provide lifelong support for survivors of sexual assault and childhood sexual abuse (although, notably, not other forms of childhood abuse), this is yet to be matched with funding for long-term therapy (NHS England, 2018). Such therapy is needed by many survivors, in parallel with capacity-building in the survivor sector, which often provides the most nuanced, specialist support that is most trusted by survivors (Bond, Ellis & McCusker, 2018). My time as a psychotherapist in one such agency left me concerned that the struggling charitable survivor sector is being used by GPs and statutory mental health services as a referral route for people experiencing complex trauma, without any follow-through money, effectively covering up enormous failures in statutory provision and putting these already struggling organisations under intolerable strain.

In addition to this systemic incapacity to respond in a timely and appropriate way to the scale of human need being uncovered, I am concerned that the increase in help-seeking is not being met with a skilled and competent workforce that can bear to hear the details of trauma without falling foul of potentially retraumatising approaches and responses. In more than 25 years of seeking therapy to recover from my abuse, I have been harmed and retraumatised on several occasions due to basic incompetence of (mostly) well-meaning therapists, some of them specialist 'trauma' therapists. It has contributed significantly to setbacks in my recovery.

From listening to hundreds of survivors in our Survivors' Voices peer groups, I know I am not alone. Many of us are being repeatedly failed by therapists across the private, NHS and third sectors. To add insult to injury, some have been blamed by their therapists for the 'failure' of therapy. It was partly the learning I have gained from these experiences and the deep wisdom of fellow survivors that led me to train as a therapist.

Added to the accounts of unhelpful therapy are the disturbing experiences of trauma survivors caught up in the mental health system, crashing against the hazards of misdiagnosis and misuse of medication emanating from a biomedical model that is focused on 'What is wrong with you?' rather than asking, 'What has happened to you?' (Watson, 2019). Alternative, relational models of responding to mental distress that recognise the significance of power imbalances and societal and environmental influences on mental wellbeing are emerging, such as Open Dialogue (Seikkula, 2003) and the Power Threat Meaning Framework (Johnstone & Boyle, 2018). However, what I perceive as the pernicious biomedical approach dominates, placing the 'abnormality' in the individual and their 'symptoms' rather than with, first, the perpetrators who caused the harm and, second, the social systems that dismiss, deny, blame and continue to support perpetrators so they continue to live with impunity. When distress and symptoms are rooted in the trauma of abuse, such pathologising responses merely perpetuate the legacy of the original abuse.

One of the most significant moments for me was when a skilled and deeply compassionate therapist put Judith Herman's *Trauma & Recovery* in my hands and encouraged me to educate myself about my trauma 'because knowledge is power' (Herman, 1997). How right he was. I am deeply grateful to him for both this intervention and the equalising way he worked with me, seeing me as a partner in the process rather than as the unwell client and himself as the expert who was going to 'cure' me.

Reading Judith Herman's book changed me by lifting the heavy label of 'abnormal' from my shoulders. I finally understood that what I had been experiencing internally since my teenage years was not because there was something wrong with me; rather that the wrongness lay in the harm that had been done to me; that my mind and body were (cleverly) having completely normal, protective responses to years and years of threat and trauma that were still activating my nervous system due to the lack of a safe place to let the trauma out. I was 32 when I finally found a therapist with whom I felt safe and who helped me make sense of what had happened in my life. Sadly, the constraints of a time-limited NHS service (20 sessions) meant that the work of processing my trauma in this safe therapeutic space with this wise, kind man was not possible, adding another layer of grief. I was sent back into the wilderness in search of a good-enough therapist but continued to amass a sad catalogue of unhelpful therapeutic experiences.

If prevalence statistics are an indicator of the numbers of 'disclosed' and 'undisclosed' survivors coming through our counselling rooms (ONS, 2019), being competent to respond helpfully is not just the remit of specialist services and trauma therapists, of which there are not enough to meet the huge need. Survivors have much to teach our profession about what works, what helps and what hinders. This is an area that we at Survivors' Voices have begun researching (Melvin & Perôt, 2018) and we are currently working on a version of the Charter for Engaging Abuse Survivors specifically for counselling and psychotherapy.

In line with our ethical professional principles of beneficence and non-maleficence (BACP, 2018), practitioners need to be aware of, and desist from, interventions that are harmful to survivors and be able to give a helpful response to people with abuse experiences. However, if the anecdotal evidence we hear at Survivors' Voices is anything to go by, something is clearly amiss in our professional training and supervision. It is time for our professional counselling and psychotherapy bodies to enter meaningful dialogue with survivor organisations and survivor counsellors in order to, first, research the nature and scale of harmful therapy that is occurring for survivors and second, agree changes in training curricula to include core competencies for responding to survivors of abuse, in order to prevent harmful responses and promote helpful ones.

Building more lighthouses

In my 20s I began the task of writing down my own story, simply because I needed to externalise the mountain of violent and abusive experiences within me. This difficult task remains unfinished, partly for the lack of safe therapeutic space to hold me while I write. As a way of beginning to build a lighthouse from within my culture, I will give the last part of this chapter to the voice of my 20-something self, written in 2000, way before #MeToo. I describe an event that occurred just before I ran away, aged 16 and very vulnerable due to years of suffering and observing abuse and extreme control in my home just outside London.

> While I toyed with the desire to run away, a chance encounter with a young woman galvanised my resolve. Her father was a '*paesano*,' a fellow Sicilian. He came around to our house one day with her in tow. I didn't know her, can't even remember her name, just that she was of a similar age to me. He and Dad were talking business in the living room. She sat on the sofa, silent. I was ordered to the kitchen to make Italian espresso coffee for Dad and the man. I came back in and served the coffee in little espresso cups. Still she sat, silent, subdued. I remember looking at her and being shocked, thinking, 'My God, she is like a blank piece of paper.' I also observed and felt a palpable dynamic between her and her father. It was as though she herself didn't exist but was merely a puppet who responded to the tugs and pulls from her father's hand. Looking at her was like looking in a mirror at myself in two years' time – no struggle left, just compliance. The image and feel of her sitting on that sofa seared into me. 'I do not want to become like that and if I stay I will.'
>
> The glimpse of what could be if I didn't leave gave me some strength. I am thankful to that girl, in a guilty kind of way, since I wonder what happened to her life – to the life inside of her. When I think of her, I also wonder how many other Italian/Sicilian daughters there are like her in British society. How many women from my culture are there who understand this experience of having your very self taken from you by a warped father's desire and 'right' to own and occupy 'his' daughter? 'Colonisation' is one term I have heard used to refer to such a state of psychological ownership – where the abuser's own thoughts and feelings have been expertly internalised into the victim to the extent that he doesn't need to be present to control her. His voice is so strong inside of her (and often indistinguishable from her own) that his ownership of her life continues, regardless of distance, time – or even death.
>
> This possessive attitude to women is something we more readily associate with some modern-day Arab/Asian cultures or more distant British history. Yet in modern day Sicily/Southern Italy (which is, after all, part of Europe) and, more extremely, in the immigrant communities abroad, this treatment of Italian/Sicilian women persists,

> hidden, unexamined, unchecked. Such socially sanctioned, ignored and condoned ownership (slavery?) of one human over another, combined with bad power and immigrant insularity (and add some psychological pathology), has created dark, secret places where abuse thrives. It is akin to the 'secret' yet corporately sanctioned power abuses in the prison cells of apartheid South Africa, except that there is no recognisable liberation movement and little or no cultural narratives about the experience of this oppressive social and family system.
>
> When the narrative comes, the light begins to shine. Until then, the badness will thrive in the dark places and the victims who dare to speak out will be ostracised as mad or bad. Is the sad, blank, puppet-daughter still out there, hungry to hear another's story that validates her own and helps her in her struggle to heal and own herself? Is she desperate to tell her own story but can find no one within her culture who is willing to stand with her and say, 'Me too', thus giving her the courage to break her silence? Perhaps she has died psychologically, so that the part of her that was born to sing and grow into her own uniqueness is just a distant ghost in her memory. Or maybe she didn't survive at all.

When I re-read those words of my younger self, particularly my clearly articulated need for someone to whom to say 'Me too', I am saddened that, years later, I am still seeking. The process of continuing to write my story remains precarious, since the emotional impact and the risk of putting my head above the parapet by speaking out requires skilled, long-term therapeutic support that, until now, has sadly been lacking for me.

Indeed, our task as therapists may involve supporting survivors who engage in what Judith Herman refers to as 'survivor mission', including protesting, researching, helping others professionally or through peer support, writing, social media campaigning and public speaking. It is imperative that we do not pathologise survivors who engage in such actions by viewing their abuse history as a weakness, and instead support and honour their desire to change the world with what they have experienced. For the world desperately needs more survivors, particularly those of us from hidden and silenced communities, to speak out. Without such survivors' voices in the public narrative, there is no #MeToo and no lighthouse to guide us home.

Conclusions

As therapists, we may have the privilege of accompanying clients on their journeys, from first daring to whisper 'Me too', to slowly describing the details of their abuse and, if they wish it, speaking more openly or publicly about their experiences in order to bring their abusers to account or to help others. At every stage, our work must entail intentionally developing safety with our clients to support all levels of disclosure. We must work with awareness of the metaphorical rocks that surround us, and are sometimes within us, as we respond to what is evoked by the #MeToo movement. In particular, we must open our eyes and ears to the more hidden places and silenced cultures where abuse thrives unchecked, so that we may support the millions of whispers, words, calls and shouts that still need to be uttered.

Response from Clarinda Cuppage

I find your metaphor so apt – #MeToo and the lighthouse effect supporting survivors to safer harbours, yet the rocks and 'communal dissociation', both from professionals and society more generally, being massive barriers to responding helpfully to survivors.

During my time as a NAPAC helpline volunteer, I too was shocked to discover how poorly survivors have been supported. To have suffered such abuse and not to be effectively, professionally helped is a double tragedy. The associated trauma manifestations of abuse are not widely understood, and survivors may be diagnosed and labelled as mentally ill in mental health services while the trauma of sexual abuse remains untreated. Is it enough to treat people for their presenting conditions, 'eating disorders,' 'substance abuse', 'self-harm' and so forth without making the link with underlying trauma and referring them to specialist support? We are only treating half the issue.

I, too, would like to see our profession become more engaged and I support your recommendation for a meaningful discussion between survivor organisations and professional bodies. I think some form of routine inquiry is appropriate, and not only within the counselling profession. The findings from work based on the Adverse Childhood Experiences (ACE) studies (Felitti et al, 1998) are a good starting point. If carried out appropriately, routine inquiry could relieve survivors of the burden of disclosure by offering them an invitation and language to talk about their experiences, and would enable therapists, where needed, to refer on. Some experienced therapists prefer not to work with survivors, which should not be judged.

My journey with professional support was also not straightforward. After attempts with kind but unskilled therapists, I nearly gave up trying. When I finally met a professional who understood abuse within a power and trauma framework, I started releasing the shame and self-blame that permeated my life and began to make sense of my trauma responses. Survivors don't necessarily know what they need, but they hope that we professionals are better informed. It is the voices of lived experience that create change and the charter for organisation on engaging abuse survivors will be an excellent, much-needed resource.

Your account of the shocking honour bond in Sicilian families illustrates the power used to silence, and the situation for silenced groups and communities. It will, I hope, inform survivors from similar cultures and families and highlight for therapists some of the dangers clients face if they disclose. It takes courage to speak up and break the code. The power of personal testimony to reach others cannot be underestimated. It is a beacon of light that starts to dissolve the isolation and loneliness that many survivors experience.

Although there is a long way to go before we get beyond dismissing, denying and blaming, I am seeing small rays of light. The NHS Sexual Assault and Abuse Strategy (NHS England, 2018) recognises that the consequences of sexual abuse are often misunderstood and neglected and that survivors of non-recent abuse need therapeutic care that acknowledges the 'lifelong consequences on mental health and physical and emotional wellbeing' (p10), and includes involving victims and survivors in the development of services as one of its core priorities.

Like you, I wanted to challenge the limited understanding of the impact of sexual abuse and developed an awareness-raising project, also called Survivors' Voices, with the charity One in Four.[2] This work aims to educate and inform others and is based on survivors' accounts about the impact of abuse on their lives. The first project focused on people abused in the family context, and the second on addiction and childhood sexual abuse as the underlying trauma. By sharing these survivors' accounts with professionals in the learning environment, we aim to prepare them to listen to and support those who they doubtless will encounter in their work.

#MeToo provides a unique opportunity, but you are right, we need more voices to speak out, including from within our profession, where there must be many, if we are to overcome the barriers and communal dissociation. Without them, countless people will continue to suffer unnecessarily.

---

2. www.oneinfour.org.uk/survivors-voices-uk

References

APPG Adult Survivors of Childhood Sexual Abuse (2019). *Can Adult Survivors of Childhood Sexual Abuse Access Justice and support? Part one: achieving quality information and support for survivors.* London: APPGSurvivorsCSA.

BACP (2018). *Ethical Framework for the Counselling Professions.* Lutterworth: BACP.

Bond E, Ellis F, McCusker J (2018). *I'll Be a Survivor for the Rest of my Life.* [Online.] Ipswich: University of Suffolk/Survivors in Transition. www.uos.ac.uk/sites/default/files/'I'll be a survivor for the rest of my life' Report FINAL.pdf (accessed 3 September 2018).

Codice Penale. *Articolo 587* (Undated). Available at: www.altalex.com/documents/news/2014/10/28/dei-delitti-contro-la-persona (accessed 8 September 2018).

Feder G, Agnew Davies R, Baird K, Dunne D, Eldridge S, Griffiths C, Gregory A, Howell A, Johnson M, Ramsay J, Rutterford C, Sharp D. (2011). Identification and referral to improve safety (IRIS) of women experiencing domestic violence with a primary care training and support programme: a cluster randomised controlled trial. *The Lancet* 378(9805): 1788–1795.

Felitti VJ, Anda RF, Nordenberg D, Williamson DF, Spitz AM, Edwards V, Koss MP, Marks JS (1998). Relationship of childhood abuse and household dysfunction to many of the leading causes of death in adults: the Adverse Childhood Experiences (ACE) study. *American Journal of Preventative Medicine* 14(4): 245–258.

Halliday J (2015). Sex abuse charity funding crisis sees up to 10,000 in UK wait a year for help. *The Guardian*; 11 August. www.theguardian.com/society/2015/aug/11/sex-abuse-charity-funding-crisis (accessed 12 September 2018).

Herman JL (1997). *Trauma and Recovery.* New York, NY: Basic Books.

Johnstone L, Boyle M, with Cromby J, Dillon J, Harper D, Kinderman P, Longden E, Pilgrim D, Read J (2018). *The Power Threat Meaning Framework: towards the identification of patterns in emotional distress, unusual experiences and troubled or troubling behaviour, as an alternative to functional psychiatric diagnosis.* Leicester: British Psychological Society.

Melvin K, Perôt C (2018). *The River of Recovery: reflections from a gathering of survivors.* [Online.] Survivors' Voices. Available at https://survivorsvoices.org/riverofrecovery (accessed 12 September 2018).

NHS England (2018). *Strategic Direction for Sexual Assault and Abuse Services.* London: NHS England. www.england.nhs.uk/publication/strategic-direction-for-sexual-assault-and-abuse-services (accessed 10 September 2018).

ONS (2019). Child Abuse Extent and Nature, England and Wales: year ending March 2019. Newport: ONS. www.ons.gov.uk/peoplepopulationandcommunity/crimeandjustice/articles/childabuseextentandnatureenglandandwales/yearendingmarch2019?hootPostID=3266e3b1c996e0dc1c36e0bbe70da235 (accessed 1 March 2020).

Perôt C, Chevous J (2018). *Turning Pain into Power: a charter for organisations engaging abuse survivors in projects, research and service development.* [Online.] Survivors' Voices. http://survivorsvoices.org/charter

Porges S (2011). *The Polyvagal Theory.* New York, NY: WW Norton & Co.

Read J, Hammersley P, Rudegeair T (2007). Why, when and how to ask about childhood abuse. *Advances in Psychiatric Treatment* 13(2): 101–110.

Read J, Harper D, Tucker I, Kennedy A (2018). How do mental health services respond when child abuse or neglect become known? A literature review. *International Journal of Mental Health Nursing 27*(6): 1606–1617.

Read J, Harper D, Tucker I, Kennedy A (2017). Do adult mental health services identify child abuse and neglect? A systematic review. *International Journal of Mental Health Nursing 27*(1): 7–19.

Scott S, Williams J, McNaughton Nicholls C, McManus S, Brown A, Harvey S, Kelly L, Lovett J (REVA team) (2015a). *Guidance for Trust Managers: implementing and sustaining routine enquiry about violence and abuse in mental health services.* Responding Effectively to Violence and Abuse (REVA project). Briefing 2. North Dalton: DMSS.

Scott S, Williams J, McNaughton Nicholls C, McManus S, Brown A, Harvey S, Kelly L, Lovett J (REVA team) (2015b). *A Briefing for Commissioners: what survivors of violence and abuse say about mental health services.* Responding Effectively to Violence and Abuse (REVA project). Briefing 4. London: NatCen. www.natcen.ac.uk/media/1057981/REVA_Brief-4_Guidance-for-commissioners_FINAL_071015.pdf (accessed 10 September 2018). www.dmss.co.uk/pdfs/REVA-Brief-2-Guidance-for-Trust-managers-FINAL-071015.pdf (accessed 5 September 2018).

Seikkula J (2003). Open dialogue integrates individual and systemic approaches in serious psychiatric crises. *Smith College Studies in Social Work 73*(2): 227–245.

Smith N, Dogaru C and Ellis F (2015). *Hear me. Believe me. Respect me. A survey of adult survivors of child sexual abuse and their experience of support services.* Ipswich: University Campus, Suffolk/Suffolk and Survivors in Transition. www.uos.ac.uk/sites/default/files/basic_file/Focus-on-Survivors-Final-Copy-Logo-Blk.pdf (accessed 3 September 2018).

Watson J (ed) (2019). *Drop the Disorder! Challenging the culture of psychiatric diagnosis.* Monmouth: PCCS Books.

Young M, Read J, Barker-Collo S, Harrison R. (2001). Evaluating and overcoming barriers to taking abuse histories. *Professional Psychology: Research and Practice 32*(4): 407–414.

Chapter 4

How we talk to girls about 'sex'

Taylor Broughton, with
Sarah J. Wilson

In this chapter, I will explore how we might combine sex-positive conversations with the realities of sexual assault, encouraging nuance when we talk with girls about 'sex'.

Research on adolescent sexuality reveals that 70% of young people have 'had sex' by the age of 19 (Harden, 2014). A sex-positive approach sees women as sexual subjects and aligns with 'pro-sex feminism' (Glick, 2000: 20). It regards consensual sexual activities among teens as healthy and potentially positive, rather than socially problematic, morally wrong or a health concern (Harden, 2014). While I can align myself with the benefits of this, because I believe teens would be hugely empowered by an educated, healthy view of their sexual body sooner rather than later, I am concerned that it can mean the prevalence of sexual assault is ignored or underplayed. Research also shows that one in four girls experience sexual violence, and up to one third of adolescent girls report their first sexual experience as forced (World Health Report, 2002). While there is research aligning the feminist sex-positive movement with politics and wider societal issues, there is limited attention to how it aligns with adolescent sexual education.

Drawing from the ongoing movements of #MeToo and #TimesUp, and my own history of sexual assault, I argue that current feminist sex-positive conversations are not addressing all of the difficulties girls face as they form their sexuality/sexualities. Here, I define 'sexuality' as the potential for positive, healthy development into a 'self-motivated sexual actor' (Tolman, 1994: 20). I refer to 'sexualities' to recognise the variety of ways in which sexuality may be expressed – or not. I argue that feminist sex-positive education is important for forming sexuality, but only alongside the realities of sexual assault stories.

We need to speak about the complexities of sexuality today. This includes sexual assault stories as well as sex-positive conversations. To me, these topics often seem polarised, just as sexual assault and open-minded sex conversations are not integrated. Although I believe speaking out about sexual assault is aligned with the sex-positive movement, I wonder if sexual assault taints the sex-positive approach? Kaplan's book *Sex Positive Law* (2014), for instance, does not mention rape or sexual assault until the last three pages. I argue that we can't be prepared for consensual, safe formations of sex without first being educated about sexual assault.

When I was a trainee therapist, a client brought her story of sexual assault. I spent the following week reliving my own story. To varying extents, I will always relive my trauma when I hear the stories of others, whether they be from a client, friend, a news article or a television programme. Healing is not linear; it is a process worked through repeatedly and often unexpectedly. Therapy did not erase sexual assault from my life story. Commonplace conversations around sexual assault are terrifying. There is often a casualness to them, when actually something very dark and complex is being talked of.

What upset me was not that I was shocked by my client's story – the act of sexual assault is still shocking to me and must continue to be; I would worry if we ceased to be shocked about terrible things happening. I was not shocked by the story. I have heard wave after wave of such stories. They are always tales of not being listened to, of feeling stunned and of guilt. I've heard them from friends, sisters, acquaintances, colleagues, strangers on the internet, not just as a therapist. The content varies: men in bars, partners, friends of friends. The narrative is very familiar.

A young woman sits across from me and shakes with tears; she has bruises all over her body. She huffs about what a major inconvenience this is to her life. I cry because both of these things are true: surviving sexual assault is unspeakably terrible, and then we have to survive beyond the interruption. I cry because she apologises for telling me. I write this in the hope that women will no longer feel they have to apologise for telling their story, now or in the future. This chapter is me being unapologetic for my own story in hope of inspiring further conversations. My story exists in a greater narrative about how female sexuality is viewed. My context is growing up in America and being fearful of how current politics dismiss sexual assault. I write because the pain and frustration and confusion all exist together. There is ambivalence after trauma.

As an American woman and a working therapist, I am often asked how I feel about our current president, Donald Trump, and about #MeToo and #TimesUp. Girls growing up in Trump's world, in America and elsewhere, are, I believe, inspired by the fight for women to have a sophisticated voice about their sexuality: to be listened to and believed about injustice and the historical, gendered battle for survival against violence. The #MeToo movement has created a space for women to reclaim a sexual identity post-sexual assault by generating a new narrative about how sex, and the existence of rape, are discussed publicly. There are girls among us still fighting for our voice in this world. The girls of tomorrow will, I hope, hear our voices and be able to craft their own truths. When they/we use their/our voices, I hope they/we will do so unapologetically. Women do not need to apologise for someone deciding to sexually assault them. Women do not need to apologise for speaking about it. The #MeToo and #TimesUp movements are testimony to this.

Too often sex research is split into sexual assault prevention *or* sex-positive research. I am writing this chapter to call for an exploration of what falls between the cracks in this distinction. Breanne Fahs (2014) wrote a beautiful paper that advances the sex-positive movement to include not only women's right to *freedom to* expand their sexual expression, but also women's need for *freedom from* doing what others require of them. The conversation has to include 'orgasm, rape and sexual coercion, body hair as "personal choice", sexual satisfaction, and treatment for sexual dysfunction' (Fahs, 2014: 1). Fahs begins a sex-positive conversation that celebrates the exhilarating freedom of sexuality but also discusses the regressive attacks on women's rights. The sex-positive movement has trumpeted 'positive liberties' for female sexuality but often ignores 'negative liberties', such as oppression and social requirements about female sexuality (Fahs, 2014: 1). Deborah Tolman has written widely on the power dynamics in young women's sexuality, such as in *Doing Desire* (1994), showing that these discussions are not new but unnervingly stagnant. Tolman (1994) fears that if sexuality for girls is culturally problematic, they lose the ability to be empowered by their desire.

So how do we talk about sex to girls? This may sound like a very simple question. But the more I write, the more ambiguous the question feels. I think this is because often sex isn't really talked about with girls – at least, not in an informative way, like the sex-positive approach suggests, or in a way that informs girls about the differences between pleasure, coercion and violence (such as sexual assault realities).

Right now, I feel many people are speaking but not enough questions are being asked. There's a lot to be curious about. Why is sexual assault talked about so easily, without question? It is a shocking thing, but it's become normalised. Why are we not questioning how sexual assault and an over-sexualised culture exist together? There seems to be a contradiction in the growing number of sexual assault prevention programmes on university campuses when more than one in four women will experience sexual assault while attending university (Association of American Universities, 2019). American culture contains a strange mix of aggressive sexuality in the music industry, reality television shows and on Instagram, yet a complete lack of sexual education beyond pregnancy prevention. We live in a culture that screams how empowering it is to be a sexy woman while the sexual assault statistics and testimonies escalate around us. It's surreal, and women's consent and pleasure don't seem to feature in the conversation at all.

We need to connect these cultural ideas of what 'sexy' is with how 'sex' is taught in schools. Sexual education in the US school system is basically about abstinence, and yet the country boasts how much sex sells through the film industry, advertisements on TV and social media, and through mainstream music. If there is no dialogue, rape culture is left unchecked and there is no space for girls to ask questions. Kate Harding (2015) has written about how eager present-day America is to make excuses for rapists, rather than believe victims. Has this reached the place where it may do most damage – where young people are taught about sex?

Sexual assault is currently not normally included in sexual education, either at home or in school. A movement in the 1990s introduced education on 'dating violence' in American schools. More recent studies showed that middle-school relationship violence rates were so high that such interventions were coming too late, suggesting dating violence should be taught at a primary level (Taylor et al, 2013). Unsurprisingly, this hasn't happened. Sexual violence is a subject nobody wants to talk about, especially with young children. But if we don't include sexual assault in abstinence-only education, girls who are sexually active or who have been sexually assaulted can feel worthless (Lynch, 2017).

It may feel daunting to know your teenage daughter is having sex, let alone imagine her being sexually assaulted. But this is exactly my point. Without your teenage daughter knowing what sexual assault is, she may form her notions of sexuality from negative sexual experiences that she assumes to be 'normal'. She will assume painful sex, boring sex, or any sex that isn't fun and exciting will be 'sex'. There's a chance that, with more experience and partners, her framework of 'sex' could evolve, which is the best-case scenario. However, there's also a chance that she will never experience healthy, enjoyable, safe sex.

Girls will be unable to learn by comparison if they can't talk to anyone about it. In my opinion, the worst way we can talk about sex is to instil shame. If a girl is taught that anything 'sexual' is 'bad,' we are already teaching her that her sexuality is 'wrong'. The development of sexual feelings (or not) and sexual preferences is natural, but female sexuality is still particularly controversial (Bass, 2016). Male sexuality has typically been accepted and applauded; women's sexuality is often suppressed or reduced down to the issue of family planning. These are very mixed messages for girls: your purpose is to make babies, but you should not be having (let alone enjoying) sex. These are contradictory messages, full of uncompromising double standards (Lees, 1993).

I was the youngest of four daughters and was taught about sex after my parents found out I was having sex with my then boyfriend at the age of 17. My sexual education was having my phone, car and computer access taken away. My parents told me they were upset with me for lying about my sexual activity. If I kept going at this rate, I was told, imagine how many people I would sleep with by the time I was 20. I was rushed to a gynaecologist to be tested for pregnancy and STDs. The doctor insinuated I wouldn't know I was safe from STDs, even if my partner told me I was his first, because he could be lying. I remember feeling very confused, angry and humiliated. I was a full-time athlete preparing to leave for college, I had rock-star grades, I was on the birth-control pill and was having consensual sex with a long-term partner, using condoms. Why was this – one of many big choices I had to make for my body – not a choice *I* was allowed to make? My sexual education is not one I would wish upon girls. It taught me to be scared and it taught me that my decisions around sexuality didn't matter.

That year I was raped by my boyfriend. I didn't call it that. We called it 'the bad night'. I did not tell anybody. I knew what happened was terrible and wrong. I felt terrible. I felt wrong. I stayed with my boyfriend for years. I didn't feel I had a voice around my sexuality. Like many other people who experience sexual assault, with hindsight I wondered why I didn't handle it differently. Why didn't I ask him to leave and immediately tell my parents when they got home? The answer is really sad. I was embarrassed. It was my fault my sexuality existed, whether the experience was positive or negative. I had been warned not to have sex. Even though sexual violence was not a subject of conversation in our house, the message was clear. I was mortified by how powerless I felt.

How could I have been empowered in my sexuality? Guarding girls' innocence around sex or punishing their innate interest in their sexuality leaves them under-educated and de-powered. Girls need a safe space to explore and understand sexuality, to be curious, to ask questions and to feel secure. 'Sex-positive' conversations are meeting '#MeToo' stories head on. If we are to empower young girls to accept, explore, consent and be educated about their sexuality, we have to educate them on what sexual assault is.

Sex-positive conversations encourage girls to discover their sexuality in an unashamed, educated way. The sex-positive movement began with research by Wilhelm Reich (1971), and his work is still relevant today. There has even been movement to institute a statutory sex-positive framework, which would influence family law, rape law and sex work and prostitution (Kaplan, 2014). Harden (2014) describes using a sex-positive model to research adolescent sexuality, which would introduce an open-minded approach rather than the current focus on abstinence or sexual deviancy.

Melanie Beres is publishing incredible research on consent and anti-sexual violence activism and education for young people within a feminist framework (for example, Beres, 2014). Her description of how to tackle miscommunication between sexual partners offers a sound foundation for reforming our sexual education programmes (Beres, 2010). She (Berers, 2014) focuses on sex as something that is negotiated, requiring a clear understanding about the capacity to consent. Her work is bridging the gap between how to communicate willingness (or not) to engage sexually and how people already think about consent. In terms of future sexual education, this approach creates context for a lot of new conversations for young people to have about ethical sexual relationships.

There is a lot of teaching to do before girls start making choices about having sex or not. If young people are choosing to have sex, they are simply encouraged to have safer sex. This usually means using condoms. But it assumes safer sex is heteronormative; the goal is not to impregnate the girl. This is old-fashioned and barely skims the surface of what should be included in sexual education. It's outdated and unimaginative, given the realities of sexual experience. It's heterosexual sex for a man.

Even when discussing birth control, there are so many options for girls that the choice is as much to do with lifestyle as it is about pregnancy prevention. There are IUDs (coils), the pill, patch, Nuva Ring, each with their own health benefits and risks. Throwing on a condom while having sex is hugely important for STI prevention and overall sexual health, as well as pregnancy prevention, regardless of other personal birth control decisions. However, it's equally important to educate girls to make decisions around birth control and their sexual health that work best for them. Many people are not heterosexual, meaning that wearing a condom for 'safer sex' may not even apply. Implying safer sex is any sex that doesn't end in pregnancy is not touching on either sex-positive conversations or the realities of sexual assault. It does not regard the gender identification or sexual orientation of the young person.

My maths for talking to girls about sex is as follows: protected sex + consensual sex + personal enjoyment of sexual activity = the ONLY safe sex.

If we only teach one of these, we leave room for misconstruction of what sex is. We want young people to accept that they may or may not want to be sexual with others, to explore their sexuality in a normative way at their own pace, and to be able to talk about it with friends, family and definitely their potential sexual partners. If, when we talk about sex to young people, we have conversations about pleasure, orgasms, comfort and safety, we can then educate them that anything less, such as not enjoying sex, or it hurts but their partner won't stop, or feeling that they want it to be over, is not safe sex just because a condom is used. Studies show that more communication and discussion about sex results in greater sexual pleasure, intimacy, sexual health and relationship satisfaction (Vanwesenbeeck, Bekker & Lenning, 1998).

By including sex-positive ideas and sexual assault realities, girls can be empowered to make physically, emotionally and psychologically safer sexual choices of their own. The fear tactics of abstinence-only sexual education just stifle or shame female sexuality by using inaccurate sexual information or religious fear (Lynch, 2017). It may teach girls to fear their own sexuality. Girls who are already too fearful and ashamed to advocate for their own body and safety could be at even greater risk of harm.

Brison (1997) wrote that we are the keepers of each other's stories. I often feel this as a therapist, but even more so as a woman. I hold so many stories. I have my own stories, some spoken and some silent. I hold the stories of my sisters, my mother, my friends, my clients. They are stories of girlhood and womanhood and what it means to be female in this generation and beyond. The #MeToo movement has unleashed stories that echo around the world. It has prompted conversations about sexual assault with friends, families and colleagues that typically wouldn't have happened before. Reactions to the movement are varied, and passionately so. It can be a shocking conversation for people who have experienced sexual assault, and for those who haven't. Some women have been shocked; others have supported the movement with an almost silent nod. Some celebrate that these stories are being voiced at last. Others have become almost paralysed by the constant reminders in the media. For many of those who have experienced sexual assault, this period has been hugely triggering. My experience is that most women have found some camaraderie within the movement, recognising themselves or their friends in these stories, whether silently or publicly. The stories of the #MeToo movement should be kept by women and girls and passed through generations. We should hold each other's stories for safekeeping with strength and dignity.

Sexual assault has happened and is happening. Someone commits rape in America every seven seconds (Harding, 2015). But what comes next? I hope girls reinvent 'sexy' on their own terms. I do not mean sexy in the way that sex is shown on the TV, or talked about by male politicians, or shouted by men from their cars as I walk down the street. Sexy, to me, means feeling sexually empowered. Sexual empowerment does not have to come from any person other than ourselves. Sexuality should be a natural part of our individual, expressed identity.

Sexy can be complicated. Sexy comes from education and intimate knowledge about our bodies, what we like, what we don't like, and being able to communicate this confidently. We all have women in our life, whether they are daughters or mothers or sisters or friends. If we learn to talk honestly to each other about sex, including the realities of sexual assault, we will learn how to grow into the complexities of individual sexuality in a transparent, reparative way. Sexy is not just being empowered to say no but being able to say yes. Sexy is communicating why and how. This is how we should talk about sex to girls.

Response from Sarah J. Wilson

Someone recently asked for my thoughts on how to raise conversations with her daughter around sexual assault. The young woman had been given sex education at school, but that didn't cover it and so she sought my advice.

My response was along the lines of: 'Just let her know that she can tell you if she feels uncomfortable in any way through what someone says, how they look at her, or touch her, or any other behaviour.'

I was left feeling dissatisfied with my response, without quite knowing why.

In reading Taylor's work, I realised I hadn't acknowledged some of the huge complexities such a question, and responses to it, can raise.

I am grateful to Taylor for prompting me to reflect more on these issues and become clearer about the unease I was left with at the end of my conversation.

Taylor's chapter left me with the urgency of the question: 'How can we keep young people safe from sexual assault?' I felt myself wanting to be able to protect and keep all young people safe, each and every one, especially those close to me.

This was quickly followed by the pain in acknowledging that harm and unsafety have been a reality for the majority of women I know, if not all, in some way or another. And the pain that yet another generation is experiencing this harm and unsafety.

I can feel hopeless about what can really be done. I also recognise that things *are* changing, that people *are* speaking up and there is the possibility of change within our society.

I want to know how conversations about sex and sexual assault can happen now, moving from what we need to do to how we do it. How explicit do things need to be made to give girls a framework and language to be able to have conversations about sex and sexual assault? As a society, we struggle to find words, particularly for girls to name their genitals. There's a proliferation of words – from the euphemistic to the medical. I notice my own difficulty and discomfort with the language. Is the word I have chosen, 'genitals', the most useful one?

The chapter left me with greater compassion towards the younger me. My own 'sex education' consisted solely of a pamphlet published by the Catholic Church, with a couple of line drawings of genitals, which explained that sex happened between a man and woman who loved each other and were married. It was hard for me later to make any sense of a totally bewildering world with no means to understand or communicate my experience. There was just no way to join up any of the dots in any meaningful way. Today, I wonder what is there for our young girls to enable them to do this?

As a body psychotherapist, I recognise how essential it is to include the body, and that a conversation using words alone is limited and limiting. As embodied beings, our 'yes' and 'no' get encoded in the body. The whole issue of consent becomes complex, as does what feels OK or not. A 'no' becomes encoded as a 'yes' when it is culturally validated – for example, 'Give your granny a kiss' or 'Go and sit on Daddy's knee.' How can a child work out what is comfortable for them when it is either implicit or explicit that they should behave in particular ways, without the possibility of saying 'no'?

We need to recognise how the body is infringed upon and transgressed, and how we learn to say nothing when something doesn't feel OK. We need to recognise how differences in cultures – cultures of all sorts: for example, family, regions, spiritual communities – influence the extent and nature of touch, its absence, its intrusion and its negotiation. We need to understand how cultural messages relating to gender and/or age instil encoded messages – for example, having to defer to someone who is male or older. We need to support the understanding that the body can respond in ways that feel pleasurable to experiences that are unwanted and uncomfortable; to realise that people will say 'yes' in order to receive affection, attention, approval or anything else that they need ; to understand how trauma can cause the body to freeze as a natural response to a perceived threat, which can then become a conditioned reaction. Again, there can then appear to be a 'yes' when it is, in fact, a 'no.'

With all these complexities in mind, how can we support children and young adults to be embodied, when we live in a culture where we are profoundly disconnected with our bodies?

There is an increasing influence of porn on young peoples' sexuality. There needs to be more support for boys and men to own and manage their sexuality. Responsibility has at times been abdicated for men and boys, excused by a belief that their sexual impulses are 'too powerful' not to be acted upon. There needs to be recognition of the complexity of sexuality in our society and other issues related to power, such as isolation, low self-esteem and misogyny, and how these all contribute to the potential of sexual assault. How to offer positive guidance for boys with regards to their sexuality is another huge piece of the work. Men need to be involved in these conversations in the hope that they can support boys in their rites of passage to manhood. I have a concern about the focus of these conversations on girls, that this could somehow implicitly continue to perpetuate the placing of responsibility on them for preventing or avoiding sexual assault, which feeds into the way our society blames the female victim. The possibility of the inclusion of boys and men in these conversations somewhat alleviates my concern. We need to make absolutely sure that responsibility for sexual assault is placed firmly where it belongs.

Girls and women are disproportionately the victims of male violence. It is also really important to me that, as in the #MeToo movement, the conversation includes the possibility of girls experiencing sexual assault from other girls or women, and boys who are assaulted by girls or women, or boys or men. This has to be both explicit and visible so that their experiences do not get missed or denied – which I have seen happen – and the individual becomes further isolated.

How far will our conversations about sex and sexual assault go? What about the places in which these conversations can't happen at all? What about those who still experience sexual assault, even so? My hope is that there will be a more open climate in which people can speak out and be believed. I think we have only just started this process.

References

Association of American Universities (2019). *Report on the AAU Campus Climate Survey on Sexual Assault and Misconduct*. Chicago, IL: AAU. www.aau.edu/sites/default/files/AAU-Files/Key-Issues/Campus-Safety/Revised%20Aggregate%20report%20%20and%20appendices%201-7_(01-16-2020_FINAL).pdf (accessed 1 March 2020).

Bass TM (2016). Exploring female sexuality: embracing the whole narrative. *NC Medical Journal* 77(6): 430–432.

Beres MA (2014). Rethinking the concept of consent for anti-sexual violence activism and education. *Feminism & Psychology* 24(3): 373–389.

Beres MA (2010). Sexual miscommunication? Untangling assumptions about sexual communication between casual sex partners. *Culture, Health & Sexuality* 12(1): 1–14.

Brison S. Outliving oneself. In: Meyers DT (1997). *Feminists Rethink the Self*. Boulder, CO: Westview Press (pp12–39).

Fahs B (2014). Freedom to and freedom from: a new vision for sex-positive politics. *Sexualities* 17(3): 267–290.

Glick E (2000). Sex positive: Feminism, queer theory, and the politics of transgression. *Feminist Review* 64(1): 19–45.

Harden KP (2014). A sex-positive framework for research on adolescent sexuality. *Perspectives on Psychological Science* 9(5): 455–469.

Harding K (2015). *Asking For It: the alarming rise of rape culture and what we can do about it*. Boston, MA: Da Capo Lifelong Books.

Kaplan M (2014). Sex-positive law. *NYU Law Review* 89: 89–164.

Lees S (1993). *Sugar and Spice: sexuality and adolescent girls*. London: Penguin Books.

Lynch MN (2017). *Abstinence-Only Sex Education in the United States: how abstinence curricula have harmed America*. University Honors Theses. Paper 380. Portland, OH: Portland State University.

Reich W (1971). *The Invasion of Compulsory Sex-Morality*. New York, NY: Farrar, Straus & Giroux.

Taylor BG, Stein ND, Mumford EA, Woods D (2013). Shifting boundaries: an experimental evaluation of a dating violence prevention program in middle schools. *Prevention Science: The Official Journal of the Society for Prevention Research* 14: 64–76.

Tolman DL (1994). Doing desire: adolescent girls' struggles for/with sexuality. *Gender & Society* 8(3): 324–342.

Vanwesenbeeck I, Bekker M, Lenning A (1998). Gender attitudes, sexual meanings, and interactional patterns in heterosexual encounters among college students in the Netherlands. *The Journal of Sex Research* 35(4): 318–327.

World Health Organization (2002). Sexual violence. In: *World Report on Violence and Health*. Geneva: WHO (pp149–181).

Chapter 5

Sexual abuse and surviving with(in) psychology

Jemma Tosh, with Fionnuala Dempsey

At 14 years old I walked away from a suicide attempt and directly to the door of a counsellor. It remains one of the proudest moments of my life. Counselling turned my life around, not by changing it or making me any safer but by giving me the tools to survive the abuse. Simply put, I would not be here today had it not been for that counsellor: her empathy and the skills she taught me, such as thinking creatively about how to lift my mood even on my worst days, or how persistently making small changes would eventually help me to dig myself out of the deep hole[1] I had found myself in. I would use those same skills many times, saving my own life over and over again.

With such a heartwarming introduction to therapy, you might assume that my view of the psy professions would be a positive one. But, while many of the therapists I encountered over the years (as colleagues and as my own therapists) were supportive and helpful, there were also those who caused more harm than good. They traumatised and re-traumatised people who had experienced sexual abuse. I was lucky, at age 14, to have had a counsellor who made me feel valued and heard and who helped me come up with practical strategies for survival, rather than fill my head with rape myths, victim-

---

1. I tend to refer to my personal experiences of very low mood and suicide attempts as a 'dark/deep hole' or a 'pit of despair' because this best reflects how it physically felt, both in terms of feeling lost and low and also how difficult it was to 'climb' out of it.

blaming theories and pathologised narratives of disorders and 'abnormality.' This was necessary, not only to avoid the harms of pathologisation but because the therapy occurred while the abuse was still ongoing.[2] A practical focus on surviving was essential. The time for healing from the long-term impacts of sexual trauma would come later. What I needed to know then, more than anything else, was how to stay alive.

When I entered my psychology training, I was greeted with a focus on women's 'risk-taking behaviours' and the 'natural' 'normality' of aggressive and sexually violent men. Survivors were often framed as 'broken' or 'damaged', with 'poor outcomes', if they were considered at all. I sat in lecture halls bewildered by how academics could think that such a reductionist and pathologising overview of sexual abuse could explain or heal anything, let alone my own complex and recurrent experiences as a survivor of rape. I was angry, insulted and disappointed that the 'helping professions' were so unhelpful (see also Tosh & Golightley, 2016) and seemingly permeated with gendered tropes and rape apologism. As a result, I have dedicated much of my academic career to debunking these problematic narratives of rape. Instead, I shine a light on the violent, abusive and coercive aspects of psychology itself (eg. Tosh, 2011, 2014, 2020), and work to make changes for survivors.

In this chapter I describe my experiences as a queer and genderfluid survivor growing up in Northern Ireland, and how those experiences influenced my career as a psychologist who specialises in the topics of sexual abuse and violence. I use the terms queer and bisexual to describe my sexuality. I define bisexual as having an attraction to people with the same gender as me, as well as those with a different gender from me. It is transgender, genderfluid, nonbinary and intersex inclusive. This term best represents my sexuality as it positions my gender as central to the definition (rather than a term like pansexual), which is important to me and my relationships. I use the terms genderfluid and nonbinary to describe my gender. I define genderfluid as having more than one gender and I use nonbinary to refer to genders that encompass more possibilities than a binary of male/female allows. This can include multiple genders as well as no genders (ie. agender). I use the terms survivor and victim to describe my experiences of sexual abuse. This is because they recognise both my strength in overcoming violence and the pain and suffering that it caused.

This positioning, and my unique intersection of personal and professional identities, is particularly relevant because of the promotion of harmful ideas

---

2. My counsellor did try to get details of my experiences to confirm her suspicion that I had been abused, but because I was unable to describe or verbalise my experiences at that time, I was unable to make a disclosure that would have legally required her to get other agencies involved.

about sexuality both in therapy texts and in Northern Ireland. As with any personal account, the experiences of others may be very different to mine. I share my story not to offer *the* reality of being a queer, genderfluid, survivor within psychology, but to offer *my* reality. I hope others find it helpful, regardless of whether their experience is similar or not. I outline the complex intersections of gender, sexuality, race, place and historical context and show why these intersections should be central to therapeutic approaches that aim to help survivors heal from sexual trauma.

Growing up a survivor/surviving growing up

Northern Ireland provides a unique context to be a survivor of sexual abuse. In addition to the lack of consideration of its border and the peace process in the event of the UK leaving the European Union (Sloat, 2018), Northern Ireland has recently garnered international attention for its discriminatory laws that are incongruent with the UK and European human rights legislation. This includes a ban on same-sex marriage[3] (Halpin, 2018; NIDirect, 2018a), ongoing challenges to LGBT anti-discrimination legislation on the grounds of 'religious beliefs' (Bowcott, 2018; McDonald, 2015), one of the strictest abortion laws in the European Union (Cuddy, 2018; Kelly, 2016), an outdated and paternalistic process for gender recognition[4] (NIDirect, 2018b), and continued arguments for creationism[5] to be taught in schools (Mann, 2017).

My schooling was influenced by this context – my science books were confiscated and replaced with the Bible on the day we were due to learn about

---

3. At the time of writing, same-sex marriage remains illegal in Northern Ireland. However, there are repeated attempts to introduce legislation that would make marriage legal for LGBT individuals, with the main barrier being the views of the Democratic Unionist Party (DUP) and their use of the 'petition of concern' that enables them to veto legislation they disagree with (Duffy, 2015). Civil partnerships were introduced in 2004 for same-sex couples only and they do not have all the same rights as married couples. While there is legal protection from discrimination in relation to marital status and sexual orientation (and, vaguely, to 'gender reassignment'), there is strong opposition to this because of Northern Ireland's protection of political opinion and religious beliefs. Members of unionist parties, such as the DUP, argue that LGBT rights impose on their religious and political rights, and this is currently being contested in court (Bowcott, 2018; McDonald, 2015).

4. Trans and nonbinary individuals are required to undergo an assessment by a Gender Recognition Panel, which requires medical and legal evidence, such as a diagnosis of gender dysphoria (see Tosh (2016) for the problems with this diagnosis), having lived in their gender for at least two years (a problematic requirement due to the hostility that trans people face in Northern Ireland, and also their inability to access body modification procedures and hormones, as well as having to live up to the doctor's expectations of that gender expression), and a commitment to live in that gender permanently (which excludes nonbinary, genderfluid, genderqueer and agender people).

5. Creationism is defined as 'a package of anti-evolutionist beliefs held by religious believers, most often Christian, and usually evangelical/fundamentalist and Protestant. Biblical creationism argues that Genesis is an accurate and clear record of the beginning of the world' (Coleman & Carlin, 2017: 4).

the big bang. I was told by teachers that I was going to hell for being pro-choice, and my sex education consisted solely of reading a poem that was written from the perspective of a baby being aborted. There was no teaching on homosexuality or LGBT issues, because it was as if LGBT people did not exist. From this perspective, which paradoxically promoted both procreation and abstinence, sex and sexual anatomy should remain a mystery to young people. It is unsurprising then, that when I was a child and I told adults of the sexual abuse I had experienced, the response was, 'Don't worry about it, dear, God will punish him.'

The aim of such emotive and uncompromising strategies in the school appeared to be the promotion of fear and guilt in young people contemplating sexual relationships. It certainly did not empower young people to be assertive about their sexuality (eg. Friedman & Valenti, 2008; see also Fine, 1988 and Fine & McClelland, 2006); nor did it provide a context where talking about abuse was possible or safe. Much like the victim in the infamous Belfast rugby case, who accused two professional rugby players of rape and faced sexist and slut-shaming messages both in court and in the media (Freeman, 2018), disclosing rape in Northern Ireland results in being labelled a 'whore', with all its religious connotations of sin and punishment. Despite my young age, I experienced this phenomenon of blame and shame too – when I was only six years old, my abuser called me a 'slut'. I had never heard the word before, and I did not know what it meant. From the reactions of others, I could tell that whatever a 'slut' was, it was 'bad'. I was a 'whore' who had no idea what sex was. It was rape culture wrapped up in sectarian sexism.

Each time I witnessed someone experience violence and speak out about it, I saw that they were violently silenced with humiliation, social exclusion and verbal and emotional abuse by the majority – by family and friends, teachers, religious leaders, journalists, politicians and local 'gossipers'. Northern Ireland is not just made up of small towns, it is a small country. At a mere 5,460 square miles, the entire country could fit into the New York Metropolitan area twice, with room to spare. With a population of around 1.9 million, it makes up less than three per cent of the UK population.[6] That 'small-town' feeling is everywhere, and everyone knows your business. Privacy can be rare, particularly regarding 'scandalous' accounts of sex or rape, in a context where the population of a town is so small that going unnoticed or unknown can be difficult.

As I got older, the response to disclosing sexual abuse changed from the view that it was an aberration that would be punished by God to simply 'that's life as a woman'. Over and over again, when I described being raped by my

---

6. Not including Northern Irish people residing in other UK countries or the Northern Irish diaspora (Northern Ireland Statistics and Research Agency, 2017; Office for National Statistics, 2015).

partner, I was told that sex was horrible and that no woman liked it. I was informed that it was a key part of the female role to participate in (unwanted, painful, coercive, violent) sex for the sake of her (male) partner, otherwise she would be unloved and alone, reaffirming the patriarchal and homophobic notion that women are incomplete without a man. Growing up a survivor in Northern Ireland, those were the choices on offer to me: enjoy sex and be a 'whore' or be raped and be a woman.

These gender 'norms' of Northern Ireland are tied to ideas of national identity within a context of conflict (Meaney, 2011; Thapar-Björkert & Ryan 2002), where rape is often used as a metaphor to describe British colonialism of the 'virgin' Irish land (Sharkey 1994; Tosh, 2015), and colonial violence and military conflicts are played out over women's bodies (Farwell, 2004; Synder et al, 2006). Thus, the 'norms' of violence in Northern Ireland are unique within the UK. For example, in 2011 riots broke out across England, sparked by the shooting of a young black man, Mark Duggan, in north London and ongoing concerns about institutional racism in the UK police system (Elliott-Cooper, 2017). This led to intense speculation over the causes of what was regarded as atypical behaviour, from criminal 'gangs' to anti-capitalist revolts (Hallsworth, 2016). This concern and theorising was done without recognition that riots were a common feature of life in Northern Ireland,[7] along with bomb threats, shootings, and the odd bonfire (Leonard, 2009; Silva & Mace, 2015). This shows that the extent to which violence is deemed 'acceptable' differs depending on the context – for example, the Northern Ireland marching season may be framed as either a parade or a riot, depending on your viewpoint (Ferman, 2013), just as the word 'rape' is used both to refer to a serious crime and the punchline of a 'joke' (Kramer, 2011).

In England, terrorism, bomb threats and riots receive worldwide attention and are viewed as inconceivable and requiring immediate attention. In Northern Ireland, however, such events can be seen as 'life as usual'. For example, in the early 2000s I was waiting in Belfast for a flight to England. An announcement was made that there was a bomb in the car park and that the army were on their way to disarm it (Bradley, 2001). When the announcement finished, I resumed reading my magazine and wondered how big the bomb was. I did not call or text my family to tell them I loved them. The airport was not evacuated. It was not the first time I had heard those words, nor the last (for a more recent example, see Donaghy, 2018). The difference between the local Northern Irish and the tourists was stark: the calm and matter-of-fact aura of the locals versus the panic and fear of those who did not grow up around army tanks, guns, and bombs. With such violence and the constant

---

7. With a long history, see Farrell (2009).

threat of violence deemed 'normal',[8] it is possible to see how this context would impact on the dismissal and minimising of experiences of interpersonal violence. In other words, if bombs don't scare you, why would you be scared of your boyfriend?

A punishment from God

The normalisation of violence in Northern Ireland is inseparable from the role of religion, which goes far beyond a personal relationship with God or an individual's faith. Every part of those 5,460 square miles is divided into Protestant and Catholic areas, symbolised by the flags flown from streetlights and the painted kerbs – red, white and blue for the Protestant and/or British areas, and green, white and orange for the Catholic and/or Irish areas. Even schools are segregated by religion rather than gender. A 'mixed' school in Northern Ireland means that it accepts both Catholic and Protestant students. Some areas are divided by large walls between communities (Geoghegan, 2015). It is an impenetrable binary of 'us' versus 'them' based around various markers of religion.[9] You are categorised by your name, where you live, the colours you wear, how you pronounce a word, what you call a city,[10] who you know and even your passport. The most common question I was asked on a night out was 'Which one are ya?' – and they were not asking about my gender. Everything is viewed through the lens of religion, whether you subscribe to that perspective or not.

One of the consequences of viewing everything in this way, and of being told that God punishes rapists, is that it can represent God as a vengeful and powerful being. This resulted in me developing a deep fear of God when I was a child. It was further complicated by the shame that can coincide with sexual abuse (Kennedy & Prock, 2016; Weiss, 2010). At that age, I did not understand what had happened to me, I did not have the words to describe it, so I felt that *I* was bad because something bad had happened to me.

At the age of six I began dissociating[11] regularly. With the imagination and understanding of a child, I believed that my small body was being dragged

---

8. A context of violence imposed on a population due to longstanding sectarian and colonial conflict should not be conflated with the stereotype of Irish people as inherently violent and aggressive. See Walter (2001), Ghaill (2000) and Curtis (1984) for more on the stereotypes of Irish people and anti-Irish racism.

9. Which also erases the lives and experiences of Irish travellers (Hayes, 2006).

10. Such as the tension surrounding the city of Derry and/or Londonderry, depending on your position. The long history of conflict and colonial oppression around this city, which began as a plantation established by English and Scottish settlers in the 1600s (Ó Dochartaigh, 2005), is reflected in this emotive and divided name.

11. Defined here as feeling 'out of body' and/or being separate to oneself. For an analysis of the genealogy of trauma discourse, see Leys (2000).

into hell to burn for an eternity for a sin that I did not understand. The fear of being rejected or cast out for my sins meant that for years I told no one. How else is a child to understand the mind's complex response to trauma? With everything explained through religious discourse, how else are children in Northern Ireland to understand their experiences of abuse other than through the narrative of sin?

For a queer and genderfluid youth, the shame of sexual abuse can become entangled with the shame of being LGBT (Walker et al, 2012). Again, this occurs in a context where often the only visibility of non-straight relationships is in debates about equal marriage (and how homosexuality is not seen as valid) or how homosexuality is a sin and an 'abomination' (Duffy, 2015; Duggan, 2010; Staples, 2018). Other sexualities (eg. bisexuality, pansexuality, asexuality and so on) remain relatively invisible (Quiery, 2007), and transgender and nonbinary individuals are also fighting for understanding, recognition and visibility in Northern Ireland.

As a teenager, I was told that 'homosexuality was a punishment from God' and that my gender nonconformity made me an 'ugly dyke'. There was no support or advice available around gender nonconformity in the isolating landscape of rural Northern Ireland at that time, so this was the only explanation available to me: that my gender was a result of my sexual orientation and that both were sinful and grounds for ridicule. As a result, I was pushed further into the closet and grew up believing that I deserved every hit, every rape and every cruel word, because of who I was. This was an easy lie to believe, as abusers often tell their victims that they deserve the violence they give. This form of psychological manipulation, or gaslighting, makes any attempt to define the relationship as abusive seem unreasonable and makes disagreement with the abuser's perspective (ie. that it was deserved, 'normal', or your fault etc) seem impossible (Abramson, 2014).

I was told that I deserved the abuse on more than one occasion and, having heard for so long that rape victims were 'whores' and queer people were sinners, I believed it completely. It stopped me from speaking out and fighting back, and it twisted an already painful experience into something even more devastating. It made possible the small step from 'I deserve to be hurt' to 'I don't deserve to live'. I would advocate for anyone else who was a victim of abuse, as the harm it caused seemed so painfully obvious to me. Yet for decades I was unable to defend myself because I thought I deserved it, that it was 'normal' and 'justified'. This is one way that the harmful narratives of slut-shaming,[12] homophobia and

---

12. Slut-shaming is defined as 'the public exposure and shaming of individuals for their (perceived or actual) sexual behaviour' and 'a form of cultural suppression of female sexuality that has been practiced since antiquity' (Webb, 2015; para 1).

transphobia can exacerbate sexual abuse and put children and young people at further risk of violence.

Training, mansplaining and victim-blaming

Following the success of my therapy in adolescence, I wanted to help others the way that I had been helped as a teenager. This made a career in psychology an obvious choice. While religious discourse in Northern Ireland around sex and abuse had obscured the reality of rape, psychology and its claim to scientific authority seemed like a worthy alternative to understanding why rape happened and how to stop it. I moved to England and started my training, becoming a chartered psychologist with the British Psychological Society after years of study at university and working in the NHS and a wide range of private and charitable mental health organisations. Unfortunately, much of those same problematic narratives remained, albeit dressed up in academic and psychologised language:

- from 'homosexuality is a sin' to 'homosexuality is abnormal' (eg. Acosta, 1975; Bieber et al, 1988; Byrd & Nicolosi, 2002; Hadden, 2006; James, 1978).
- from coercive, painful or 'unwanted' sex being seen as part of the 'female role' to the pathologisation of women who experience pain or fear when penetrated and the insistence that penetrative heterosexual sex is required to be 'normal' (see Tosh & Carson, 2016 for a critique).
- repeatedly framing men as 'naturally' aggressive, especially during sex (eg. Freud, 1949; Thornhill & Palmer, 2000).
- from the conflation of gender and sexuality in the insults of 'dyke' and 'fag' for gender nonconformity to the pathologisation of transgender and gender nonconforming people in the *Diagnostic and Statistical Manual of Mental Disorders* (American Psychiatric Association, 2013) and the ongoing conflation and/or fascination with sexuality (eg. Blanchard, 2005; Lawrence, 2017).

This change in context, moving to a different country and learning from a different perspective, revealed numerous contrasts between religious and psychological discourse. Yet they were discouragingly similar in many ways in their constructions of rape. The justifications for violence and abuse I had learned at home were reframed as reasons for 'treatment', such as electro-shock treatments for homosexuality (Bancroft & Marks, 1968; MacCulloch & Feldman, 1967). The history of psychology was full of examples of therapeutic abuse deemed 'acceptable' for certain groups of people, including those who were minoritised because of their gender and sexuality and those who had experienced sexual abuse. Instead of telling me I was 'bad' and going to hell, psychology could easily have led me to believe that there was something wrong with me for being who I was and what I had survived. Psychology turned out to be a disappointing alternative to religious discourse – to say the least.

I spent years in training, watching psychologists with little to no understanding of sexual abuse apply inappropriate and victim-blaming interventions to survivors. They focused on 'risk-taking behaviours' and how victims could prevent further violence, even though they were not responsible for the abuse that happened to them. I watched as children were referred back and forth from charities to specialists because no one felt qualified enough to deal with them. I worked in a range of high secure psychiatric wards filled with women who had spent years, and sometimes decades, being dosed up with antipsychotic medication while their reports of rape were categorised as 'delusions' and seen as further evidence of 'mental illness'. Once this happened solely on the opinion of the psychiatrist, who knew the perpetrator personally and declared that 'he was a nice man, who would never do something like that'.

As a part of my training, I observed a child who had been referred for neuropsychological testing; even though the tests revealed she had serious difficulties with language, she was considered to be lying about sexual assault because she used the wrong word in her statement. Even though she continued to draw pictures and write about monsters in her room at night, this one linguistic error was used time and time again to discredit her. My concerns and objections were harshly silenced when I spoke out against physically restraining young children who had been sexually abused. The emotional and traumatic impact of being repeatedly forced to the ground by a group of adults for minor infractions of the rules was completely dismissed. As a survivor of sexual abuse, I experienced my training in psychology as heartbreaking.

Becoming my own therapist

The physical toll of long-term and chronic stress from sexual abuse and trauma can be overwhelming (Randomsky, 2014; Wilson, 2009). My flashbacks increased in frequency as I got older until I was no longer able to leave my home. Specific sounds, smells, sensations, words, images and so much more triggered me.[13] The more I was triggered, the more often I would

---

13. I refer to 'triggered' here as a neurological and embodied response to traumatic stimuli and their reminders, rather than the problematic conflation of 'triggering' as 'being offended' in ableist and sanist discussions regarding 'free speech' (Lockhart, 2016; Rae, 2016).

have flashbacks and the bigger they would get. The stress of it all made me so physically unwell that I was bedridden for months.

That might sound a little depressing but I view it as one of the key turning points in my life, like a suicide attempt in my teens. For me, it was my body's way of telling me that I needed to stop and address the trauma – that it was simply no longer possible to continue to function as I had been doing and denying that the abuse had a lasting and devastating impact on my body, my health and my wellbeing. For the first time in my life, I started standing up for myself. I said no to exciting new projects. I let colleagues down. I failed to deliver papers and projects that I had committed to. I started to tell people the truth: 'No, I can't do that, because I'm not well.' When people responded with further demands to complete the work when I 'got better', I still told them no, because I had no idea when that would be. This was not a bad head cold; you do not heal from trauma after a week in bed drinking lemon and honey tea.

After spending many years as a psychologist helping survivors of sexual abuse, and many before that as a volunteer and support worker, I finally started to help myself. It may be cliché, but you really can help other people better if you help yourself first. It is even better if you can heal together. There were those who were supportive of me prioritising my healing, and those who were not. When you begin this process, it quickly becomes apparent who values their deadline more than your health. Again, I view this as a positive step towards surrounding yourself with supportive people who share in your aim of healing from trauma and removing influences that would derail or sabotage that process.

I started re-reading books I had on sexual abuse from the perspective of a survivor rather than a psychologist. I started with *The Courage to Heal* (Bass & Davis, 1994) and *The Body Keeps the Score* (van der Kolk, 2014). I drew on feminism, I was critical of pathologising perspectives and I held embodied experience and emotional wellbeing as paramount. I devised my own personalised healing approach based on my years of expertise. I used dialectical behaviour therapy (DBT) to hone my skills in coping with the painful emotions arising in the other therapies I used (McKay, Wood & Brantley, 2007). I used internal family systems therapy (IFST) to get a better understanding of how childhood sexual abuse influenced who I am and how I respond to stress and trauma (Schwartz, 1995). I used both of these as a foundation for eye movement desensitisation and reprocessing (EMDR) therapy (Shapiro, 2001), which can be a difficult approach when used with complex and chronic trauma, as things can get worse before they get better (such as increases in flashbacks, being emotionally overwhelmed and exhaustion). To further support this process, I used a range of activities from narrative therapy, art therapy and relationship therapy. It was an eclectic mix of approaches that each addressed an area of healing for me. It was also an organic process, in that I did not lead it: I followed what was needed at the time. For example, I spent many months working on body memories[14] as I hit a bump in the road with my EMDR. I was unable to access emotions connected to a memory, but I could not stop shaking during sessions. So I changed the focus of my therapy to address the embodied emotions and trauma and, once the shaking lessened, I was able to return to EMDR with much more success.

It is an ongoing process, and most likely a continuation of a lifelong process of healing from violence and abuse. However, rather than view this solely as a painful and difficult journey, I have also experienced it as an exciting adventure in getting to know myself better. Starting therapy and seeing the positive changes was wonderful, not only because it felt like I was slowly getting my life back but because it also showed me something I had never thought possible – that you *can* heal the trauma from sexual abuse.[15] The journey from being unable to leave my bed or my home to seeing triggers and realising that they no longer had any effect on me was so beautifully freeing that it empowered me to continue the hard work of facing my own trauma and helping others to heal theirs.

Critical psychology and feminism

Key to my healing was more than a decade of study and training in psychology, including critical and feminist psychology. Reading feminist books in the university library was the first time that I felt someone understood what I had been through. I had finally found answers to questions I had been looking for since I was a child. It provided an alternative analysis of rape and the 'norms' of men and women as socially constructed and unnecessarily limiting and offered new ways of thinking about sex, sexuality and gender.[16] I embraced feminist psychology and found support through the Psychology of Women Section (POWS) of the BPS. I met others who shared my outrage at the pathologisation of women and gender nonconformity, at the atrocious narratives and justifications for rape within psychology, at the reparative 'treatment' of transgender children, and more. I found critical psychologists

---

14. Body memories are trauma (ie. emotions, feelings, sensations and memories) that is stored in the body, such as in the muscles and the nervous system. They can result in a wide variety of related health issues (van der Kolk, 2014).

15. I am also aware of the complex tension between the (class) privilege of being able to access resources to heal (in this case, my support, knowledge and education), as well as the ableism (Campbell, 2009) and sanism (Perlin, 2016) of arguments that also view necessary self-care and unavoidable life changes for healing as a privilege.

16. Although not without its own problems. It took me time to find resources that were anti-racist, trans-inclusive and moved beyond the binary of men as perpetrators and women as victims, which was important as some of my abusers were women.

who shared my concerns about the role psychology played in promoting harmful concepts around gender 'norms' and heteronormativity (Pyne, 2014; Sedgwick, 1991; Ussher, 1991; Winters, 2008), as well as the role of power and coercion in psychological and psychiatric approaches (Rose, 1985; Szasz, 2007).

This knowledge and support made it possible for me to navigate the available resources and literature and tell the difference between harmful victim-blaming approaches and those that were grounded in lived experience and were more effective at healing trauma. It meant that I could sidestep the longstanding pathologising narratives and labels and, with new theories and research, I had the skills to be able to tell whether they were 'friend' or 'foe.' My work in critical and feminist psychology introduced me to the complex intersections of sexism, racism, ableism, sanism, biphobia, and cisgenderism, so I knew that my healing journey would be a distinctive mix of approaches that best suited me, my identities and my unique experience. It required the addition of specific approaches on gender identity and how my gender fluidity impacted on my experience of sexual abuse, as well as how the abuse impacted on my experience of being queer and bisexual (Walker et al, 2012). This meant drawing on queer, trans and nonbinary affirmative perspectives or, more often, rewriting already available sources in affirmative language to make them meaningful and helpful to me (rather than continuing the harm of erasing my experiences from dominant perspectives on sexual abuse). Having had several sexually violent experiences that were motivated by my being Irish in England, my journey also included healing work around my identity as Irish and its relationship with broader intergenerational trauma and colonial violence within the context of Northern Ireland.[17] It is this nuanced, situated and personalised approach, one that includes this range of experience and personal identity, that is essential to healing from sexual abuse.

Conclusions

Healing from sexual abuse requires not just a comprehensive array of therapies and supports to respond to the various ways that the body and mind can react to trauma but an equally comprehensive range of approaches to address the intersections of sexual abuse with other axes of oppression and identity. This is so the survivor can heal, not just from the sexual abuse but from its impact on their experience and understanding of themselves. Therefore, it must be socially situated, yet individualised. We must understand the context in which the abuse occurred as well as the experience and identities of the individual.

---

17. However, it is important to note that my experiences of being Irish in Northern Ireland are very different from being Irish in Ireland, England (Hickman, 1995), and North America (Walter, 2001).

Shamed into silence for decades for my experiences of rape and sexual abuse, as well as my gender and sexuality, I'm acutely aware of the emotional and physical pain that results from a coerced silence, as well as how silence can enable abuse to continue and isolate survivors. At the same time, breaking silence has risks, particularly in a context where violence towards oppressed and marginalised groups is prevalent. A supportive and understanding therapist, as well as self-therapy, helped me develop the skills necessary to survive and heal from sexual abuse and the resulting trauma, but it was feminist and critical psychology that helped me find my voice and gave me the courage to use it.

Jemma Tosh in conversation with Fionnuala Dempsey

Fionnuala: Your reality overlaps with mine in many ways, which is a big part of the foundation of our more than 20-year friendship. I would like to discuss a little more three points you explained in your chapter, where our experiences overlap the most.

As an autistic person with a special interest in psychology, I have researched talking therapies intensely. As an abuse survivor, I have experienced a range of talking therapies, such as cognitive behavioural therapy (CBT) and psychodynamic therapy. I have had some positive experiences, some negative and a few very damaging interactions. Most frustratingly, my autism was not acknowledged or identified throughout my treatment, and since being aware of it, I have struggled to find appropriate support. Like you, I had to learn how to become my own therapist and be alert to unhelpful approaches. However, without any formal training or the wealth of experience and expertise you have worked to build throughout your career, I am sure there is more I could learn about how to support myself and heal. I also believe that becoming your own therapist is something anyone can learn to do and could benefit from. This could be learning the approaches and applying them yourself, as you did, or being the lead within a team of support. Would you agree and would you add any words of caution before beginning?

Jemma: I will begin with a cautious, *it depends*. Learning how to be your own therapist can be difficult and potentially harmful for two reasons. One, there is a wealth of research and theory that is unhelpful. It draws on a long history of sexist, victim-blaming and rape-apologetic perspectives within psychology. As a beginner, it can be difficult to travel this complex and highly debated terrain without direction or support. This is especially the case for survivors who may find what they read upsetting or triggering. It can also be easy to find a single piece of information that fits with your experience, but it can be more difficult to see the context in which that information was produced. For example, approaches that focus on 'risk-taking behaviours' can feel empowering at first, as it can feel as if you have control over the situation. You may say to yourself, 'If I just avoid these behaviours, I won't get hurt again,' but research repeatedly shows that this approach is ineffective at preventing violence and over time can lead to shame and self-blame.

The second reason is that things can get worse before they get better. With trauma (especially if your coping strategies have included numbing, dissociation and amnesia and so on), when you start the healing work, a lot of very difficult and painful feelings and memories can come to the surface, which can be overwhelming. So, I agree that becoming your own therapist can be a good option for survivors, but I would encourage them to find support first, whether that is a therapist or a support group, or family and friends who really support and understand what you are going through. If the abuse is complex and over a long period of time, I would recommend working with someone who is qualified to make sure that you are well supported on your healing journey.

Fionnuala: I think it will be incredibly validating for some survivors to read about a qualified therapist who has had harmful treatment by a professional. It may possibly allow them to acknowledge the re-traumatising experience of being blamed for the abuse they survived. Is there anything you would add, or advice you would offer, to anyone with that experience?

Jemma: Don't give up. My first therapist was literally a lifesaver, but I was lucky I found her. I have had several negative experiences with professionals when I have reached out for help, including being raped by them. I also had one therapist in England who told me to 'just go home' when I talked about two sexual assaults that were motivated by my being Irish. These two examples were deeply traumatising and have made it extremely difficult for me to develop trusting relationships with health professionals, which has understandably impacted on my overall health and wellbeing. It continues to be an everyday struggle, whether I am simply going to the dentist for a check-up or going for a PAP smear test, but it is important to keep trying as a part of my self-care. I would recommend prioritising your emotional wellbeing as much as your physical health during these times, and to try your best to find those who can support you in attending appointments (and potentially act as an advocate for you), and help comfort you if you have experienced a 'bad one'. Reach out to knowledgeable people in your community or professionals for advice on where to go if you are not sure where to find the help you need.

Fionnuala: I wholeheartedly believe that intersectional feminism is necessary to achieve sustainable wellbeing. It took recognising both the challenges and privileges of my identity to fully understand the traumatic experiences of my life and find a way through to acceptance of what happened and why it happened the way it did. Usually the traumatic events worsened over time as the instances of violence and abuse were followed by experiences of victim-blaming and shaming of my very existence. Being white, English-speaking and able-bodied, while also being non-binary (but often read as female), queer, autistic and Irish Catholic in Northern Ireland, my intersections of identities are numerous and complicated. Without an understanding of how these intersections affected my life, I was at a loss to explain why I so often experienced violence and abuse. It took self-discovery, diagnosis and a self-led review of a vast quantity of writing on sociology, religion and culture, psychology, feminist theory and more, as well as engaging in my own activism, to understand where my story fitted in. You have helped me throughout this journey, both through your supportive friendship and by providing links to so many of the resources I have read, and I am incredibly grateful for both.

Jemma: As you know, my experience has been very similar to yours. I spent so many years asking 'Why me?' because I could not find a way to explain why I had been victimised so often, by so many, and in so many different contexts. When I talked to people and disclosed my experiences, which to me were 'normal', I was confused by their reactions of shock, horror and tears, always with the question, 'What is it about *you* that makes this happen so often?' I wasted years over-analysing myself, trying to answer that question, and it took more than a decade of study and becoming an academic to finally answer it – that my experiences exist within a complex matrix of intersecting axes of oppression and they had much more to do with the context that I was abused within than some internal 'flaw' within myself. The other realisation was that this information would have been not only lifesaving to me as a child but protective against and preventative of further violence, but it was inaccessible to me in an elitist system of education and a social and cultural context where gender norms, heteronormativity and the normalisation of violence thrived.

References

Abramson K (2014). Turning up the lights on gaslighting. *Philosophical Perspectives 28*: 1–30.

Acosta F (1975). Etiology and treatment of homosexuality: a review. *Archives of Sexual Behaviour 4*: 9–29.

American Psychiatric Association (2013). *Diagnostic and Statistical Manual of Mental Disorder* (5th ed). Washington, DC: American Psychiatric Association.

Bancroft J, Marks I (1968). Electric aversion therapy of sexual deviants. *Proceedings of the Royal Society of Medicine* 61: 797–799.

Bass E, Davis, L (1994). *The Courage to Heal: a guide for women survivors of childhood sexual abuse.* New York, NY: Harper Collins.

Bieber I, Bieber T, Dain H, Dince P, Drellich M, Grand H et al (1988). *Homosexuality: a psychoanalytic study.* London: Jason Aronson Inc.

Blanchard R (2005). Early history of the concept of autogynephilia. *Archives of Sexual Behaviour* 34: 439–446.

Bowcott O (2018). Gay marriage cake row reaches UK's supreme court in Belfast. *The Guardian*; 12 May. www.theguardian.com/uk-news/2018/may/01/gay-marriage-cake-ashers-bakery-northern-ireland-uk-supreme-court (accessed 12 July 2018).

Bradley M (2001). Car-bomb left at Belfast airport. *The Irish Times*; 2 August. www.irishtimes.com/news/car-bomb-left-at-belfast-airport-1.320688 (accessed 3 March 2020).

Byrd D, Nicolosi N (2002). A meta-analytic review of treatment of homosexuality. *Psychological Reports* 90: 1139–1152.

Campbell F (2009). *Contours of ableism: the production of disability and abledness.* Basingstoke: Palgrave Macmillan.

Coleman S, Carlin L. The cultures of creationism: shifting boundaries of belief, knowledge and nationhood. In: Coleman S, Carlin, L (eds) (2017). *The Cultures of Creationism: anti-evolutionism in English-speaking countries.* London: Routledge (pp1–28).

Cuddy A (2018). Which European countries have the strictest abortion rules? *Euronews*; 30 January. www.euronews.com/2018/01/30/which-european-countries-have-the-strictest-abortion-rules (accessed 12 July 2018).

Curtis L (1984). *Same old story? The roots of anti-Irish racism.* London: Information on Ireland.

Donaghy G (2018). Security alert at Belfast City Airport amid fears of 'serious disorder' from UVF in East Belfast. *The Irish Post*; 11 July. www.irishpost.com/news/security-alert-belfast-city-airport-amid-fears-serious-disorder-uvf-east-belfast-157228 (accessed 3 March 2020).

Duffy N (2015). Northern Irish Assembly votes for equal marriage, but DUP vetoes it. *Pink News*; 2 November. www.pinknews.co.uk/2015/11/02/northern-ireland-assembly-votes-in-favour-of-equal-marriage-but-dup-vetoes-it/ (accessed 12 July 2018).

Duggan M (2010). The politics of Pride: representing relegated sexual identities in Northern Ireland. *Northern Ireland Legal Quarterly* 61(2): 163–178.

Elliott-Cooper A (2017). The struggle that cannot be named: violence, space and the re-articulation of anti-racism in post-Duggan Britain. *Ethnic and Racial Studies* 14: 1–19.

Farrell S (2009). *Rituals and Riots: sectarian violence and political culture in Ulster, 1784–1886.* Lexington: University Press of Kentucky.

Farwell N (2004). War rape: conceptualizations and responses. *Affilia* 19: 389–403.

Ferman D (2013). A parade or a riot: a discourse analysis of two ethnic newspapers on the 2011 marching season in Northern Ireland. *Journal of Media and Religion* 12(2): 57–70.

Fine M (1988). Sexuality, schooling, and adolescent females: the missing discourse of desire. *Harvard Educational Review* 58(1): 29–51.

Fine M, McClelland S (2006). Sexuality education and desire: still missing after all these years. *Harvard Educational Review* 76(3): 297–437.

Freeman H (2018). What does the Belfast rape trial tell women? Make a complaint and you'll be vilified. *The Guardian*; 4 April. www.theguardian.com/fashion/2018/apr/04/what-does-the-belfast-trial-tell-women-make-a-complaint-and-youll-be-vilified?CMP=fb_gu (accessed 12 July 2018).

Freud S (1949). *Three Essays on the Theory of Sexuality.* London: Imago Publishing.

Friedman J, Valenti J (2008). *Yes Means Yes! Visions of female sexual power and a world without rape.* Berkeley, CA: Seal Press.

Ghaill MM (2000). The Irish in Britain: the invisibility of ethnicity and anti-Irish racism. *Journal of Ethnic and Migration Studies 26*(1): 137–147.

Geoghegan P (2015). Will Belfast ever have a Berlin Wall moment and tear down its 'peace walls'? *The Guardian*; 29 September. www.theguardian.com/cities/2015/sep/29/belfast-berlin-wall-moment-permanent-peace-walls (accessed 3 March 2020).

Hadden S (2006). Treatment of homosexuality by individual and group psychotherapy. *American Journal of Psychiatry 9*: 810–815.

Hallsworth S (2016). What the 2011 summer riots were really about. *Vice*; 6 August. www.vice.com/en_uk/article/kwkbde/england-riots-2011-five-years-later (accessed 29 May 2018).

Halpin H (2018). Northern Ireland same-sex marriage bill passes first stage in House of Lords. *The Journal*; 28 March. www.thejournal.ie/northern-ireland-same-sex-marriage-bill-3927701-Mar2018/ (accessed 12 July 2018).

Hickman M (1995). Deconstructing whiteness: Irish women in Britain. *Feminist Review 50*: 5–19.

James S (1978). Treatment of homosexuality II. Superiority of desensitisation/arousal as compared with anticipatory avoidance conditioning: Results of a controlled trial. *Behaviour Therapy 9*: 28-36.

Kelly J (2016). Why are Northern Ireland's abortion laws different to the rest of the UK? *BBC News*; 8 April. www.bbc.co.uk/news/magazine-35980195 (accessed 12 July 2018).

Kennedy A, Prock K (2016). 'I still feel like I am not normal': a review of the role of stigma and stigmatization among female survivors of child sexual abuse, sexual assault, and intimate partner violence. *Trauma, Violence & Abuse 19*(5): 512–527.

Kramer E (2011). The playful is political: the metapragmatics of internet rape-joke arguments. *Language & Society 40*: 137–168.

Lawrence A (2017). Autogynephilia and the typology of male-to-female transsexualism. *European Psychologist 22*: 39–54.

Leonard M (2009). What's recreational about 'recreational rioting'? Children on the streets of Belfast. *Children & Society 24*: 38–49.

Leys R (2000). *Trauma: a genealogy.* Chicago, IL: University of Chicago Press.

Lockhart E (2016). Why trigger warnings are beneficial, perhaps even necessary. *First Amendment Studies 50*(2): 59–69.

MacCulloch M, Feldman M (1967). Aversion therapy in management of 43 homosexuals. *British Medical Journal 2*: 594–597.

Mann T (2017). What DUP in government would mean for the LGBT community in the UK. *Metro*; 10 June. https://metro.co.uk/2017/06/10/what-dup-in-government-would-mean-for-the-lgbt-community-in-the-uk-6699460/ (accessed 29 May 2018).

McDonald H (2015). What is Belfast's 'gay cake' case? *The Guardian*; 26 March. www.theguardian.com/uk-news/2015/mar/26/what-is-belfasts-gay-cake-case (accessed 12 July 2018).

McKay M, Wood J, Brantley J (2007). *The Dialectical Behaviour Therapy Skills Workbook: practical DBT exercises for learning mindfulness, interpersonal effectiveness, emotion regulation and distress tolerance*. Oakland, CA: New Harbinger Publications Inc.

Meaney G (2011). *Gender, Ireland, and Cultural Change: race, sex, and nation*. Abingdon: Routledge.

NIDirect (2018a). Guidance on civil partnerships in Northern Ireland. [Online.] *NI Direct*. www.nidirect.gov.uk/articles/guidance-civil-partnerships-northern-ireland (accessed 29 May 2018).

NIDirect (2018b). Gender recognition. [Online.] *NIDirect*. www.nidirect.gov.uk/articles/gender-recognition (accessed 29 May 2018).

Northern Ireland Statistics and Research Agency (2017). *2016 Mid-Year Population Estimates for Northern Ireland*. Belfast: NISRA. www.nisra.gov.uk/news/2016-mid-year-population-estimates-northern-ireland (accessed 7 July 2018).

Ó Dochartaigh N (2005). *From Civil Rights to Armalites: Derry and the birth of the Irish Troubles*. Basingstoke: Palgrave Macmillan.

Office for National Statistics (2015). *The Countries of the UK*. [Online.] London: ONS. https://webarchive.nationalarchives.gov.uk/20160108051201/http://www.ons.gov.uk/ons/guide-method/geography/beginner-s-guide/administrative/the-countries-of-the-uk/index.html (accessed 7 July 2018).

Perlin M (2016). Infinity goes on trial: Sanism, pretextuality, and the representation of defendants with mental disabilities. *QUT Law Review 16*: 106-126.

Pyne J (2014). The governance of gender non-conforming children: a dangerous enclosure. *Annual Review of Critical Psychology 11*: 79–96.

Quiery M (2007). *Invisible Women: a review of the impact of discrimination and social exclusion on lesbian and bisexual women's health in Northern Ireland*. Ballymena: Lesbian Advocacy Services Initiative (LASI).

Rae L (2016). Re-focusing the debate on trigger warnings: privilege, trauma, and disability in the classroom. *First Amendment Studies 50*(2): 95–101.

Randomsky N (2014). *Lost Voices: women, chronic pain, and abuse*. London: Routledge.

Rose N (1985). *The Psychological Complex*. London: Routledge.

Schwartz R (1995). *Internal Family Systems Therapy*. New York, NY: Guilford Press.

Sedgwick E (1991). How to bring your kids up gay. *Social Text 29*: 18–27.

Shapiro F (2001). *Eye Movement Desensitisation and Reprocessing (EMDR): basic principles, protocols, and procedures*. New York, NY: Guilford Press.

Sharkey S (1994). *Ireland and the Iconography of Rape: colonization, constraint, and gender*. London: University of North London Press.

Silva A, Mace R (2015). Inter-group conflict and cooperation: field experiments before, during, and after sectarian riots in Northern Ireland. *Frontiers in Psychology 6*: 1790.

Sloat A (2018). Sacrificing peace in Northern Ireland is not acceptable price for Brexit. *Washington Post*; 20 December. www.washingtonpost.com/opinions/2018/12/20/sacrificing-peace-northern-ireland-is-not-acceptable-price-brexit/?noredirect=on&utm_term=.e1573815d73d (accessed 3 March 2020).

Staples L (2018). Stories of LGBTWQ coming of age and fighting for equality in Northern Ireland. *Dazed*; 30 April. www.dazeddigital.com/life-culture/article/39668/1/stories-of-lgbtq-coming-of-age-fighting-for-equality-in-northern-ireland (accessed 3 March 2020).

Synder C, Gabbard W, May J, Zulcic N (2006). On the battleground of women's bodies: mass rape in Bosnia-Herzegovina. *Affilia 21*: 184–195.

Szasz T (2007). *Coercion as Cure: a critical history of psychiatry*. New Brunswick: Transaction.

Thapar-Björkert S, Ryan, L (2002). Mother India/Mother Ireland: comparative gendered dialogues of colonialism and nationalism in the early 20th century. *Women's Studies International Forum 25*(3): 301–313.

Thornhill R, Palmer, C (2000). *A Natural History of Rape: biological bases of sexual coercion*. Cambridge, MA: MIT Press.

Tosh J (2020). *The Body and Consent in Psychology, Psychiatry, and Medicine: a therapeutic rape culture*. London: Routledge.

Tosh J (2016). *Psychology and Gender Dysphoria: feminist and transgender perspectives*. London: Routledge.

Tosh J (2015). Rape me, I'm Irish: an analysis of the intersecting discourses of anti-Irish racism and sexual violence. *Intersectionalities: a Global Journal of Social Work Analysis, Research, Polity, and Practice 4*: 59–81.

Tosh J (2014). *Perverse Psychology*. London: Routledge.

Tosh J (2011). The medicalisation of rape: a discursive analysis of 'Paraphilic Coercive Disorder' and the psychiatrisation of sexuality. *Psychology of Women Section Review 13*: 2–12.

Tosh J, Carson K (2016). A desire to be 'normal'? A discursive and intersectional analysis of 'penetration disorder'. *Intersectionalities 5*: 151–172.

Tosh J, Golightley S (2016). The caring professions, not so caring? Bullying and emotional distress in the academy. In: Burstow B (ed). *Psychiatry Interrogated: an institutional ethnography anthology*. New York, NY: Palgrave Macmillan (pp143–160).

Ussher J (1991). *Women's Madness: misogyny or mental illness*. Hemel Hempstead: Harvester Wheatsheaf.

van der Kolk B (2014). *The Body Keeps the Score: brain, mind, and body in the healing of trauma*. New York, NY: Viking.

Walker M, Hernandez A, Davey M (2012). Childhood sexual abuse and adult sexual identity formation: intersection of gender, race, and sexual orientation. *American Journal of Family Therapy 20*: 385–398.

Walter B (2001). *Outsiders Inside: whiteness, place and Irish women*. London: Routledge.

Webb L (2015). Shame transfigured: slut-shaming from Rome to cyberspace. [Online.] *First Monday 24*. https://firstmonday.org/ojs/index.php/fm/article/view/5464/4419 (accessed 1 March 2020).

Weiss K (2010). Too ashamed to report: deconstructing the shame of sexual victimization. *Feminist Criminology 5*: 286–310.

Wilson D (2009). Health consequences of childhood sexual abuse. *Perspectives in Psychiatric Care 46*: 56–64.

Winters K (2008). *Gender Madness in American Psychiatry: essays from the struggle for dignity*. Colorado: GID Reform Advocates.

Chapter 6

Therapists' lived experience in counselling and psychotherapy training

Liz Smith and Sara Teresa Mollis

Notes about the conversation process

When we first received the brief for this chapter, we thought writing it would be straightforward – Liz would interview Sara and write the chapter based on the interview and both our lived experiences. In practice, however, the chapter turned out quite differently. It has evolved as a series of conversations between us, and the writing became a fully collaborative, experiential and even therapeutic process. We both felt a sense of ownership over its direction and, as such, the author's voice here has turned out to be 'we', because we realised it was more powerful to describe our experiences in a collective voice, rather like the #MeToo movement itself. The importance of shared experience, solidarity and hope for change are at the heart of the movement and of our chapter.

Excerpts of our conversations are included throughout to show some of the processes we went through at each stage in the writing. We felt this might give our readers some insight into our discussions and emotions and to us as individuals, as well as a sense of the time and place in which we were writing – a sense of authenticity, perhaps, that cannot always be conveyed through analytical prose alone.

We began our conversation by talking about what it is like for us, as women, to bring our own #MeToo experiences in the age of #MeToo to our training as therapists. We hope that this chapter will resonate with other women who have either recently trained, are going through their training or are about to start training and are wondering how the counselling and therapy professions relate to #MeToo, and to therapists (including those in training) with lived experiences of sexual violence. As we wrote, we realised that there are many areas where our experiences are aligned with our professional training and ethics and others where there is friction, which we explore in the course of this chapter.

Introduction

In one of our early conversations, Sara came up with the phrase 'digital reckoning'. This builds on the idea of #MeToo as the zeitgeist of the digital age – an internet-based public calling out of the prevalence of sexual violence and abuse. This has stayed with us as a succinct way of also describing and understanding the force of societal resistance to #MeToo. In our training, we both experienced strong resistance among both our trainers and our student peers to engaging with the sheer scale of #MeToo and its implications for the counselling and psychotherapy profession we are entering. Our training has never dealt with the enormity of the problem and the emotions that this might bring up for trainees, other than in a perfunctory and academic way, with a focus on how 'they' (victims of sexual abuse and assault) might present to 'us' in the therapy room. But for us, #MeToo confirmed that it wasn't '#JustThem' (Lee, 2018); it was all of 'us'.

Never once has this been discussed in our lectures and seminars. It has never been openly acknowledged that there could be women in our cohorts with their own #MeToo experiences who are both 'we therapists' and 'them, our clients'. In our experience, there is still a strong assumption that the two are separate; that any of us might hold a dual identity is implicitly denied through its absence from the content of our training, beyond what might emerge in the mandatory personal therapy we undergo.

In the academic spheres we inhabit as trainees, it is almost as if #MeToo has never happened, despite the fact that the overwhelming majority of students in both our cohorts are women, reflecting the predominance of women among practising counsellors and psychotherapists. This deafening silence about personal experiences of sexual violence has at times made us wonder if it is seen as a source of shame, and this has made it hard for us to speak about it.

A handful of female therapists have spoken out publicly about the pathologising of female survivors of sexual violence, both before and since

#MeToo. We acknowledge that their tireless work has allowed us to speak as freely as we are doing now. Therapists such as A Disorder for Everyone founder Jo Watson, some therapists in Psychotherapists and Counsellors for Social Responsibility (PCSR) and individuals such as Dr Jay Watts and our programme director Dr Gillian Proctor have spoken out against the psychiatric labelling of women who have been sexually abused or assaulted (notably, Gillian has supported us in writing this chapter and by critiquing our training process). We should not forget, of course, the co-editors of this book, Dr Deborah Lee and Emma Palmer, who, with many others, have influenced and inspired us along the way.

We have also been strongly influenced by Carl Rogers and the person-centred approach, since we are both peer support workers trained in survivor-led organisations that resist narratives of pathology and labelling. But there is still much work to be done to engage trainee counsellors and psychotherapists on academically led training courses like ours with contemporary social issues like #MeToo.

Rogers' (1961) seven-stage process provides a framework that has helped us to understand how such change might happen and to share this learning. We subscribe to Rogers' concept of self-actualisation: the idea that the human organism has a natural tendency to seek to thrive and does the best it can with the conditions it is given. Rogers' (1961) self-actualisation process moves the profession away from imposing therapist understandings and interpretations on clients and instead encourages them to create their own. In focusing on human process, rather than human failings, he created a framework that enables us to understand how change happens and how the therapeutic process can facilitate such change.

We are critical of our profession in some respects, and in this chapter we highlight its shortcomings with regard to #MeToo. Nonetheless, we want this chapter to carry a message of hope. Whenever we feel less than hopeful at, say, a difficult point in our client work, Rogers' process reminds us that there is a way forward and that, given the right conditions, change will happen. Even though the seven-stage process is not fixed, it may be a bumpy road and we may have to re-engage with it several times over.

We have divided the chapter into seven sections to match each stage of the process. The questions we ask in our conversations and the feelings and perceptions we unearth are personal; we do not intend them as evidenced truths. This is an experiential journey towards growth, which we hope others may draw on for their own thinking and behaviour. We hope that other women in or contemplating entering the profession will find some solidarity and comfort in conversation, as we have.

Stage 1: In which the organism remains fixed and rigid and resists all forms of change

According to Rogers (1961), in the first stage the client sees things in binary terms, displays a fixed, rigid thinking style and focuses all their energy outwards. They blame others for their difficulties and are unable to see their own contribution. They are somewhat passive in this part of the process and have no desire for change.

Sexual violence is so often spoken about in the passive voice, particularly when discussing women's experience of sexual assault. The embedding of implicit victim blaming in language is one example of this.

> We talk about how many women were raped last year, not how many men raped women. We talk about how many girls… got pregnant last year, rather than how many boys and men impregnated teenage girls. So you can see how the use of the passive voice has a political effect. It shifts the focus off of men and boys and on to girls and women… when you look at that term 'violence against women', nobody is doing it to them. It just happens to them. Men aren't even a part of it. (Keren, 2012)

Indeed, when you go on social media and find yourself involved in debates about #MeToo, you might well wonder where the perpetrators are. Why should those who have had the harm done to them have to answer for their experiences, especially for daring to speak about them, as Christine Blasey Ford[1] was forced to do in the courtroom? And why is there such insistence on shifting or deflecting blame, whether by asking what the victim was wearing, what their sex lives were like prior to the assault or how much they had been drinking, or simply by questioning the narrative? These defences relate to deeply held societal myths, which Lonsway and Fitzgerald (1994) call 'rape myths'. They might include, for example, the belief that women frequently lie about rape, or that rape only happens to women who are already sexually promiscuous. Lonsway and Fitzgerald's paper extensively cites the work of Martha Burt (1980), who, 14 years previously, was discussing the prevalence of these myths and their function in denying the extent of the problem of widespread sexual violence.

If this sounds familiar, that is because it is. Burt was writing in 1980, Lonsway and Fitzgerald in 1994, Keren in 2012. The current iteration of #MeToo

---

1. Christine Blasey Ford accused Supreme Court Justice Brett Kavanaugh of sexually assaulting her at a party when she was 15 years old. Since her testimony, she has reported receiving death threats and harassment, as well as media vilification, and has been forced to leave her home for her own safety (Baker, 2018).

went viral on social media in late 2017. The following year, the same tired, toxic myths were used to discredit Blasey Ford to justify the 'denial and trivialization of a crime that affects a substantial proportion of the female population' (Lonsway & Fitzgerald, 1994: 136). As Burt wrote, and it still rings true now, 'the world is indeed not a safe place for rape victims' (Burt, 1980: 229).

In terms of our personal experiences of #MeToo, we have both experienced the anger that is directed towards those who refuse to stay silent about sexual violence, instead of towards perpetrators. Women who, like us, have spoken up about #MeToo are an inconvenience to those – men and women – who would rather not engage with this problem or do not think anything needs to change. As Lonsway and Fitzgerald suggest, 'the belief that only certain types of women are raped functions to obscure and deny the personal vulnerability of *all* women by suggesting that only *other* women are raped' (1994: 136).

One of the main accusations against #MeToo advocates and anti-abuse activists is that they revel in their victim status. The strongest criticism – and indeed, abuse – has come from the men's rights activist (MRA) movement and the mainly online Men Going Their Own Way (MGTOW) community, some of whose proponents reject involvement with women altogether. Many MRAs see women as 'programmed to ruin men's lives' (cited in Lamoureux, 2015) and as using men for their financial gain. MRAs frequently fearmonger about false allegations. #MeToo, for them, is further proof that women cannot be trusted (ie. that women routinely lie about rape and assault) and that men live in constant danger of being falsely accused. Burt's ideas about adversarial sexual beliefs – ie. that 'sexual relationships are fundamentally exploitative' (1980: 218) – are perhaps best exemplified by the MRA and MGTOW movements' deep distrust of and lack of respect for women.

Their fear of false accusation is, however, greatly exaggerated (Beaulieu, 2012). The false accusation rate in the UK, for instance, stands at around three per cent of reported cases (Burton et al, 2012), lower than for all other crimes. Moreover, it is almost always female victims who are accused of making false or malicious allegations. The British press, for instance, applauded the male victims of youth coach Barry Bennell,[2] who was convicted in 2018 of 36 sex offences against 10 boys (BBC, 2018). Much was made of their decisions to waive anonymity and face their abuser in court: the *Mirror* described Gary Cliffe as 'brave' (Dunn, 2018); the *Buxton Advertiser* declared Chris Unsworth a 'voice of hope' (Ball, 2018), and the *Guardian* described Andy Woodward as having 'great courage and eloquence' (Taylor, 2016). Compare this with the coverage of Christine Blasey Ford. Lionel Shriver (2018), writing in the

---

2. Barry Bennell was a youth coach at several high-profile English football clubs. He was convicted in 2018 of 36 sex offences against 10 boys. www.bbc.co.uk/news/uk-43050466

Spectator, described her as 'a deferent and visibly fragile academic with a high mousy voice… a lousy role model for young women today'. Donald Trump mocked Blasey Ford at a Mississippi rally,[3] parodying her account of the incident and declaring 'a man's life is in tatters'.

This hostile media coverage of women who have dared to speak out makes uncomfortable reading for us and for other therapists like us. This is an excerpt from one of our early conversations:

Sara: I feel like in our profession #MeToo has the most potential to be damaging, because we're viewed as these people who are supposed to be helping people who aren't well, so we're meant to be well. Not only are we meant to be well, but we are *not* supposed to be 'damaged'.

Liz: Our profession often talks about victims of abuse in terms of the damage done to them. But if we are also victims, survivors, whatever we want to call ourselves, what does that mean we are? How will our clients see us? Or our mentors? Or our supervisors?

Sara: What are we supposed to tell ourselves – that we have to deal with this ourselves? That it's more of a risk to be part of the conversation than not to be?

Liz: I've worked a lot with clients who have experienced sexual abuse, assault and rape. I'm afraid to be too 'out there' about my own experiences in public, even though I also have something of a public profile as a writer. What if a client or a manager Googles me, finds that, and then assumes things about me because of it or calls my competency into question? At this stage of my career, before I've even built a reputation for myself, that feels too risky.

Stage 1, therefore, does not just apply to 'society out there' – it applies to our own profession and its orthodoxies. We suspect that counselling and psychotherapy has yet to fully embrace therapists with lived experience. But if we are too afraid to participate in the debate around #MeToo, are we colluding with the deniers and disbelievers? As we talked, we wondered if we might also be letting other women down if we refuse to engage:

Sara: How much should we be loyal to our work and how much to our identities as women? Even if we feel we have resolved our past traumas privately in therapy, do we have a duty to womankind?

---

3. A video of Donald Trump mocking Blasey Ford at the rally was posted by *The Guardian* on 3 October, 2018. www.theguardian.com/us-news/video/2018/oct/03/i-dont-know-laughter-as-trump-mocks-fords-sexual-assault-testimony-video

Liz: You know, I hadn't even thought about that tension in terms of loyalty to the profession versus our loyalty to our sisters. Am I ducking out of some responsibility here because I put self-preservation first, my career first, instead of my identity as a woman?

Sara: Yeah, I noticed that a lot of my friends, when they posted on Twitter, they just put the hashtag and that was it.

Liz: I did the same! Just posted it with something very vague, so nobody could really tell what had happened to me. I didn't even fully trust some of the people on my Facebook friends list with that information, to be honest. Even though they're not therapists, they have certain views on what a therapist is, or should be. What if I don't measure up? I worry constantly if things I say on social media might be considered not right for a therapist to be saying. I've even shut my social media down for periods of time because I get paranoid about it.

It feels to both of us that therapists are expected to conform to a higher standard of behaviour than other professionals and are expected to have a higher level of emotional control. As female therapists, we feel this is even more the case: if we are seen to be 'overly emotional' about #MeToo – or even women's issues in general – we might be regarded as having insufficient emotional control to be taken seriously.

This might be an exaggerated fear – after all, we mentioned earlier the many female therapists who have and are speaking out. Nonetheless, we cannot help feeling that it is somehow not acceptable for us to do so, especially at this stage in our careers, while we are still trainees. Perhaps this is because it is simply not spoken about in our training – it is not yet a part of the everyday discourse of counsellors, therapists and trainees. Most of those women, inspiring though they are, are not our contemporaries; they are not our peers. Although we can read their articles and books, we cannot sit down with them and have the kind of conversations we have had with each other during this writing process.

Stage 2: In which expression begins to flow, but the organism remains fixated on others

In stage 2, the client begins to talk about their preoccupations, but still tends to externalise them.

Here, we will focus on our experiences as trainees in the counselling and psychotherapy world. In our training, we readily theorise about what clients' experiences might be and how they affect them, in a detached, clinical way, but – in our experience – the last thing anybody wants to say is, 'This is how it affected me'.

We have included here part of a conversation in which we talked about our own preoccupations during training, both with our own experiences and with how these might be interpreted by our peers and mentors:

Sara: For women, is there 'acceptable trauma' and 'unacceptable trauma?' What I mean is, you could probably tell your fellow students and your lecturer that you had a traumatic birth with one of your kids, and people would probably be quite empathic. But sexual assault or abuse – that's too uncomfortable for others to talk about and to hear and it has different implications for how people might view you.

Liz: There's the idea that you wouldn't be able to come back from it in a professional sense. Look at Christine Blasey Ford, it's going to affect the rest of her working life.

Sara: I can become unspeakably angry thinking about those high school boys [the group who assaulted Christine Blasey Ford], where that sense of entitlement came from – and what we do that may contribute to it. Does our silence, as psychotherapists, in itself perpetuate it? Do we need #TherapistsToo?

Liz: Yeah, there's still this idea that abuse and assault is something our clients experience but we don't. Even if we have actually experienced it, the process of training dissociates you from it because it's too difficult to confront that dual identity and then, if you do, you don't know what to do with it.

There is a huge implication in therapists' externalisation of this problem – if we feel too much shame or doubt to be comfortable with owning 'unacceptable trauma' in the training process, what does that say about how we feel about our clients? If we deny 'unacceptable trauma' through fear that we may be seen as too wounded to work with clients, are we really embodying the belief in our clients' potential for growth and healing that is so central to our training? We have found that 'us and them' language is rarely challenged in class, group supervision and so forth, and there is little acknowledgement that we might all share these experiences, especially among women:

Liz: I vividly remember one student in my class saying something like, 'You've got to remember, they don't think like we do' – referring to clients – and I remember thinking, 'Who is this "we"? Who are "they"? If you knew certain things about what I've experienced, would you think I was a "we" or a "they"?'

In pausing to think about what this actually means in practice, we are reminded of the numbers of female victims of sexual trauma who are given the label of borderline personality disorder (BPD) or its modern equivalent, emotionally unstable personality disorder (EUPD). The second a woman receives that diagnosis, regardless of anything that has happened to her beyond her control, she is viewed as unstable, unreliable – a liar, even. Yet the common factor in this diagnosis is so often abuse and trauma (Shaw & Proctor, 2005); the BPD diagnosis 'conceals sexual abuse by categorising, blaming and "treating" the survivors' (2005: 487). It's another way to shift the focus and, importantly and more weightily, the responsibility.

It is hard for us not to make the link when we are confronted in training with case studies that resonate with our own experiences. We recognise, however, that our socio-economic privilege has made it easier for us to navigate the mirrored halls of psychiatric services than it is for some of our clients, and we have evaded the label ourselves. We could take up the rest of this chapter critiquing the use and even existence of the BPD/EUPD label; it is for another book. Nonetheless, it made us wonder: if you knew your therapist had ever been given a BPD/EUPD label, would you continue to see them?

Stage 3: When experience begins to flow

In this stage, Rogers (1961) notes that the client may begin to accept past feelings, but emotions, and indeed the self, are still highly intellectualised. Nonetheless, he characterised this stage as the beginning of an awakening of sorts – an increased sense of awareness of oneself in the world. It is often the stage at which clients are more likely to present for therapy.

Once we opened the floodgates here, our experiences did indeed begin to flow freely. For us, this section represents the beginning of a move away from the intellectual to the personal and experiential. One of the reasons for using a person-centred framework to write this chapter was to give space to our own emotional experiencing. Hyper-intellectualisation often functions as a defence against vulnerability, which we had recognised in others around us, but also in ourselves.

So many individual stories have been obscured by demands for hard evidence in the form of numbers and conviction rates. We have heard many people suggest that #MeToo does not equal 'proof'. Deniers also seek to minimise the problem, making fun of 'social justice warriors' and 'snowflakes', asserting that #MeToo is just a phenomenon for oversensitive millennials obsessed with trigger warnings and safe spaces. Displacement often follows, in that instead of confronting the sheer numbers of people, mostly women, who have come forward to say they have experienced some form of sexual violence in their lives, the focus is all too often brought back to men. What about false accusations? The men's lives that would be 'ruined' by allegations of 'minor indiscretions'? What about the victims? They're probably lying anyway, especially if they are women. What about the men?

In other words, 'What about the perpetrators'?

But what about them? We already have a justice system that is stacked against rape and assault victims. Brock Turner, for example, served a mere three months in jail, while his victim, Chanel Miller, was grilled in court about her sex life, her clothing choices and, most notably, her drinking habits, as if alcohol were the rapist and not Turner.[4] As Miller said in her statement, 'alcohol was not the one who stripped me, fingered me, had my head dragging against the ground, with me almost fully naked' (cited in Buncombe, 2016). That she spoke so graphically in court about what Turner did to her that night and still received abuse speaks volumes about where we are as a society when it comes to believing victims and recognising that they also have a right to justice. Women have to weigh up whether it is worth coming forward, knowing how they are likely to be treated.

Liz: After an assault in a bar a few years ago, I knew there would be no point in reporting it. I didn't have any trust that anybody would care and I just thought I'd be blamed for it because I'd had a few drinks. I just thought, 'What's the point?' The saddest thing is, I considered myself lucky that I wasn't actually raped. The guys who did it could have been worse; there are worse men out there.

We have been angry, we are angry and, not only that, we accept that we are angry.

Stage 4: In which we begin to recognise and accept our inner experiences

In stage 4 there is greater acceptance and willingness to explore 'here and now' feelings and the internal world. Rogers (1961) asserts that most of the work of therapy takes place in stages 4 and 5.

In this section, we turn from our external environment to ourselves. As we

---

4. Brock Turner was convicted in 2016 of the sexual assault of 'an unconscious woman outside a fraternity house' (Buncombe, 2016). The leniency of the sentence prompted criticism that Turner's privileged status as a college student and athlete counted for more than the suffering of the victim in the eventual sentencing and the judge was widely criticised. Chanel Miller subsequently chose to reveal her identity and has since published her own book about what happened, *Know My Name* (Miller, 2019).

realised that we shared similar experiences, both in our lives and within our training process, this opened up a space for a deeper exploration of our relationship with each other, with other survivors and trainees, and with ourselves.

In this part of the process, having experienced the anger we mentioned in stage 3, we began to explore how we were in the present, although it remained hard for us to trust our feelings about it. The 'higher authority' of our future profession still loomed large – but did it really present the obstacles we thought it did? The questions we began to ask ourselves here were around the responsibilities we might hold as therapists and individuals. We discussed these responsibilities and the risks with respect to our identities as women, as survivors, as therapists, and as members of society and contributors to the post-#MeToo world.

Sara: It's fear of the loss of what we've worked for. If we're seen as damaged, will we still be trusted?

Liz: It's also a fear of the unknown – I don't know what it would be like if psychotherapists were more open about their own experiences, because to a certain extent I feel like we're expected to be extremely private, like closed books.

Sara: It's not fear of judgement exactly, it's also about having a choice. We shouldn't have to talk about it. If a woman says she doesn't want to discuss it or support anyone else with it, then she shouldn't have to, any more than we should judge those who do discuss it in public. But then how does that fit with a sense of responsibility? I see it like the activist paradox. One person who doesn't want to speak about it might think it doesn't matter because other people who are able to will do it. They might think that, as one person, they can't accomplish anything anyway. But then if everybody felt that way, nothing would shift.

Liz: This is the individualism in our profession, though, isn't it? We mostly do one-to-one work. We are isolated to some degree because of the nature of the work. It doesn't feel connected for me sometimes with my community, the society I live in. I often feel helpless in the face of systemic injustice as a therapist, whether it's #MeToo, poverty or the removal of disability benefits. Sometimes it feels like all I do is sit in a room and talk but I don't do anything with it, because I'm afraid of the potential ramifications. So this for me is where we have to think, really think, about how political therapy is for us and what we do with that.

Sara: Do we as female psychotherapists with lived experience have a responsibility to address this power dynamic that we're so involved with? Is that what we're talking about here?

Liz: I know other female therapists and psychologists, like Jay Watts, who speak out about political stuff and their own lived experience, but they're protected to a degree by the fact that they're established.

Sara: So are we having this conversation because we're trainees, we're not established and #MeToo is happening now, while we're at this place in our training, in our lives?

The conclusion we came to is that it is our trainee status, more than the profession itself, that made us feel fearful. It may not, of course, be true in practice – we acknowledged in the discussion we had after this conversation that other female therapists are already speaking out and may be risking much by doing so. Being professionally established may not offer the protection we think it does at this point, but for us it still feels like our position is more tenuous.

The major risk for us is that in training, we are still on trial. Those who have the power to assess us could find us too challenging of their orthodoxy and as such find us lacking. If we fall too much out of line, we might not get our seat at the table, which is a double bind for us as women fighting for a place in a profession that has traditionally been dominated by men at the top, despite higher numbers of female practitioners overall (Brown, 2017).

Stage 5: In which we begin to recognise and express where we are in the present

In stage 5, according to Rogers (1961), the client begins to understand their own incongruences and moves towards a state of greater congruence. This stage is also characterised in terms of increased self-awareness, trust in one's own decision-making processes and a more defined sense of personal responsibility. Clients in this stage feel more confident to express their emotions in the present and feel that they are likely to be heard and understood.

In stage 4 we identified our trainee status as being a key source of anxiety. Within that, however, we also identified a sense of responsibility for each other and for other survivors. The excerpt below records some of our discussions about the risks and barriers, and about the responsibility we felt to break the silence within our profession.

Sara: Is there any other profession where you'd disclose 'I was raped' either recently or a long time ago, and you would be immediately asked if you were fit to do your job? I think that's quite unique about therapy. But it's got to the point where it's undeniable; when so many people have said #MeToo, of course there will be therapists who have gone through this, especially women.

Liz: It's implicit because there are just so many of us. This is where we're starting to break down the denial, isn't it? We can't just say 'Oh, it's not us,' or pretend it's not us.

Sara: It's always been there, it's always happened, it's just not been talked about. Maybe we're being given permission, because it's everybody – or almost everybody.

Liz: Wow – so are therapists the final frontier of #MeToo? If we come out and say it, then it really is everybody?

Our silence would mean nothing changes, either for us or for them – or it simply means we expect others to do the work for us.

During the process of writing this chapter, we both began working in a peer support service, providing person-centred peer support to people experiencing mental health crisis. The kind of peer support that we both practise in our current workplace has been instrumental in building our own resilience during the process of training as therapists and as women with lived experiences of sexual violence in the #MeToo era. Being in relationship with each other in the process of writing this chapter, as well as the multiple connections we have made with others in training and within the #MeToo movement, has helped us begin to feel seen and heard, as in a therapeutic relationship. This has given us confidence and more trust that others might see and hear us too, as our readers are hopefully doing here. If the next generation of millennial therapists were to say #TherapistsToo, might that be the shift we are looking for?

Stage 6: A dramatic turn of events?

Rogers (1961) sees this stage as one of a movement towards wholeness and greater integration of the self. He states that it can be a powerful stage, where beliefs about self and others may dramatically evolve and current emotions are fully experienced and accepted.

In terms of our journey, this stage involved the realisation that we were not alone and we did not need to be. There are many counsellors and psychotherapists and trainees like us – mostly women with lived experience – who are out there practising competently but may never have disclosed. The counter-argument might be that personal therapy is the place for counsellors and psychotherapists to 'work through' such things. #MeToo is not about therapy, however. It is about bringing out into the open conversations that typically take place behind closed doors. Without this open dialogue, the therapy room could be another secretive location that may even turn into yet another 'shame space' – one that reminds us that we are not allowed to talk about these things in public, these things that are not nice, and that others do not want to know about them.

Below is part of a conversation we had about why it feels important to have both public and private spaces to discuss #MeToo experiences, both in our training and outside it.

Liz: So are we saying that we need both? That we need the private spaces, but we also need the public conversations?

Sara: The public conversations help to deprive the victim blamers of oxygen. We can still have the therapeutic spaces – you can't do that work in 280 characters on Twitter – but this public sharing allows people to feel less alone. Maybe we need that as therapists, too – to feel less alone in having lived experience and not to feel like we are less competent.

Liz: Yeah, I've definitely felt alone at times. I've felt like I'm the only one in the room going 'What the hell?' when, because of my experiences, I've felt a reaction to something we've done in class, and because of that I might see it as stigmatising or even victim blaming. I've certainly felt that victim blaming was present in some of the case studies and lectures I've heard while training. But nobody called it out, so neither did I. But it has helped to know that, as time has gone on, there are other students sitting with the same feelings.

Sara: I do not see my lived experience at all as a weakness, not at all. I wonder how people can do this work, actually, without at least some knowledge of what it might feel like to be a client who we might work with one day.

In the process of training, not only did we feel that clients were 'othered' by some of the teaching; we also felt that we had begun to 'other' ourselves. The 'us and them' language has rarely been problematised, so if there is an 'us' and a 'them', how can we be both? Our training seemed to imply that we have to choose which camp we sit in. If we choose to sit with 'we therapists', how much are we allowed to have in common with 'them' and still be trusted to work with 'them' effectively?

As yet, nobody has answered that question for us – or pointed it out as a problem.

Throughout the process of writing this chapter and sharing our emotions and experiences, we have felt despondent at times, and we have also felt angry. We also moved towards greater acceptance of our dual identities and felt less anxious about needing to fit into the narratives offered to us during our training, or even to accept them as absolute truths. We allowed ourselves the space to feel compassion for ourselves and each other in navigating our training and our contributions to #MeToo, including the decision to contribute to this book. Our contributing to the book also felt like a contribution to the therapy trainees of the future. Our hope is that open discussion about women's lived experience of sexual violence may one day be an integral part of training, instead of being avoided and pathologised.

It is that hope that keeps us here – that keeps us having these conversations and thinking about what it all means.

Stage 7: What next?

In stage 7, the client begins to effect change for themselves and the need to be in therapy becomes largely redundant (Rogers, 1961).

When we started to write this chapter, we began by talking about everything around us and how it had affected us and continues to do so. But as we went on, like any good therapeutic process, it became less about others' attitudes and much more about us and our own experiences, our feelings about them, and how to reconcile these with the training process in which we find ourselves now.

In an interview in *The Cut*, in October 2018, #MeToo founder Tarana Burke[5] talked about the 'unifying language' of #MeToo (Rowley, 2018): 'You have a built-in group of people who automatically get you, who automatically believe you.' There was some relief and some solidarity for us in the process of writing this, but it also left us with a sense of cognitive dissonance. As counsellors, we have plenty of unconditional positive regard for our clients with #MeToo experiences, but do we have enough for ourselves and each other? Do we talk about this enough on our courses, amongst ourselves, in our professional community? Where is our group of people that 'gets' us? We felt that this sense of communal emotional holding that Burke wanted to create through #MeToo is largely missing from our training process and our profession. This goes back, for us, to the tension between the individual, private level of the therapeutic process and the fact that

---

5. Burke first coined the term 'Me Too' in 2006. Between 1998 and 2015, she ran 'healing circles' in Philadelphia and Alabama. #MeToo did not become a viral movement on social media until October 2017.

we cannot always separate the private from the public, the individual from their socio-political context.

In the same interview, Burke discusses public expectations of #MeToo, which we link to the current obsession with measurable results in therapy. Expecting perpetrators to be named and shamed, for example, could be one such desired result and even ostensibly herald the end of the movement. However, the 'results' of #MeToo – and of counselling and psychotherapy, come to that – are not so tangible. At its core, the movement (and its key meaning for us personally) is about people holding up their hands, feeling supported, and not being expected to provide 'results' or 'outcomes' – that is not the job of a victim or a survivor. The need for hard outcomes is something we resist in our therapeutic work and that we also resisted in the process of writing this chapter – there are no neat conclusions to be made.

There is a reason, however, why this book was even needed to shed some light on psychotherapists and counsellors in relation to #MeToo. For us, that reason was the victim blaming and shame, both external and internal, implicit in our reluctance to be open about our experiences of sexual assault and abuse. Naming that in itself has been therapeutic for us. If this book, and our chapter, makes a small difference in terms of shifting how we talk about these issues, we will feel that we have been 'good enough' therapists. Surely that is what we all aspire to, and perhaps all we can aspire to in a process-driven profession that continues to resist hard outcomes, despite growing socio-political pressure?

It was also timely that Burke's interview came just as we were coming to our own (lack of) conclusions while writing this chapter – so perhaps we should leave the last word to her:

> If we shift how we talk about it, we can shift how we respond to it, we can shift how the entire culture understands it... It's going to make a difference in the way people respond to survivors of sexual violence and that difference is really everything.

References

Baker S (2018). Christine Blasey Ford still can't live at home because of unending death threats after her Kavanaugh testimony, lawyers say. *UK Business Insider*; 8 October. http://uk.businessinsider.com/christine-blasey-ford-cant-move-home-kavanaugh-testimony-death-threats-2018-10 (accessed 13 September 2018).

Ball L (2018). Barry Bennell victim bravely speaks out as voice for hope. *Buxton Advertiser*; 22

February. www.buxtonadvertiser.co.uk/news/barry-bennell-victim-bravely-speaks-out-as-voice-of-hope-1-9029641 (accessed 15 September 2018).

BBC News (2018). Ex-football coach Barry Bennell guilty of sex abuse. *BBC News*; 13 February. www.bbc.co.uk/news/uk-43050466 (accessed 14 September 2018).

Beaulieu S (2012). *The truth about false accusation*. [Blog.] Sarah Beaulieu. https://sarahbeaulieu.me/the-truth-about-false-accusation (accessed 13 September 2018).

Brown S (2017). Is counselling women's work? *Therapy Today 28*(2): 8–11.

Buncombe A (2016). Stanford rape case: read the impact statement of Brock Turner's victim. *Independent*; 2 September. www.independent.co.uk/news/people/stanford-rape-case-read-the-impact-statement-of-brock-turners-victim-a7222371.html (accessed 18 September 2018).

Burt M (1980). Cultural myths and supports for rape. *Journal of Personality and Social Psychology 38*(2): 217–230.

Burton M, McLeod R, de Guzmán V, Evans R, Lambert H, Cass G (2012). *Understanding the progression of serious cases through the Criminal Justice System: evidence drawn from a selection of casefiles*. [Online.] Ministry of Justice Research Series 11/12. London: Ministry of Justice. https://assets.publishing.service.gov.uk/government/uploads/system/uploads/attachment_data/file/217471/understanding-progression-serious-cases.pdf#page=35 (accessed 15 September 2018).

Dunn A (2018). We can only hope there is closure for brave men abused by Barry Bennell and football pays for their awful betrayal. *The Mirror*; 22 February. www.mirror.co.uk/sport/football/news/can-only-hope-closure-brave-12072130 (accessed 19 September 2018).

Keren R (2012). The language of gender violence. *Middlebury Magazine*; 15 March. www.jacksonkatz.com/news/language-gender-violence/ (accessed 13 September 2018).

Lamoureux M (2015). This group of anti-feminist men is banishing women from their lives. *Vice*; 25 September. www.vice.com/en_uk/article/7bdwyx/inside-the-global-collective-of-straight-male-separatists (accessed 19 September 2018).

Lee DA (2018). If it's #MeToo, it can't be #JustThem. *Asylum 25*(1): 8-9. http://asylummagazine.org/2018/03/if-its-metoo-it-cant-be-justthem-by-deborah-a-lee/ (accessed 4 February 2019).

Lonsway KA, Fitzgerald LF (1994). Rape myths: in review. *Psychology of Women Quarterly 18*(2): 133–164.

Miller C (2019). *Know My Name*. New York NY: Viking.

Rogers CR (1961). *On Becoming a Person*. Boston, MA: Houghton Mifflin.

Rowley L (2018). The Architect of #MeToo says the movement has lost its way. *The Cut*; 23 October. www.thecut.com/2018/10/tarana-burke-me-too-founder-movement-has-lost-its-way.html (accessed 19 September 2018).

Shaw C, Proctor G (2005). Women at the margins: a critique of the diagnosis of borderline personality disorder. *Feminism & Psychology 15*(4): 483–490.

Shriver L (2018). Why Christine Blasey Ford's testimony didn't make me cry. *The Spectator*; 24 December. https://blogs.spectator.co.uk/2018/12/why-christine-blasey-fords-testimony-didnt-make-me-cry/ (accessed 13 September 2018).

Taylor D (2016). Andy Woodward: it was the softer, weaker boys he targeted. *The Guardian*; 16 November. www.theguardian.com/football/2016/nov/16/andy-woodward (accessed 19 September 2018).

Chapter 7

Survivors of sexual violence training as psychotherapists in the UK

Deborah A. Lee, with Peggy, Sam and Phoenix

On reading my review of *Zen and Therapy* (Bazzano, 2017a; Lee, 2018a), in which a broken combi boiler starred, Bazzano (2017b) observed some similarity with the writing of Miranda July. He didn't say why but, intrigued and on meeting July (2015a) for the first time, I felt deeply connected and honoured by the comparison.

For Christmas 2017, a new friend who had watched from afar gave me a DVD of *The Breakfast Club* (Hughes, 1985). She saw me as Claire, eating sushi; I'd thought I would be Allison making a sugary crisp sandwich. I sought to see the confidence that was, apparently, being admired.

The audio book of another July novel (July, 2015b) now draws me back again and again: falling asleep while listening, you hear something new every night; it's a tapestry that may finally weave together, but why *should* everything make sense at once, or even at all?

When July reads, every word seems licked, tasted, devoured, enjoyed; there's such pleasure in words, language, the act of speaking. I might have said I'd like July to read my work aloud, but in the journey of life, yes, I *am* increasingly learning to be confident in my own voice and in my own connections with others (because of/in spite of psychotherapy training?)

* * *

It's early Spring 2018, and I'm in my house on the hill, watching the horizon as moon-landing machinery whizzes back and forth, winking knowingly, and the green fields unravel. It was so beautiful, so serene; it grounded me from the moment I moved there. I never believed its demise was coming, that the builders would finally arrive.

> All night we stay up together speaking of Sappho. Then at dawn we dig a grave and lay the body in… Then before we go to bed, we visit the brooder and signal the intent to begin a baby. (Piercy, 1978: 161–162)

I turn my eyes away from the departing view, and return to my desk, my books, my computer, my writer's block, but there's something shifting; the baby is coming, after so long…

* * *

The story (sort of) starts in the academic year 2015/16, with a proposal (Lee, 2017a): a qualitative, person-centred study of women survivors training as psychotherapists; an (intended) grounded theory exploration of post-traumatic growth and unconditional positive self-regard.

A 'yes!' from the Ethics Committee led to a long, stormy engagement.

Something Bad Happened… But it's not the time for that.

Artistic differences, then; we grew apart.

Well, not entirely… Feminism's 'interpretive framework' and its 'ontological, epistemological and methodological beliefs' (Creswell, 2013: 37) stayed close.

But I was unsettled by studies of unconditional positive self-regard ('measures were administered… ' (Flanagan et al, 2015: 194); I'd challenged pathology-creep in 'post-traumatic growth' (Lee, 2017b), and the grounded theory approach I'd planned to use became irksome. Even Glaser and Strauss didn't last forever (Creswell, 2013: 84). No matter how often Charmaz (2014) came compassionately to coax me with her constructivist approach, I feared how scientific it seemed.

The passion wasn't there; I wanted, wanted… to study *what it's like* to be a survivor in training (while being a survivor in training). Moustakas (1980: 14) explains that heuristic research 'demands the total presence, honesty, maturity and integrity of a researcher who not only strongly desires to know and understand but is willing to commit endless hours of sustained immersion and focused concentration on one central question, to risk the opening of wounds and passionate concerns, and to undergo the personal transformation that exists as a possibility in every heuristic journey'. That sounded like my heart's desire.

* * *

#itsnotok week, February 2018. My friend and I arrive at a screening of The Hunting Ground *(Dick, 2015).*

We're offered popcorn: 'It's free!'

When we reject the free condoms/wristbands as well, the organiser shrugs: 'Enjoy the film!'

In the interval, there's an advertisement for a 'mental health' campaign. A Post-it note saying 'OCD' twitches on a woman's forehead.

'Great idea,' say people, murmuring and nodding seriously about Prince Harry.

When the lights go up, a man shakes with anger: 'Women make false allegations! Where's the wristband for that?'

(The massive three per cent).

The man grabs free condoms and rushes away (to do what?).

* * *

Joy (2017: 1) observes that television shows can make violence against women secondary to 'the complexities of hegemonic masculinity'. When a man rapes a woman in *Breaking Bad*, Joy (2017: 9) points to a lack of attention to rape's 'impact and after-effects', a lack of attention to women in comparison with men. Indeed, the media frequently denigrates/simplifies women victims/survivors as 'broken hysterics or vengeful harpies' (Thompson, 2017: 67). All of this depoliticises men's violence and contributes to individualising and silencing women victims/survivors.

These sorts of processes are played out constantly in our everyday lives. The processes of sexual violence are part of the fabric of our lives. Whether explicitly recognised or not, sexual violence is presented as rare and entertaining; it's fine to watch real women (not actresses) steeling themselves to say on-camera that they've been raped, while enjoying popcorn with your friends; responses are encouraged to be tokenistic, simplistic, unaware. It doesn't matter if messages about safer sex and sexual violence are confused; concern is fleeting anyway.

There are distinct parallels, of course, with the field of 'mental health', where women victims/survivors are often located, often unwillingly, frequently with 'borderline personality disorder' diagnoses that pathologise and 'other' women's pain, trauma, anger and sadness. As Sen (2016: 27) asserts, in 'mental health' campaigns '[the] use of the word "stigma" is deliberate, because if they used the word "discrimination" instead, it would be a whole different ballgame'.

What might it look like, and mean, if 'mental health professionals' refused victim-blaming discourses about sexual violence, and that we led the way? This chapter offers some thoughts.

* * *

Typing up ideas in March 2018, I heard Belinda Carlisle's song (2007), 'Goodbye, Just Go'. Sometimes it felt empowering to sing while writing goodbye to psychotherapy training; at other times, it was desperately sad.

Brisola and Cury (2015) conducted a heuristic study of singing. It seemed apt to be reading when singing had become part of my writing landscape.

But when the poetic creative synthesis was written up in their paper, it was hidden, in favour of 'two experiential categories' (Brisola & Cury, 2015: 402) – a more 'academic' presentation. When I saw that, I experienced confusion and sadness that the creative had been so neatly boundaried.

The poem refuses to stay secret forever. In a later paper (Brisola & Cury, 2016: 101), it 'blossoms'. It's but a day rose, though, petals shed in a half-page – and you can find parallels of this approach in psychotherapy studies by Atkins and Loewenthal (2004: 506-507) and Stephenson and Loewenthal (2006: 499-450); it's certainly not rare for the creative synthesis of heuristic studies to be short.

But it's the creative synthesis that I want to be singing, song after song, not just a catchy chorus.

I'm enjoying fusing academic and conversational registers, experimenting with style and content (following my earlier work (Lee, 2017c; 2019)). Heuristic research processes (Moustakas, 1980) call to me, but I'm also going to be travelling beyond heuristic work's individualism by drawing in the autoethnographic, appreciating its cultural focus (see Meekums, 2008: 288-289). Then I'll be coming back to heuristic research in reaching 'a point of illumination' (McLeod, 2011: 212). I'll be juxtaposing everyday and traumatic *auto*/biography (or autoethnography) ('when academics write about themselves but acknowledge the significance of others' (Brennan & Letherby, 2017: 157)). I'll also be the auto/*biographer* ('writing about others but recognising the subjectivity of the biographer' (Brennan & Letherby, 2017: 157)) of three co-researchers – three other women survivors training as psychotherapists. The #itsnotok week scenario you've just read had largely non-fiction ingredients but a fictional presentation (indicated throughout by the different font). As Watson (2016: 437) observes, the fictional may widen the 'consumption' of academic analysis. Later, the fictional will be science fiction. Reider (2007: v) comments that life-writing and science fiction seem divergent, one being 'witnessing', the other 'escape'; however, they have similar 'tropes and strategies'. I want to be playful with both. I'd originally thought about writing fairy stories: Cinderella-the-survivor going to the ball (*actually* being welcome in a clinical placement, imagine that (see Lee, 2018a)). I love following leads, and I travelled to feminist science fiction, to academic analyses of Piercy (1978), and then to re-read the book.

I first read Piercy (1978) in 1993, the year after a man with whom I was staying while studying abroad repeatedly attacked me. We meet Piercy's (1978) protagonist in a 1970s mental institution that miserably resonates with the present day (see Sen, 2016: 1). Piercy is not just part of my herstory, then, but speaks to my present person-centred passion for meeting 'people' not 'diagnoses'. As I read and re-read, the book felt increasingly evocative of some of my own experiences of psychotherapy training, which prompted this research.

Curtis (2005: 161) says that Piercy is 'working to outline the foundations for productive, non-coercive, human communities'. A utopia of group process (a space where students converge and create their own agenda)? Yes, sometimes I felt met in group process, like nowhere else, ever; Schmid (2015a: 107) talks of how groups can promote warm self-acceptance.

Trainor (2005: 33) says that when there is conflict in Piercy's imagined community of Mattapoisett, 'in this there is no privacy. The individuals involved are expected to work through their emotions in a semi-public ceremony or to part company'. A dystopia of group process? Yes, at times I experienced feeling drawn and quartered while the crowd of fellow psychotherapists-in-training and tutors watched. As Rose (2008: 4) says, 'groups can be dangerous places'.

Eichler (1981: 52) points to science fiction's sexist history, but Liang (2015: 2037) notes it has 'infinite possibilities'. Corrigan (1996: 89) remarks that 'there seems to be an approximate correspondence between periods of social unrest and the production of utopias'. The science fiction scenarios of this chapter resonate deeply for me, with #MeToo (its past, present and potential future): a passionate desire for everything to be different.

* * *

I wrote most of the above in April 2018, waking up at 4am to complete sentences queuing in my head, demanding to be typed. But that's not where the process began.

There are strong roots – many creative syntheses emerging from many heuristic processes (published 2017–2018). I've 'come out' as a survivor (Lee, 2017c), experienced the terror of self-disclosure, and written poetry about it (Lee, 2017d), objected to being asked intrusive questions about survivor-status in placement interviews (Lee, 2018b), called for mental health professionals to write more #MeToo testimonies (Lee, 2018c), and written a collagist personal testimony of rape (Lee, 2018d).

These pieces make a patchwork of 'self-dialogue[s]' (Moustakas, 1980: 27); they were also about asking of myself what I might be asking of co-researchers – 'congruence' (Rogers, 1979: 9).

Of their heuristic study of singing, Brisola and Cury (2015: 99) say, 'Once the theme was determined, the researcher began to "live" it, paying close attention to everything related to singing.'

Like July's Cheryl to the baby (2015b) (a scene that has stayed in my head), I whisper internally, over and over: 'For them, the living of it "began".'

The words sound outlandish; imagine, if you can choose when to 'begin', you can choose when to 'end': 'That's a wrap, folks, thank you! Singing's just for fun now!'

There is no beginning and ending, neatly wrapped, here.

One day, violence was everywhere, inescapable, UNBEARABLE.

BACP (2004: 11), in the research ethics guidance in place at the time of this study, advised 'careful consideration of the personal challenges and vulnerabilities involved in undertaking… research', saying there should be 'support' to 'overcome challenges posed'.

Some would just advise you: 'Research something else then' (you can almost see them rolling their eyes), silencing people who don't think in this language.

Kelland (2016: 731) draws attention to 'harmful canonical narratives that serve the interests of patriarchy'. We can see how 'overcoming' becomes privileged by looking at the titles of rape memoirs: for example, Freedman's (2014) *One Hour in Paris: a true story of rape and recovery*.

Get. Over. It. Write when you've Got. Over. It.

What about saying: what's wrong with *feeling* the messiness of rawness, *conveying* the messiness of rawness?

* * *

Music plays.
Standing in the wings, in a strapless, red-satin, bouffant ball-gown, I growl (an echo of something from long ago in a psychotherapy training room, where too much seemed to be demanded), 'You want another piece of me?'
The audience waits expectantly. (It does.)
I step forward and sing.
In Basset and Lee (2017), we were there for each other.
Then I'm alone again, feeling vulnerable (Lee, 2018a).
Brennan and Letherby (2017: 159) sing (encouragingly): 'There's a "moral imperative to speak out".'

And exactly what happened to me (Lee, 2018d) is now out there for all to see.

But when people ask me what I'm writing now, it's 'about psychotherapy training'.

('What about it?')

(Crossing my fingers that they *won't* ask.)

Turner (2016: 79) laments: 'It's research you cannot talk about.'

'Thanks, guys, that's a wrap!'

(No it isn't!)

And as I sweep off stage, someone taps my shoulder: 'We've read "On coming out as a rape survivor", and we'd love you to give the keynote address at the International Congress of Gynaecology.'

* * *

Writing about being raped apparently makes me a world expert on vaginas. The spam emails you get when you've written something fall between embarrassing and hilarious (depending on what sort of day I'm having). Someone suggested recently that I should take up one of these keynote speech offers, take an all-expenses-paid trip to somewhere-or-other, to talk about vaginas.

I've certainly been characterised at times for what I have said, and what I have written. People (including me) aren't always generous or diplomatic. Reviewers such as Alter (2015) pity July's Cheryl; she doesn't fit with 'normality', whatever that is. I'm glad I 'met' her before reading the reviews; she's not pitiable, no more than anyone is.

* * *

August 2016: Something Bad Happened at a psychotherapy CPD event: a #MeTooPsychotherapyTraining moment.

I experienced terror, blamed myself, minimised it, forgot it (see Kelly (1988: 144) for a discussion of what can happen when men commit sexual violence).

Speechless.

Frozen.

Shouldn't have put my thigh there

Oh, it's nothing

'So, are you looking forward to the CPD?'

In October 2016, I was riding in a taxi. As we passed all the side roads leading to my destination (psychotherapy training), I protested, with rising panic, 'We're going the wrong way.'

The driver mansplained.

'Remembering almost always involves some sort of trigger' (Kelly, 1988: 144), and there it was: I was terrified of what might happen next.

* * *

In talking of science fiction, McBean (2014: 39) observes that 'the future becomes generated… through re-engaging with the past as partial and incomplete – as productively interrupting the coherence of the present'. In the science fiction scenarios that follow, this chapter grapples with sexual violence in the past, present and imagined futures, drawing on Marge Piercy and Carl Rogers. I seek to always recognise, rather than always resolve, overlaps, complexities, confusions, hopes and fears. Fiction, like life itself, isn't straightforward.

* * *

I wake looking at a pink sky (they sounded comforting (Piercy, 1978: 73)).
'We knew your time was like that, that men thought they could paw women whenever they liked, but it's still shocking seeing it,' says a woman, stroking my hair gently.
'Where am I?'
'Tomorrow, 2237,' she smiles. 'I'm Carla, "Person of Tomorrow" (Rogers, 1979: 262).'
(Well, if Kirschenbaum (2012) can have a posthumous conversation with Carl!)
Bazzano (2017c: 306) appears: 'Rogers was not immune to the temptation of describing a desirable human prototype.'
Carla objects: 'We Persons of Tomorrow aren't fully-functioning. Rogers knew that no one would ever reach that. What we are is the next step after Piercy's Woman on the Edge of Time. There was violence in her imagined community of Mattapoisett, but we don't have violence now, here in 2237.'
'#MeToo worked?'
'Not the first time.' ('When was the first time?')
'Do you still need therapists?'
'We recognise that intergenerational trauma takes a long time to heal. Fromm's (2012: 218) book – remember Jane Fonda, her body remembering what happened to her mother? We still see all sorts of outcomes of what was happening in the past. We're "suspicious of the professional 'helpers'" (Rogers, 1980: 351). We value "imagination and creation" (Richman, 2014: 130-131).'
That's not quite an answer, and I want to ask why I'm here, but my energy fades.

* * *

I wake in the GP's surgery in February 2017. No one's stroking my hair.

The sexual violence in my 'past' is converging with the sexual violence in my 'present'.

I pause seeing clients.

'The actualising tendency is robust and resilient: the drive for growth is difficult to thwart completely' (Wilkins, 2006: 10). Back at my clinical placement a few weeks later, bullying – requests to know 'exactly' why I had time off, the sudden appearance of a minutely-detailed medical questionnaire; the usual threats of withholding clients/annual reports/sign-off of clinical hours.

* * *

At this point in writing this chapter (April 2018), I started to describe how I recruited my co-researchers. But it didn't seem the right time to write about something so precious, straight after thinking about the awfulness of some placements. I wasn't in the right place to receive them.

Moustakas (1980: 103) observes that there's 'freedom' in the heuristic research process; my (dusty) learning journals – the 'record of [my] developing self-as-counsellor' (Johns, 2012: 130) – were calling.

After reading them, I realised 'with fresh energy' (Moustakas, 1980: 51) that I wanted to focus on the one from arguably the worst year of my training. As the cleansing white sage burned, this 'individual depiction' (Moustakas, 1980: 51) emerged.

> 9/15: When I told her about the weekend, my clinical supervisor encouraged me to remain with my independence... I am doing a good job keeping afloat...
>
> 10/15: I did really well to get there... It felt an intimate, intense and comfortable setting... Thinking about research ideas – the highlight of what's coming...
>
> 1/16: I've learned to be independent... I feel I have a place in the group... It was an achievement to talk about my research...
>
> 2/16: I felt encouraged to stay with my own way of being... I have been more creative...
>
> 4/16: I have to go with what I'm thinking and leave open whether it is permanent... 5/16: I felt I made a new friend...

I realised that I wasn't always *The Breakfast Club*'s Allison-the-outcast; sometimes we all raced round the corridors.

* * *

In October 2017, I advertised for co-researchers, identifying as a fellow survivor. I agree with Wise and Stanley (1993: 160) that my 'personhood cannot be left behind… it must be capitalised upon'; I'm not 'disqualified' (Wise & Stanley, 1993: 167) by insider status. What matters is making my 'actions, reasoning, deductions and evidence' apparent (Wise & Stanley, 1993: 168), so that others can decide if they agree. My process, my workings, are being privileged in this unfolding chapter.

When women made contact, they received project details. No materials positioned them as 'vulnerable'. I like Downes, Kelly and Westmarland's (2014: 2.8) observation that violence/abuse is so prevalent that survivors are everywhere. I felt and expressed care for co-researchers and worked with the potential emotional impacts of participating.

I advised that people would need to be careful with other people's material, consistent with group contracts/ethical codes (eg. BACP, 2018). As I've been writing, I've been drawn back to Brennan and Letherby (2017: 159) talking about the 'moral imperative to speak out' – an ethics of needing-to-know.

Three women – Peggy, Sam, and Phoenix (all self-chosen pseudonyms) – agreed to participate. They are training at three UK universities. None (unlike me) is studying purely person-centred psychotherapy, but all express a strong affinity with person-centred approaches.

After the interviews, I didn't rush to write; I felt/feel considerable anxiety about working with co-researchers' voices because much of my work is *auto/biographical*; I only have my own exposure to experience.

* * *

Some interesting quotes, to which we will return.

> The primary responsibility and task of the psychotherapy training institution is to provide a 'safe-enough' environment. (Sullivan & Goldenberg, 2015: 82)

> Members of personal development (PD) groups generally wish to create a fair and just society within their groups where everyone has an equal voice. Unfortunately, translating this wish into reality will be a great struggle. (Rose, 2008: 88-89)

> During my person-centred training, it was assumed that using 'I' as a self-referent indicated self-responsibility, maturity and autonomy… these messages… lacked any validity within my Punjabi (home) culture… In PD, my words were construed to be generalisations about the group,

> prompting irritated glances and criticisms. (Sembi, 2006: 55-57)

> ... I took my concerns to my personal tutor... I felt that much of what I said was attributed to my being a lesbian, ie. I was paranoid about homophobia. (Peachey, 2006: 64)

> The professional development of the therapist is a primary aim and the placement environment is expected to support this. (Oldale & Cooke, 2015: 5)

> [S]ome of the hardest times for many of us who have worked in the [rape crisis] movement have been the moments when the caller on the line is talking about something that happened to her, but where she could be describing your own experiences to you. (Jones & Cook, 2008: 49)

> I enjoy being able to be myself and when I feel that I can't, I know that I tend to disappear... I did not want to *start* my relationship with a supervisor by having to explore my own disappearance. (Herwig, 2007: 13, original italics)

* * *

In what follows, I listened to/read recordings/transcripts, and then I carefully pruned down the typed interview transcripts to 'individual depictions' (Moustakas, 1980: 51), seeking to hear/convey their essences, not just the 'stresses' of psychotherapy training (as Truell (2001) explored), but also the positives (as described by Pascual-Leone, Rodriguez-Rubio & Metler, 2013: 587). In keeping with a collaborative approach, we also hear what co-researchers made of their portraits (their 'validity checking' (McLeod, 2011: 67)). Co-researchers' words are represented in another font, to distinguish their contributions to the chapter.

* * *

Conversation with Peggy

November 2017

> I got involved in a group... I learned a lot...

> ... Then I got into therapy and my therapist... was kind of saying... after a few months... 'You'd be great as a therapist'... I'd love to be... I want to help people who have had these experiences...

> ... I was... recognising the people that I shouldn't be around... doing

stuff about that, and it was just life changing as well… especially going to [university], that was even more so…

… Just being on this journey… I decided to… prosecute… while I've been doing the course… I don't think, if I didn't have the support or the knowledge of what I know, I would have done it…

… it could have been the first workshop… something came up… caught me off guard… I said… 'I'm a survivor'… I felt everyone go [intake of breath]… They didn't really check it out with me…

… I don't think it's just me and my situation… there's been times when people don't respond appropriately… I think that's just group process… it all acts out there… it's all stuff you're going to see in the therapy room… everyone's there on the same mission…

… I've said to them… some clients are going to have horrendous trauma… you're going to have to respond in a better way…

… I told them… when I first went into therapy… she told me… 'put it in a box, close the lid, lock it up… put it at the back of your mind'… Never went back… I went into hiding for many, many years…

… I had the court case… people really avoiding it, and avoiding me… I think it was their own shame, or whatever it was…

… I don't know whether it's because of that, or because it's the final year, I've kind of backed off from it…

… I'm struck by the lack of their curiosity…

… I feel quite warm to every individual in the group…

… I went to my first placement… interview… I was totally open… she said… 'Peggy, you've done a really good job, but… what's happened to you must impact your work;' she was pointing at me…

… She did a long email saying: 'At this moment in time… maybe come back in the third year.' I thought, 'Bog off'…

… mortified… My tutor… 'Maybe I shouldn't be more forthcoming with my personal experiences'…

… subsequent to that, every placement I have been on I have not told them…

… One of the clients… wished she could have more sessions… support worker: … 'She'll be inviting you into her bed next'… just throwaway comments to them… I couldn't even smile

… I just thought… I've got to get out of here… the fight's too big… just move placement…

… no matter what the system is… I know my work is OK…

… the people are really good, supportive… I think that if someone asked me, I would be truthful…

… you've got to bring yourself into the essays… It was a risk, again…

… I remember some of her feedback was, 'Really appreciate what you're saying to me here, Peggy'…

… it's almost as if I'm going to lose respect if I let it out… I don't think it's down to just individuals, it's society as a whole…

… I haven't fully said… I was sexually abused… it's a placement isn't it?! … it just may influence their interactions with me… I don't know if it's me or them, or…

… I'm really strong on… being there for the person… 'This is…not you Peggy'… just a natural thing for me… I don't disclose… bat it straight back…

… Jimmy Savile… independent enquiry… they've got to do something about this now… it might take another 10, 20 years, might not be in our lifetime…

… I don't get to meet many people who have been through what I've been through, or similar kinds of experiences… it's nice to meet someone else who kind of resonates…

(When Peggy read this, she said: 'It's great how you have managed to shorten this down but still kept the content.')

* * *

Conversation with Sam

November 2017

… I… found a therapist where I felt… actually this… can work… decided to train…

… I've got no regrets… there were moments of joy… but… the first two years were traumatic… re-traumatising…

… the third year, I found my response to it…

… I have chosen the modality quite carefully…

… I would lower my expectations and hopes about how I would be met as a survivor…

… it felt like the course was designed with… a prescriptive kind of picture of what the growth of the students looks like, and what they need at each stage…

… what I needed for my process was incompatible with the process that was facilitated…

… it sits in a wider… what gets permission and what doesn't… it's very subtle…

… I needed to negotiate a safe space… I felt that was seen as my resistance…

… it's almost like it feels like if you've got a history of trauma… it's seen as the trump card and it disempowers others who deal with… cumulative trauma… if you don't set up some kind of 'This will get messy and we need to find a way to talk about it'… one group is going to have to be silenced… and what a repeat that is…

… I did try to raise it… I was not met with interest…

… how I bring things isn't perfect… nor are the others… why should I be somehow bigger than everybody else because my story has got more impact on others…?

… repeats of course…

… in the third year, there have been some real relational exchanges… I relax immediately…

… I looked for the relationships I can have…

… there was still lots of rich learning available…

… it is political, and they just don't want to go there…

… some definitely experienced me as prickly and rejecting… I also got a lot of appreciation for naming things…

… the first… group presentations we had to do… just like a fact… but not in a space where people could start therapising me… determined not to force myself to share things when it felt forced… had I done that, I think I would have not been able to finish the course…

… there was just one session where social context… an acknowledgement that that was a weakness in the selection of tutors… I just thanked the tutor for acknowledging it…

… it's always me projecting onto the tutor and it's all good information about my functioning adaptations…

… I am holding my breath underwater a bit… get through it… see what difference I can make…

… I decided in the application to disclose… to keep my clients safe…

… I found the training excruciating… 'Survivors do this', 'Survivors… will deskill you'… 'They're really manipulative!' … I said, 'Look… it's quite tough to sit in a training where I'm being told I'm manipulative… is it possible to just find another way of talking about it?' … He said: 'Really glad you shared that with me' … gave up… sat through the training…

… the manager… 'Don't you find that survivors are amazing… they think, "Wow, I survived this, I can survive anything…!" … I just said… 'I think it is a really dangerous thing to offer to a survivor as a concept'… No response…

… I think parts of me have not survived… reserve the right not to be better… it's rescuing the social responsibility… because it's good… to know that people just recover… then it takes the pressure off to do something about it…

… and of course training in therapy is an investment in people getting better…

… without a good supervisor, I couldn't have done it…

… has reinforced my wish to campaign… not something to do on your own… it was great when I saw your poster…

… the four years are sort of tailored round you… I just think we are in denial how interconnected we are…

... I'd actually rather repair being open than withholding... it's always been incredibly powerful and positive... I'm trying not to be a defensive therapist...

...it's really very powerful to know it's not just my experience, but I'd rather it was just mine...

... one of the feelings is that I'm betraying [university]... that in itself is a sort of repeat...

(When Sam read this she said: 'Ohhh, I wish I was not under such pressure to do my own work... transcript... all fine!' When I re-read this section in May 2018, I powerfully re-experienced the sadness of the interview. A theme of wanting survivors to be able to 'raise [our] expectations' has kept coming back to me.)

* * *

Conversation with Phoenix

January 2018

... as a child I saw a few therapists that were absolutely appalling... now, whether or not I was not ready to connect because of the age I was...

... people finding a calmness about... being with me...

... I thought well, I need to know if this is what I want to do... counselling skills...

... I thought, I can do this, actually...

... there was a lot of work I needed to do on myself... I took a year out... to try and find who I was and what I wanted to be... because it really had an effect... entering a world of going into people's heads...

... I was a child and I went to Crown Court...felt absolutely stripped bare...and them calling one of the other girls in, and I remember... just holding her hand... wanting to protect... That's stayed with me, massively...

... If I could just change how someone felt while they are going through that process... then that would be enough...

... I think they just drop you in it and just see how you just cope...

... some people didn't even have a therapist ever until we got there...

... it kind of annoys them that I can do it and they can't... I mean like I can talk about stuff...

... And I was re-traumatised by this situation... it affected other people as well...

... I took extra therapy... needed to piece myself back together... I doubted myself again...

... it's good to know that those triggers are there...

... there's people in our room... I know that it's been uncomfortable for them to hear on two different levels... because they don't want to listen to that sort of thing and... it's happened to me and not them... 'Do you want my shit? Because you can have it'... Almost like they are pissed off they haven't got that much drama...

... We had been doing about trauma... I sort of came into the group talking about it from a personal experience... I could have just sat there and wrote it in my journal, but what's the point?...

... I challenged these people, I felt then, like, they changed their game play and so what we had before the traumatic weekend was an attack mode...

... I ended up almost absorbing these people... took me back... I couldn't breathe...

... He [placement] said... 'Why do you want to come to work for us? ... I said... I wanted to work with young people... I felt like there wasn't anything there for me... They were OK with it, very supportive... they've been very supportive with what has happened at (university)...

... I saw my supervisor... the words I used were... emotionally raped...

... My tutor was really good...

... One of my friends... 'You're on, like, a psychotherapy counselling course. ... how the hell are you like this?'...

... Then I got angry... We are professional people... what the hell was professional about that, projecting shit onto other people...

… The damage wasn't being assessed… a bus crash… next minute fucking train coming from the other angle and then after that another car accident… being punched from more than one angle… And once you get that ultimate blow… that's going to take you down… then you are then hit again…

… people not owning their own shit…

… I had to go back even if I had to leave still…

… it was a good learning curve for me to know how I might deal with that in a therapeutic relationship…

… no one apologised…

… other people… said… there was a lack of compassion in the room…

… I have told clients that I've been there… they said they felt they trusted me more…

… I feel quite comfortable talking with you… I think the connection I feel is you've been there before…

(After reading this, Phoenix said: 'Wow, yes, I do feel you captured me – even my language and frustration.')

* * *

Maybe you're looking for an authoritative academic voice right now?
    Instead, consider: what are *you* hearing?
    Where might what you're hearing be *coming from*?
    Are there *alternative* ways you might listen?

* * *

The sky is pink again.
    '"Baker-Miller pink" (St Clair, 2016: 118-9), for keeping aggression at bay,' states a woman, who is called Carlette.
    'What happened to Carla?'
    'Not here.'
    'What's the date?'
    'Some things are timeless.'
    'Are they really?'
    'There are many different types of psychotherapy clients… in some unusual cases, it may be important for therapists to help women who have been victimised to become less sexually provocative…' (Dye & Roth, 1990: 209).

Phew, I think – we're in the past.

Then, I hear Ullman (2014) (a survivor) talking of responses from some (not all) therapists she interviewed about working with survivors.

Oh, 2014.

'One described survivors as "a mess"' (Ullman, 2014: 1148).

'One… told me she had trouble personally dealing with the larger social realities of rape' (Ullman, 2014: 1144).

Is that where we've been; where we are; where we're going?

* * *

I'm under a pink sky – a different pink.

'Amaranth. "Garlands of amaranth were used to honour heroes… they hinted, with their long-lasting blooms, at immortality" (St Clair, 2016: 130),' says a woman identifying as Carly.

She's surrounded by books. Oprah Winfrey's 2018 Golden Globes speech is blasting.

'2237 was too late, it was so far in the future that thinking about it just made you depressed and unable to write,' she smiles, taking a pencil from behind her ear, 'so I changed it for you.'

I wonder if I should ask what the date is, and if Carlette was but a fantasy.

'Did you know that "the most transgressive moments have occurred on TV talk shows when the splits between victim and audience and between recorder of experience and interpreter of experience are obstructed" (Alcoff & Grey, 1993: 278) and one of those examples was this woman you can hear talking?… Your era was fascinating. Back and forth, round and round…'

She continues: '"The last several years have seen protest against the identification of rape victims as seducers…" (Brodsky, 1980: 337-8).'

'Didn't we hear someone in the 1990s saying otherwise earlier?' I muse, forgetting Carly wasn't there, but she shrieks: 'Back and forth, round and round!'

'And how about this? "Interest in rape victims has already passed its prime" (Brodsky, 1980: 341)… And then there was #MeToo re-emerging in 2017: "… finally, our words mattered… This [book] is an artefact of a time when things were changing" (Phillips, 2018: 8-9).'

'Is it an artefact?'

'What's important right now is you work out what's happening in psychotherapy training, and what to do about it.'

She hands me her pencil…

* * *

I start with an analytical 'composite depiction' (Moustakas, 1980: 52):

In co-researchers' explorations we see that 'groups always mirror the outside reality' (Schmid, 2015b: 229). The outside reality has a long history of denigrating victim/survivors (see Thompson, 2017; Gavey & Schmidt, 2011), of being a rape culture (Harding, 2015), normalising violence. All this is so ingrained that it will take more than #MeToo to break it.

All co-researchers have/appreciate experiences of being heard. But we also know that, as a consequence of the societal context, we cannot take such experiences for granted; they're precarious and precious.

This precarity and the injustices (profound and subtle) that we've encountered reveal the impact of others, the vulnerabilities and struggles for safety of those not identifying as survivors – rather than (as more conventionally expected) our vulnerabilities as survivors (see Jones & Cook, 2008: 49).

The outcome is that the 'safe-enough' training environment (Sullivan & Goldenberg, 2015: 82), with supportive placements (Oldale & Cooke, 2015: 5), where supervisees don't have to 'disappear' (Herwig, 2007: 13), doesn't seem, in our exploratory accounts, as available as it might be. We're also clear we don't seek to erase training's risks.

* * *

A postcard from Tomorrow: 'A beginning, an outline, a suggestion… in all its infant awkwardness and imperfection I present it to you' (Rogers, 1980: 340).

We held close that 'working as a therapist and learning from this work can be difficult and painful' (Turner et al, 2008: 178). That never changed, nor should it.

But we explored whether we agreed that training is effective, rather than taking this claim as truth (Folkes-Skinner, Elliott & Wheeler, 2010: 83).

We looked at group process. We reaffirmed its value in readying us to be of service to others by encountering ourselves (Mearns & Cooper, 2005: 147). We agreed that so doing involves difficult experiences/feelings (Sullivan & Goldenberg, 2015: 12).

We regretted that sometimes people didn't want risk (Schmid, 2015a: 108), but we saw how often 'safety' came up for people (eg. Payne, 2001: 274; Robson & Robson, 2008: 378), so we also held that, by feeling safe, people felt able to grow.

We noticed that, while 'safety' writing wasn't specific, we were encouraged to work with 'difference' (Sullivan & Goldenberg, 2015: 15).

Some 'differences' started to be more considered; we celebrated Sembi (2006) and Peachey (2006), who had dared to speak about 'race' and sexuality.

We saw we hadn't paid attention to 'life experience' differences (Sullivan &

Goldenberg, 2015: 15); Shah's (2017: 10) positing of 'survivor-therapists' as 'another oppressed community' resonated.

We saw we'd distrusted survivors, feared ways of being that were assumed to follow (like 'borderline personality disorder'). We abolished diagnoses and our only Diagnostic and Statistical Manual of Mental Disorders (DSM) *(American Psychiatric Association, 2013) was Sen's (2016) satirical book,* DSM69.

We heard Smith (2016: 127) talking approvingly of students who 'were very aware of the real or potential impact of sharing too much with peers'.

We decided that this discourse of Too Much – and its companion, The Wrong Thing – weren't consistent with what we wanted for ourselves or our clients.

We started inquiring into the meanings of sexual violence for people. We made visible those simmering undercurrents before they burned us. With Kelly's 'continuum of sexual violence' (1988: 74), we saw we've all experienced something. And our anger about that meant we no longer permitted the 'trauma model' (Ovenden, 2012: 950) to eclipse activism.

We realised how important this work was for our practice, agreeing that 'survivors need trustworthy supporters who have examined their own attitudes, beliefs and experiences' (Hawkins, 2014: 24).

But we didn't marginalise ourselves either. Survivor-therapists(-in-training) hadn't deserved injustices; Cinderella now stocked her wardrobe with ballgowns.

We looked deeply, embraced complexity. Following Schmid (2002: 61), we recognised that to encounter involves 'confrontation', perhaps 'conflict'; for the Other 'is… an entirely different person [and only] when fully appreciating this fact of fundamental difference do encounter and community become possible' (Schmid, 2002: 60). We delighted in Bazzano's (2017c: 306) observation that there is always more.

We touched the edges of time.

* * *

'Why am I here?' I had asked Carla.

'Person must not do what person cannot do… but likewise, person must do what person has to do' (Piercy, 1978: 136).

Self-disclosing writing is, at times, excruciating. But I've experienced growthful community/solidarity here; three women (at least!) cheered me on.

There is no baby – there never was – but there is what Erikson and Erikson (1998) (cited by Richman, 2014: 216) refers to as 'generativity'. The starting point is the assertion that vulnerability isn't an inherent property of those who have been victimised. The world changes; foundations are appearing on the horizon; what will time's fluidity bring next?

In sharing a draft of this work, I was gifted the idea of it connecting with 'incongruity' (Berliner, 2010: 3) in 1970s Hollywood cinema. Berliner (2010:

9) says this successful approach 'tends to nestle idiosyncratic and complicating devices within a familiar and stable structure'. In the psychotherapy world, McLeod (2011: 215) asserts that heuristic and autoethnographic work causes discomfort, that people are 'unsure about how to read it'. Yet we don't seek easy answers in the therapy room; we appreciate complexity; we live with not-knowing – even relish it. Perhaps psychotherapists can learn from watchers of Hollywood cinema?

July, interviewed by Alter (2015), says: 'I've made some whimsical stuff in my time, but nothing I've made has ever been purely light. I'm not huggy. If anything, I'm slightly prickly.'

Summer beckons, and if you listen to Belinda, you'll know what I'm singing.

(With thanks to Marge Piercy.)

References

Alcoff L, Grey L (1993). Survivor discourse: transgression or recuperation? *Signs* 18(2): 260–290.

Alter A (2015). An escape artist, unlocking door after door. [Online.] *New York Times*; 10 January. www.nytimes.com/2015/01/10/arts/miranda-july-blurs-fiction-and-reality-to-promote-a-novel.html?action=click&contentCollection=Sunday%20Book%20Review&module=RelatedCoverage&region=Marginalia&pgtype=article (accessed 10 May 2018).

American Psychiatric Association (2013). *Diagnostic and Statistical Manual of Mental Disorders* (5th ed). Washington, DC: APA.

Atkins D, Loewenthal D (2004). The lived experience of psychotherapists working with older clients: a heuristic study. *British Journal of Guidance & Counselling* 32(4): 493–509.

Basset F, Lee DA (2017). Review of *Unbroken*, by Madeleine Black. *Psychotherapy and Politics International* 15(3): e1427.

Bazzano M (2017a). *Zen and Therapy: heretical perspectives*. London: Routledge.

Bazzano M (2017b). *Zen and Therapy*. Personal communication to Deborah A. Lee; 22 November.

Bazzano M (2017c). A bid for freedom: the actualising tendency updated. *Person-Centred & Experiential Psychotherapies* 16(4): 303–315.

Berliner T (2010). *Hollywood Incoherent*. Austin, TX: University of Texas Press.

Brennan M, Letherby G (2017). Auto/biographical approaches to researching death and bereavement: connections, continuums, contrasts. *Mortality* 22(2): 155–169.

Brisola E, Cury V (2016). Researcher experience as an instrument of investigation of a phenomenon: an example of heuristic research. *Estudos de Psicologia Campinas* 33: 95–105.

Brisola E, Cury V (2015). Singing your troubles away: the experience of singing from a psychological standpoint – contributions from a heuristic research. *The Humanistic Psychologist* 43: 395–408.

British Association for Counselling and Psychotherapy (2018). *Ethical Framework for the Counselling Professions.* [Online.] www.bacp.co.uk/events-and-resources/ethics-and-standards/ethical-framework-for-the-counselling-professions/ (accessed 4 April 2018).

British Association for Counselling and Psychotherapy (2004). *Ethical Guidelines for Researching Counselling and Psychotherapy.* Lutterworth: BACP.

Brodsky A (1980). A decade of feminist influence on psychotherapy. *Psychology of Women Quarterly* 4(3): 331–344.

Carlisle B (2007). *Goodbye, Just Go.* [CD]. USA: Demon Music Group.

Charmaz K (2014). *Constructing Grounded Theory.* London: Sage.

Corrigan P (1996). Dressing in imaginary communities: clothing, gender and the body in utopian texts from Thomas More to feminist science fiction. *Body & Society* 2(3): 89–106.

Creswell J (2013). *Qualitative Inquiry and Research Design.* London: Sage.

Curtis C (2005). Rehabilitating utopia: feminist science fiction and finding the ideal. *Contemporary Justice Review* 8(2):147–162.

Dick K (dir) (2015). *The Hunting Ground.* [DVD.] New York, NY: The Weinstein Company.

Downes J, Kelly L, Westmarland N (2014). Ethics in violence and abuse research – a positive empowerment approach. *Sociological Research Online* 19(1): 29–41.

Dye E, Roth S (1990). Psychotherapists' knowledge about and attitudes toward sexual assault victim clients. *Psychology of Women Quarterly* 14(2): 191–212.

Eichler M (1981). Science fiction as desirable feminist scenarios. *Women's Studies International Quarterly* 4(1): 51–64.

Flanagan S, Patterson T, Hume I, Joseph S (2015). A longitudinal investigation of the relationship between unconditional positive self-regard and posttraumatic growth. *Person-Centred & Experiential Psychotherapies* 14(3): 191–200.

Folkes-Skinner J, Elliott R, Wheeler S (2010). A baptism of fire: a qualitative investigation of a trainee counsellor's experience at the start of training. *Counselling and Psychotherapy Research* 10(2): 83–92.

Freedman KL (2014). *One Hour in Paris: a true story of rape and recovery.* Chicago, IL: University of Chicago Press.

Fromm MG (ed) (2012). *Lost in Transmission: studies of trauma across generations.* London: Karnac.

Gavey N, Schmidt J (2011). Trauma of rape discourse: a double-edge template for everyday understandings of the impact of rape? *Violence Against Women* 17(4): 433–456.

Harding K (2015). *Asking For It.* Boston, MA: Da Capo.

Hawkins J. Person-centred therapy with adult survivors of childhood sexual abuse. In: Pearce P, Sommerbeck L (eds) (2014). *Person-Centred Practice at the Difficult Edge.* Ross-on-Wye: PCCS Books (pp14–26).

Herwig CF. Choosing a supervisor. In: Tudor K, Worrall M (eds) (2007). *Freedom to Practise, Volume 2.* Ross-on-Wye: PCCS Books (pp11–15).

Hughes J (dir) (1985). *The Breakfast Club.* [DVD.] London: Universal.

Johns H (2012). *Personal Development in Counsellor Training.* London: Sage.

Jones H, Cook K (2008). *Rape Crisis: responding to sexual violence*. Lyme Regis: Russell House Publishing.

Joy S (2017). Sexual violence in serial form: breaking bad habits on TV. *Feminist Media Studies* 19(1): 118–129.

July M (2015a). *No One Belongs Here More Than You*. London: Canongate.

July M (2015b). *The First Bad Man*. London: Canongate.

Kelland L (2016). A call to arms: the centrality of feminist consciousness-raising speak-outs to the recovery of rape survivors. *Hypatia* 31(4): 730–745.

Kelly L (1988). *Surviving Sexual Violence*. Cambridge: Polity.

Kirschenbaum H (2012). What is person-centred? A posthumous conversation with Carl Rogers on the development of the person-centred approach. *Person-Centred & Experiential Psychotherapies* 11(1): 14–30.

Lee DA (2019). '@emmyzen liked your Tweet!' (and other stories): the antidote to case studies. *Self & Society* 47(2): 11–22.

Lee DA (2018a). Review of Zen and Therapy. *Psychotherapy and Politics International* 16(1): e1437.

Lee DA (2018b). 'How would you answer if a client asked if you'd been raped?': towards a political critique of psychotherapy placements. *Psychotherapy and Politics International* 16(1): e1435.

Lee DA (2018c). If it's #MeToo, it can't be #JustThem. *Asylum: The magazine for democratic psychiatry* 25(1): 8–9.

Lee DA (2018d). Sexual violence while studying abroad: a critical, collagist personal testimony. *Journal of Gender-Based Violence* 2(1): 119–128.

Lee DA (2017a). Enter centre stage, the case study… *British Journal of Guidance & Counselling* 46(3): 304–314.

Lee DA (2017b). A person-centred political critique of current post-traumatic stress and post-traumatic growth discourses. *Psychotherapy and Politics International* 15(2): e1411.

Lee DA (2017c). Shocking revelation! There are women survivors of sexual violence training as person-centred psychotherapists. *Psychotherapy and Politics International* 15(1): e1396.

Lee DA (2017d). On 'coming out' as a rape survivor. *Psychotherapy and Politics International* 15(2): e1415.

Liang Y (2015). Female body in the postmodern science fiction. *Theory and Practice in Language Studies* 5(10): 2037–2045.

McBean S (2014). Feminism and futurity: revisiting Marge Piercy's *Woman on the Edge of Time*. *Feminist Review* 107: 37–56.

McLeod J (2011). *Qualitative Research in Counselling and Psychotherapy*. London: Sage.

Mearns D, Cooper M. (2005). *Working at Relational Depth in Counselling and Psychotherapy*. London: Sage.

Meekums B (2008). Embodied narratives in becoming a counselling trainer: An autoethnographic study. *British Journal of Guidance & Counselling* 36(3): 287–301.

Moustakas C (1980). *Heuristic Research*. London: Sage.

Oldale M, Cooke M (2015). *Making the Most of Counselling and Psychotherapy Placements*. London: Sage.

Ovenden G (2012). Young women's management of victim and survivor identities. *Culture, Health & Sexuality* 14(8): 941–954.

Pascual-Leone A, Rodriguez-Rubio B, Metler S (2013). What else are psychotherapy trainees learning? A qualitative model of students' personal experiences based on two populations. *Psychotherapy Research* 23(5): 578–591.

Payne H (2001). Student experiences in a personal development group: the question of safety. *European Journal of Psychotherapy and Counselling* 4(2): 267–292.

Peachey L (2006). Personal reflections on training as a person-centred counsellor. In: Proctor G, Cooper M, Sanders P, Malcolm B (eds). *Politicising the Person-Centred Approach*. Ross-on-Wye: PCCS Books (pp60–65).

Phillips J (2018). Foreword. In: Alma D (ed). *#MeToo: a women's poetry anthology*. Keele: Fair Acre Press (pp8–9).

Piercy M (1978). *Woman on the Edge of Time*. London: Women's Press.

Reider J (2007). Life writing and science fiction: constructing identities and constructing genres. *Biography* 30(1): i–xvii.

Richman S (2014). *Mended by the Muse*. London: Routledge.

Robson M, Robson J (2008). Explorations of participants' experiences of a personal development group held as part of a counselling psychology training group: is it safe in here? *Counselling Psychology Quarterly* 21(4): 371–382.

Rogers CR (1980). *A Way of Being*. Boston: Houghton Mifflin.

Rogers CR (1979). *Personal Power*. London: Constable.

Rose C (2008). *The Personal Development Group*. London: Karnac.

Schmid PF (2015a). Encounter-oriented learning programs for person-centred psychotherapists: some learnings from decades of experience and their theoretical background. *Person-Centred & Experiential Psychotherapies* 14(1): 100–114.

Schmid PF (2015b). Person and society: towards a person-centred sociotherapy. *Person-Centred & Experiential Psychotherapies* 14(3): 217–235.

Schmid PF (2002). Knowledge or acknowledgement? Psychotherapy as the 'art of not knowing' – Prospects on further developments of a radical paradigm. *Person-Centred & Experiential Psychotherapies* 1(1–2): 56–70.

Sembi R (2006). The cultural situatedness of language use in person-centred training. In: Proctor G, Cooper M, Sanders P, Malcolm B (eds). *Politicising the Person-Centred Approach*. Ross-on-Wye: PCCS Books (pp55–59).

Sen D (2016). *DSM69: Dolly Sen's manual of psychiatric disorder*. Eleusinian Press.

Shah R (2017). Broken mirror: the intertwining of therapist and client stories of childhood sexual abuse. *European Journal of Psychotherapy and Counselling* 19(4): 343–356.

Smith K (2016). Learning from triads: training undergraduates in counselling skills. *Counselling and Psychotherapy Research* 16(2): 123–131.

St Clair K (2016). *The Secret Lives of Colour*. London: John Murray.

Stephenson S, Loewenthal D (2006). The effect on counselling/psychotherapy practice of an absent father in the therapist's childhood: a heuristic study. *Psychodynamic Practice* 12(4): 435–452.

Sullivan MM, Goldenberg H (2015). *Cradling the Chrysalis*. London: Karnac/UKCP.

Thompson ZB (2017). Happiness (or not) after rape: hysterics and harpies in the media versus killjoys in black women's fiction. *Journal of Gender Studies* 26(1): 66–77.

Trainor K (2005). What her soul could imagine: envisioning human flourishing in Marge Piercy's *Woman on the Edge of Time*. *Contemporary Justice Review* 8(1): 25–38.

Truell R (2001). The stresses of learning counselling. *Counselling Psychology Quarterly* 14(1): 67–89.

Turner D (2016). Research you cannot talk about: a personal account of researching sudden, unexpected child death. *Illness, Crisis & Loss* 24(2): 73–87.

Turner S, Gibson N, Bennetts C, Hunt C (2008). Learning from experience: examining the impact of client work upon two trainee therapists. *Counselling and Psychotherapy Research* 8(3): 174–181.

Ullman S (2014). Interviewing therapists about working with sexual assault survivors: researcher and therapist perspectives. *Violence Against Women* 20(9): 1138–1156.

Watson A (2016). Directions for public sociology: novel writing as a creative approach. *Cultural Sociology* 10(4): 431–447.

Wilkins P (2006). Being person-centred. *Self & Society* 34(3): 6–14.

Wise S, Stanley L (1993). *Breaking Out Again*. London: Routledge.

Chapter 8

#MeToo on the internet

Tara Shennan, with Haley Clifford

I'm just old enough to remember the arrival of the internet. The camera phone hadn't yet been invented. I was 11 when we got a home computer and we had the internet by the time I turned 12, in 1999. Broadband existed, but most of us would still be using dial-up internet until around 2003.

It was that year, in 1999, that I met my first online abuser, Peter (all names are pseudonyms). We met when he sent me a private message asking me if I wanted to see a picture of him. He was 31; he knew I was a child and would think he meant a photo of his face. The picture was a full-frontal picture of him naked, aroused. He told me he knew I was a good girl who would keep 'our' secret. Very shortly after this, he would call me to talk while masturbating.

When I met Tom (21), I was 13 and Peter was beginning to make me feel increasingly afraid. He knew my home address and he wanted to pay for me to leave the country to meet him in person. Tom then breezed into my sphere, asking me to be his girlfriend, with no pressure to be sexual – at first. He promised me the illusion of control rather than being a passive witness to his arousal.

Daniel (30) approached me under the guise of wanting to be the big brother I never had. I latched onto him very quickly; I needed a safe, non-sexual confidant. Our relationship was always characterised by this pseudo-incestuous frame and I really felt like a little sister. As a result, it also meant that I felt a more profound sense of betrayal when our relationship became 'sexual'.

In addition to these three men who abused me concurrently until my late teens, my online life was littered with one-off abusive events. These were opportunistic abusers – adult men and women who were searching for immediate sexual gratification from a child. The abuse was facilitated through the medium of the chatroom environment. It became particularly prominent in my life when I began seeking out these interactions, even though I still felt ashamed about doing it.

Perhaps my biggest question afterwards was how could I not have realised this was abusive? The answer is complicated by the denial I experienced, but I also didn't know what internet sexual abuse was – not really. When the abuse began, there wasn't any information about it anywhere. Nobody had heard of it, certainly no one I knew.

In writing this chapter, I want to stress the commonalities between internet and 'traditional' sexual abuse. Sometimes the language used gives the impression that internet abuse is a uniquely different experience, and this can make practitioners and victims feel as though existing resources for healing are irrelevant to them. While there are some differences, the core of the therapeutic work is very similar. I have chosen to use the term 'traditional abuse' to describe sexual abuse without an online element, to help clarify the comparisons I am making. This should not be seen as reflecting any hierarchy of severity; it is simply that this form of abuse has been written about much more and is more widely known.

In this chapter, I will explore how internet sexual abuse is defined and understood. I will take a critical look at the concept of trust in an abusive relationship, including how professionals may be mimicking abusers when we discuss trust. I will also dissect some of the myths that surround internet sexual abuse and explore how people often 'other' this form of abuse from 'traditional' sexual abuse, despite there being areas of great similarity. I will also briefly mention some therapeutic resources that can be used in a self-help or professional capacity to help a victim to process the impact of abuse. The chapter ends with a conversation with Haley Clifford about the issues I raise.

What is internet sexual abuse?

At the most basic level, internet sexual abuse (ISA) is sexual abuse that is experienced through the medium of the internet. It is often referred to as 'grooming', a word that is increasingly commonly recognised. While there is currently no definitive term to describe this type of abuse, I've chosen to use the term ISA. In my opinion, internet 'grooming' describes the process of the offender, not the experience of the victim. I prefer to use the broader term, ISA, because it encompasses both. In the bluntest terms, ISA describes sexual abuse that often goes beyond online conversations about sexual acts to victims performing sexual acts on themselves for the gratification of the abuser.

Some definitions of ISA use the phrase 'unwanted sexual contact' (International Centre for Missing & Exploited Children, 2017). This tends to be how people define abuse of people who are legally able to consent, in order to differentiate it from consensual acts. Children and adolescents cannot consent. It is therefore a problematic phrase when trying to work with abused children and adolescents, and especially when trying to help them understand that what they experienced was actually abusive and what is meant by abusive. There may be a distinction between whether they *felt* it was wanted or not, regardless of their actual capacity to consent. An adolescent may seek out sexual experiences online, just as they naturally do offline. Nonetheless, it is very difficult for them to see that an adult responding to their curiosity is abusive and that they are being manipulated.

Therefore, simply asking children and adolescents if they have experienced 'unwanted sexual contact' may mean we miss a key opportunity to hear and respond, because we are categorising their experiences through adult filters. They might not class what has happened as 'unwanted', so why not simply ask if they've 'had any sexual contact online'? They may not feel ashamed to tell you about the exciting new love interest they have. If we are aware of it, we can start to work towards preventing further harm. If we want to know if someone is being exploited or sexually abused online, we need to explicitly ask them. Have they been approached for sexual acts or a sexual relationship? Has anyone has asked them to take pictures? Using misinformed language simply prevents us from hearing disclosures.

The grooming process

The central challenge in helping children and adolescents understand that they've experienced sexual abuse is that their abuser will have been consistently manipulating them to regard what is happening as anything but abusive. This behaviour by the abuser is referred to as the grooming process.

Grooming is perhaps seen as synonymous with ISA by those not familiar with this field. However, grooming describes the set of actions that are undertaken in order to facilitate sexual abuse. Thus it occurs in traditional as well as online abuse. An important difference between traditional and online abuse is that traditional grooming often includes significant others around a child: for example, the abuser befriends a parent to get closer to the child. Sutton and Jones (2004, cited in McAlinden, 2012: 24) describe the process of grooming as 'the abuser gradually overcoming the child's resistance through a sequence of psychologically manipulative acts'. This is true whether we look at interactions occurring face to face, online and/or during contact abuse – the physical act of the abuser touching the victim. This definition also goes some way to explain why some instances of child sexual abuse do not require any grooming to take place. If the child has no resistance, the abuser does not need to employ any tactics to overcome it. An example is a child who has already been conditioned for abuse because they have already experienced it. My own history demonstrates how easily revictimisation occurs, unless someone intervenes.

A highly effective form of manipulation by an abuser is to make the victim believe they wanted the sexual contact to happen and convince them to ignore all evidence of their own attempts at resistance. Whenever I would express the slightest reluctance, Tom would tell me that I wanted it and that I had liked it in the past. Any further resistance from me and he would start to question whether I trusted him. It can take very little grooming to make a victim feel complicit in their own abuse because their actions may be confused with genuine feelings of arousal. The contact abuse in ISA is a child being asked to perform sexual acts on themselves. This nature of contact abuse also shuts down the possibility of disclosure, especially as the acts being asked of the victim can become more depraved. At the height of my abuse, I started to think about telling the police. But how could I tell them about the man who wanted to meet me, when – as the meet date got nearer – he was asking me to perform acts to prepare every conceivable area of my body for his enjoyment? I felt so dirty and ashamed.

As discussed, 'grooming' isn't always necessary, but if an abuser wishes to establish an intimate relationship, they need to behave in ways that suggest they are trustworthy. The goal is to successfully deceive their victim into believing this false presentation of self is true (Ben-Yehuda, 2001: 6-7, 11-13). Abusers build trust through the creation of shared interests and connection. It is this sense of belonging and togetherness that makes that betrayal of trust possible. This feeling of belonging to the abuser becomes more powerful as the abuse continues and the victim is made to feel a sense of difference and otherness from their peers. Sexual abusers know that trust is supposed to be demonstrable and that they are behaving in an untrustworthy way (Leberg, 1997). This means they cannot simply let their actions speak for themselves; they have to circumvent their victim's assessment of them and the relationship. They do this, as I experienced, by challenging their victims: 'Don't you trust me? I thought you cared about me? You know I wouldn't hurt you. You can trust me. You're safe with me.'

How this affects the victim depends on a variety of factors. The victim may not want to upset their abuser or may fear being rejected by them. The victim may be well-versed in what their abuser needs and wants to hear; their responses may become automatic and they will say they feel safe or trust the abuser even if that is not how they are feeling in that moment. Automatic and learned responses may also occur if previous experiences of being honest about how they feel have resulted in a negative response from the abuser. The victim may also feel hurt by the suggestion that they do not trust the abuser, especially after they have repeatedly demonstrated that they trust them. This questioning of trust, as a tactic, tricks the victim into believing the abuser has, must have, their best interests at heart and demolishes any internal conflicts and warning instincts. It is also used throughout the abuse when the abuser starts to push on more sexual boundaries: 'It didn't hurt last time, remember? I will keep you safe. Don't you trust me?'

It is this specific abuse of the word 'trust' that has led me to remove it from my own professional vocabulary. I don't ask a client to trust me. I don't try to provoke a desired response by telling them they can trust me. It is normal for victims of abuse to struggle to trust and it is generally healthier when people do not give immediate and complete trust, depending on their developmental age. A valuable lesson for clients to learn is that trustworthy people don't spend a lot of time telling them how trustworthy they are or constantly asking to be trusted. They simply *are* trustworthy. As professionals, we can be an excellent model for that.

Furthermore, the word 'trust' can be a trigger. To victims of abuse, trust does not mean what it means to others without such histories. There was a point in my own therapy when I felt I was having to choose between my therapist and my abuser. After choosing to walk away from my abuser, I began to feel towards my therapist, 'I've proved I trust him. So when will the abuse begin?' This corruption of the meaning of trust created a challenging dynamic in my therapy. What helped me to overcome it was my therapist being steadfast in holding his boundaries. When I told him why the word trust was triggering for me, he completely stopped using it, thus proving that he valued my boundaries and was not another abusive person.

A note about opportunist abusers

Current literature has tended towards focusing on abusers who explicitly groom, and not on the opportunistic predators seeking children who appear willing to engage in sexual activity with little encouragement. In the latter, the focus appears to be on what is it about the *child* that *causes* sexual exploitation (Eaton, 2018).

Even though this type of interaction is often one-off, many abusers still need to follow a 'script'. This script is the way in which that abuser engages with their victim – how they prefer to approach the victim but also how they prefer the victim to respond. It develops as part of the abuser's rationalisation and normalisation process (explained further below). For example, most female abusers wanted me to teach them how to have sex with a girl. They needed to remain submissive and so their fantasy was that they would approach a sexualised female child (me) and praise me for how sexually experienced I appeared to be (for example). They would tell me they wanted to be as experienced as me and this would evolve into me teaching them explicitly how to do that sex act. Their sexual arousal would be framed as either accidental or proof of how experienced I must be.

Most men, however, wanted to teach me how to be in a 'grown-up' relationship. Over time, due to the many years of abuse, I became ready to respond to any suggestion that someone wanted to engage with me sexually and I was overtly sexualised. Yet, the abusers still played their roles, even when this was clearly no longer necessary, and would become frustrated or angry if I stepped out of my role.

The majority of sex offenders know that what they are doing is wrong and socially abhorrent (Webster, Davidson & Gottschalk, 2015: 74-75). In order to engage in a behaviour that is viewed so heinously, they need to normalise and justify their actions to themselves or deny a portion of reality. To face reality would be too psychologically dangerous. This is often referred to as 'self-grooming' (van Dam, 2001). It is a process that abusers undertake and maintain before, during and after sexually abusing a child. For these opportunistic abusers, any challenge to this 'script' momentarily forces them outside of their own justifications for their behaviours. If I were speaking to a man and I displayed 'too much' sexuality, this would often elicit a response of disgust – as if it were OK to teach sexual behaviours but not to know more about it than the abuser deemed was 'age-appropriate'.

This twisted logic wasn't lost on me at the time, but it was much more difficult to see it within the long-term abuse. Daniel was an abuser who stuck to an inflexible script and would often punish me if I stepped outside of that. He would react with revulsion as though suddenly remembering I was a child, and I would feel compelled to beg him to stay and apologise for being too sexual.

Challenging the myths

When working with sexual trauma, there is the potential to cause great harm to the victim, even when the professional is well-meaning. In order to work safely, it is important to understand the socialisation around abuse and the messages victims receive about the abuse they are enduring or have endured.

Working safely starts with challenging some of the myths around ISA and it continues with practitioners educating themselves on the mechanisms of abuse, especially those specific to ISA. Many of these myths are similar to those surrounding other forms of abuse. For example, why don't victims of domestic violence just leave? One of the counterarguments is that a victim is most at risk of harm when they are at the point of leaving, so it is safer to stay. With domestic abuse, people can understand that, faced with the threat of death, someone may choose to stay.

1. Why don't they just leave the conversation if they don't want it?

A common misconception, which still pervades, is that abuse that occurs on the internet is easily avoidable because it is possible to switch a device off. This ignores the very simple fact that the devices are being used by humans who have emotions and can be threatened or manipulated to prevent them from exiting the conversation or relationship. It also ignores the possibility that the abuser is known offline to the victim.

It is common to hear victims of sexual abuse say that they wanted to spend time with their abuser; they just wished the abuse would stop. The abuser could be providing support and love that the victim is lacking in their life, making it much more difficult simply to switch off and walk away.

When we imagine abusive situations, we tend to imagine that the victim and abuser are in the same physical space. As there is no physical presence with ISA, we tend to believe the abuser presents no threat. But online predators can be threatening. When I was being persistently resistant with Tom, he would threaten to move on to my sisters. It was a double whammy and highly effective – the threat to abandon me and the threat to harm my sisters. I would immediately relent and beg him to do whatever I had been resisting.

2. Online abuse is not real abuse

There is no such thing as an abuse hierarchy, with abuse ranked on a scale from mild to the worst kind. This hierarchy is used with all victims of sexual abuse and sexual violence, both as a defence mechanism (to minimise their abuse) and as a silencing tactic (their abuse is not 'bad enough' to warrant disclosure). The abuse of victims of ISA is often invalidated because online relationships are seen as less real and less meaningful. Some victims may be told outright that masturbating for an abuser is not as harmful as being 'forcibly' raped by one. They may hear how lucky they are that it was 'only online', or that it's not abuse if they 'did it to themselves'. This is simply not true. It is all traumatic and it is all abusive.

3. Victims are young, naïve and stupid

Anyone has the potential to be manipulated. There are limited statistics about how many children are victimised through ISA and none at all for adults. The NSPCC (Bentley et al, 2018) reported that, in the 12 months after it became illegal to engage in sexual communication with a child (April 2017/18), 3,096 offences were recorded by the police in England and Wales and the British Transport Police, which equates to nine offences per day. In Northern Ireland, over the same period, there were 82 recorded offences. In 2016/17, Scotland recorded 462 offences.

Prevention of ISA focuses on educating children to make better 'choices'. This is essentially blaming the victim; it assumes that the victim is in control of the abuse. It negates all the explanations we have about why children cannot simply leave a conversation with their abuser. It suggests that, having been given the information, if they are then abused, it is their fault.

At some point during their childhood, children and young people will be taught rules for safe internet use. Often these rules take the form of infographics that adults can share with children. These infographics and the prevention campaigns they link to are problematic for many reasons:

1. They are belittling – they use acronyms like SMART (Stay Safe; Don't Meet Up; Accepting Files; Reliable? Tell Someone). These suggest victims of ISA are not as smart as children who haven't been abused.

2. They are unrealistic – it wasn't realistic back in 2000 (when ISA and its prevention was first becoming more prominent in the media) to ask children not to contact strangers, and it is not realistic now that social media is so pervasive. By continually dishing out this advice, we are ignoring the nature of online friendships and how they are formed. It seems like a basic point but the move towards viewing online friendships as friendships means that no one is a stranger, thus negating all advice to ignore strangers.

3. Not all online sexual abusers are strangers; they can be relatives,

friends of the child's parents or parents of the child's friends. Even if the child has minimal physical contact with them, they may not be unknown.

Myths and victim blaming are ubiquitous in this field and extend beyond ISA to all victims of abuse in all of its forms, not just sexual. It is a response that is born out of fear; people believe that, if the victim is to blame for the abuse, then they (we) can avoid being targeted by abusers if we don't do anything that causes or provokes it. For example, if I don't wear a short skirt, walk down that alley, use that chatroom or meet up with strangers, then I will be safe from harm, and I can protect my loved ones from harm with this knowledge. It is not a new response to the prevention of abuse.

All these messages ignore the simple statistical truth that people are more likely to be victimised by someone very close to them, like a family member, than they are by a stranger.

Many of us grew up with the messages about 'stranger danger' and were taught not to get into vans with strange men. The same notion is being replicated in ISA, as information and prevention has focused for a long time on men who pretend to be children to trick children into performing sexual acts. This was never my experience of internet predators. They may have suggested they were younger *adults,* but it was always clear that I was a child and they were an adult. It was flattering to me that adults were interested in me. But it also, later, became a source of shame and self-blame because I had known they were an adult and I felt I should have known better. Looking back, it's bizarre to focus on building mistrust of what are more likely to be peer-to-peer interactions and ignore the reality of adults interacting with children. This approach still hasn't changed, despite there being more evidence of other ways that online abusers interact with their potential victims.

As counsellors, we can challenge these myths, abuse denials and the self-protecting beliefs that fuel the attribution of blame towards victims. We are uniquely placed to do so, both in and outside the counselling room. We can help a victim unpick the beliefs they hold. We can challenge misinformed colleagues and poor training. We can also be socially and/or politically vocal to challenge the oppressive culture surrounding victims of sexual violence. These are the ways we can be true allies to victims of abuse.

Recovery resources outside the counselling room

Sexual abuse can have a pervasive impact on an individual's personhood. Just like the victims of 'traditional' sexual abuse, victims of ISA can experience anxiety, depression, post-traumatic stress and complex post-traumatic stress, sleep difficulties, including nightmares, feelings of guilt and shame, feelings of otherness, suicidal ideation and suicide attempts, self-harm, dissociation, and sexual and relationship difficulties.

A person may be able to recognise some of the ways sexual abuse has affected them, but others may be outside their immediate awareness. One of the activities that helped increase my awareness was to look at a list of potential effects, like that above, and mark off the ones that I felt had affected or were affecting me. This can be difficult to do as it pushes through any denial the person may have built up to protect themself. It is not uncommon for people to feel more 'broken' after trying out this activity. It is normal to feel overwhelmed and as though our problems are greater than when we entered the therapy session. But the truth is, those problems were already there, and awareness of them makes it easier to begin healing.

Not all clients will use the term 'broken', but they may experience a similar conflict. It is a fine line to walk. Some are able to hold these two seemingly opposing concepts; others may swing between the two: 'I'm so broken, there's no hope for me' versus 'Broken is a feeling, not what I am.' I don't want to encourage the notion of being 'broken', but I do want victims to benefit from the restorative potential of recognising they have been deeply hurt. If you're interested in exploring this further, I recommend *Resurrection After Rape* (Atkinson, 2008). ISA can include the act of rape and contact abuse and many of the resources already available to professionals for use with victims of contact sexual abuse are suitable for victims of ISA as well.

I used Atkinson's book to aid my healing from rape and from ISA, and specifically the exercise 'If rape is a form of theft, what did it steal?'(p70). There is much to grieve in the aftermath of abuse. In order to grieve, clients need to acknowledge the abuse and its effects. Addressing what was 'stolen' was immensely helpful to me in identifying areas of loss. I also like it because it directly places the blame where it should be; with the abuser.

There is a follow-up question that asks, 'If rape steals something from you, what parts of you are NOT gone?'(p70). It is tempting to start with this exercise in the hope of empowering the client, but I think this reduces its therapeutic value. By this I mean that we need to feel the full weight of our grief and pain in order to feel the fullness of hope and empowerment that comes from realising that some things remain sacred and untarnished by the abuse.

Another exercise, which I devised, is the Story Aid. This is intended to help a victim to disclose their full story. Where possible, I avoid vague terminology because using euphemisms often compounds shame. But it may take time for someone to feel able to write 'They asked me to touch my clitoris/penis.' The worksheet is frank and written to avoid creating or perpetuating avoidance in victim or practitioner. These sentences often drill down into deep shame that cannot be relieved if it is kept hidden.

Although the goal is to reach a place of being able to verbalise these sentences, this exercise is most likely to be used as a journal exercise. It is OK to go at any pace that feels comfortable.

Ways abuser contacted me:
   a) Social media
   b) Instant chat/chat rooms
   c) Messaging apps such as WhatsApp, Kik
   d) Text messages
   e) Phone calls
   f) Video messaging apps such as Skype.

He/she asked me to touch [here]

He/she touched themselves [here]

He/she asked me to insert _____ into _____

He/she asked me to send them a photograph:
   a) where I was partially dressed
   b) where I was naked
   c) where I was posing in a sexually suggestive way
   d) where I was performing a sex act for them.

He/she asked me to send a video:
   a) where I was partially dressed
   b) where I was naked
   c) where I was posing in a sexually suggestive way
   d) where I was performing a sex act for them.

I found that reading materials that were explicit in this way and didn't shy away from the detail of sexual abuse really validated my experiences. I could lose some of the shame I felt because, if my experience was laid out in a book, then it couldn't be just me who went through this.

When I first started writing this chapter, my main concern was to help to bridge the perceived gap between ISA and other forms of sexual abuse. But, as the chapter came along, it became more about how we can use what we know, or can learn, not only to aid someone's recovery but also to challenge the barriers placed around victims of sexual violence. By this I mean, we should be seeking to help victims unlearn the myths they've been taught, challenge any reproduction of these myths we may find, and/or model a safe relationship to help victims explore feeling safe in a relationship. It is perhaps a tall ask for one short chapter, but I hope that, alongside this, I have also given hope to any reader that healing is possible.

Conversation with Haley Clifford

Haley: I've researched disclosures of sexual abuse/assault. I've looked at experiences of re-telling and the healing potential of expression in different forms. When we talked, you mentioned that you didn't feel able to verbally disclose but did so online – I think that's really interesting.

Tara: Verbal disclosures can be difficult for all victims and I think we all feel a certain level of shame or embarrassment. I grew up online and its anonymity shouldn't be overlooked as a factor in helping disclosure. I gained huge therapeutic value from engaging in (anonymous) online survivor communities, such as Pandora's Aquarium[1] and After Silence.[2] In fact, I credit them with helping me to remain hopeful that I *could* recover and heal.

Having said that, I am a firm believer that the most restorative form of disclosure is one that happens in person, with a safe person – someone who respects the victim. We profoundly reduce shame when we disclose to someone and their response is validating – that there is nothing to feel ashamed about because it wasn't our fault.

Before I had therapy with a therapist who understood the nature of ISA, I didn't believe they would understand that meeting Tom in person was an extension of that abuse. It felt like everyone thought it was consensual because I was 16 and just promiscuous. I wasn't ready to call it rape but I yearned for people to notice that it was – that I wasn't the girl they seemed to believe I was.

Haley: You've just said, 'I wasn't ready to call it rape but I yearned for people to notice that it was. That I wasn't the girl they seemed to believe I was.' Do you believe that this was specifically because of the nuances of online interactions?

Tara: I don't believe it's different for victims of ISA. There is a pervasive, damaging idea that a teenager is in control of their own sexual abuse. The narrative barely separates from that of abusers. My own abusers were telling

---

1. Pandora's Aquarium – https://pandys.org/forums/
2. After Silence – www.aftersilence.org/forum/index.php

me I drove them to abuse me. There was therefore no reason to believe I wasn't precocious and sexual, that I hadn't caused this reaction in them.

When I didn't come home the day I met Tom in person, my parents called the police to report me missing. I managed to call home later that same evening and a police officer asked me if I wanted to stay with Tom. I said I did. The police officer did not realise that Tom was standing right next to me – the man who held the power to decide if I could leave alive or not. The police then told my parents that, because I was 16, they couldn't force me to come home, but they also made no real effort to check if I was safe. When officers came to visit me when I returned home, they treated me like a troublemaker, not a potential victim of sexual exploitation. It was assumed I had simply met a stranger for sex. What the police officers could have done was start from a position of neutrality and not form their opinions entirely from what others had told them about me. They could have spoken to me in private, away from my parents and their anger and accusations. They could have taken the time to learn the background of what happened. I might not have called it abuse but I probably would have told them about my 'relationship' with this man.

Haley: Am I correct in saying that abusers take advantage of the trust victims place in them, or do they bully them into 'trusting' them from the start?

Tara: They definitely abuse any real trust the victim has placed in them. A victim will tell you they completely trust their abuser, but their definition and experience of trust has been warped. Their survival (including emotional survival) has become dependent on pleasing their abuser, at great sacrifice to themselves, and, as I mentioned, there's often a consequence for not saying you trust them. I would argue now that it's not trust being given but a replacement of one's own instincts with another's. It felt very much like I had to stay in this box (or script) and it became a systematic way to disconnect me from any sense of self. My existence ceased to be separate from theirs – a common experience for many survivors. This rewording can also help to explain how a victim can retain a level of distrust towards their abuser but also ignore it. They remain aware that their life is in the hands of the abuser and the abuser's capacity to end it.

Haley: I wonder if trust and the relationship are formed in a slightly different way through the medium of the internet?

Tara: This is an interesting question and one we haven't adequately answered yet. As a person who has experienced abuse both on and offline, I don't feel there was a significant difference between the two. We experience these encounters as emotionally real and I believe this is a key aspect of how internet-based abusers are able to groom so successfully. It's the emotions of their victims that they are manipulating; children are particularly vulnerable to this manipulation.

Haley: You make an interesting point about the unique nature of ISA – it is most often the abuser manipulating the victim into performing sexual acts on themselves. Does it make it harder for the victim to see this as abuse and themselves as victims? Does it also bring in an added dimension when working therapeutically with victims?

Tara: When a victim is asked to actively participate in their abuse, and this happens in 'traditional' abuse too, it creates a feeling that this act is being done *together* rather than being done *to* them. This is something that victims struggle deeply to come to terms with. There is a profound level of damage being done when victims are asked to violate themselves. It is a systematic dehumanisation process that requires of the victim a degree of dissociation. The victim is led to believe that they want the act of abuse, even if that want is to fulfil the wishes of the abuser. It is this dissonance and dissociation that the therapist needs to help unpick in the face of what seems like a very clear logic to the victim – I must have wanted it because I did it and no one physically forced me. Or they experienced sexual arousal and orgasm in doing these acts. But this too occurs in other sexual abuse.

Haley: You critique the notion of 'stranger danger' – the stranger in a van. So how do we protect ourselves in the context of the internet?

Tara: The man in the van was never the biggest risk. Both then and now, we struggle to admit that the highest risk comes from those closest to children. I predict we will start to hear of more online abuse cases where the predator was known to the child in some offline capacity. The truth is, we're not very good at preventing abuse. At the moment, we don't have any evidence-based prevention programmes to use with children. There are still local authorities that use materials that are both traumatic and victim-blaming in their attempts to prevent through education. At the very least, the materials we use should not expect a child to prevent or stop their own victimisation. One such example is the film *Kayleigh's Love Story* (Affixxius Films, 2017), which depicts the rape and murder of a child and concludes with the message 'Stop and think'. This film has won many awards and been shown in schools, but the takeaway message is, 'If you're not careful or clever enough, you could get yourself raped and murdered.'

Thank you for your thoughtful questions, Haley.

References

Affixxius Films (2017). *Kayleigh's Love Story*. [DVD.] Leicester: Leicestershire Police. www.leics.police.uk/kayleighslovestory (accessed 24 February 2019).

Atkinson M (2008). *Resurrection after Rape: a guide to transforming from victim to survivor*. Oklahoma City, OK: RAR Publishing.

Ben-Yehuda N (2001). *Betrayal and Treason: violations of trust and loyalty*. Boulder: CO: Westview.

Bentley H, Burrows A, Clarke L et al (2018). *How safe are our children? The most comprehensive overview of child protection in the UK 2018*. London: NSPCC. https://learning.nspcc.org.uk/media/1067/how-safe-are-our-children-2018.pdf (accessed 24 February 2019).

Eaton J (2018). *Can I Tell You What It Feels Like? Exploring the harm caused by CSE films*. [Online.] VictimFocus. www.victimfocus.org.uk/campaigns (accessed 8 April 2019).

International Centre for Missing & Exploited Children (2017). *Online Grooming of Children for Sexual Purposes: model legislation and global review*. Alexandria, VA: ICMEC. www.icmec.org/wp-content/uploads/2017/09/Online-Grooming-of-Children_FINAL_9-18-17.pdf (accessed 24 February 2019).

Leberg E (1997). *Understanding Child Molesters: taking charge*. London: Sage.

McAlinden A-M (2012). *Grooming and the Sexual Abuse of Children: institutional, internet and familial dimensions*. Clarendon Series in Criminology. Oxford: Oxford University Press.

van Dam C (2001). *Identifying Child Abusers: preventing child sexual abuse by recognizing the patterns of offenders*. New York, NY: The Haworth Press.

Webster S, Davidson J, Gottschalk P (2015). Understanding online grooming: findings from the EOGP study. In: Webster S, Davidson J, Bifulco A (eds). *Online Offending Behaviour and Child Victimization: new findings and policy*. Basingstoke: Palgrave Macmillan (pp55–90).

Chapter 9

Reconnection through dance movement psychotherapy

Amanda Light,[1] with Tina Johnson

Introduction

Sexual violence is a direct attack on the body, with potentially lifelong physical and psychological repercussions (Kelly, 1988). To address the consequences of sexual trauma, therapeutic approaches typically use talking treatments, sometimes in combination with prescribed medications. Yet, as arts psychotherapy research (Dieterich-Hartwell, 2017; Hodge & Simpson, 2016) increasingly suggests, therapeutic practices that prioritise language over material experience can be problematic. This is because they frequently fail to recognise the potential of nonverbal interactions as a way of addressing trauma and a means to support mind-body connectivity. There is growing recognition that sensory studies and embodied therapies such as dance movement psychotherapy (DMP) might help bring people who have experienced child sexual abuse (CSA) to a place of integration. As such, it is surprising that somatic interventions are not being more readily used alongside standard therapeutic practices.

This chapter advocates DMP as a means of enhancing the psychological interventions currently available to those who have experienced CSA. The

---

1. A note about this author's name. Amanda is referred to as Millie in her conversations with her conversation partner Tina, below, and in one of the journal reflections. Amanda wishes to retain the name Millie in these conversations, as this is an important part of her identity in this context.

chapter will consider ideas from two perspectives that call for integrated and emergent approaches. First, it draws on ideas found in feminist new materialism (Barad, 2007), in particular how language is privileged over material experience, and offers a means of rethinking the binary within a holistic approach that avoids hierarchy. Second, it references posthuman ideas (Braidotti, 2007), which decentre the human in order to foreground connections between other-than-human and human forms. Finally, it discusses how these alternative theoretical views might be used to develop new frameworks for the way we research and evaluate therapeutic interventions relating to sexual trauma.

Alternative epistemologies

A number of feminist scholars, most notably Judith Butler, have devoted much of their research to issues concerning the body. However, they have been criticised for privileging theoretical discourse over material experience (Alaimo & Hekman, 2008). Feminist new materialists argue that bodies are not only shaped by 'the forces of language, culture, and politics' (Frost, 2011: 70), but should also be regarded as formative actors that have their own unique agency, independent of human intentionality. By failing to consider the material world as agentic, human-centricity continues to value minds and language over bodies and matter, including nonhuman and other-than-human forms. Feminist new materialists are not alone in seeking to address this; a number of other approaches also 'stress the agency of more-than-human entities and make clear that the human is shaped through encounters with other agencies' (Hollin et al, 2017: 933).

A theme within the discourse and practical application of DMP, which will be highlighted in the autoethnographic sections of this chapter, is the potential of nonverbal interactions to support mind-body connectivity. However, the ways in which DMP is experienced and how these experiences might manifest can be difficult to elucidate using verbal language. This could, in part, contribute towards explaining the limited research into and (consequently) lack of funding for DMP, which means it is often relegated to the margins of recovery-based settings.

Van der Kolk (2014) notes how dance is used to good effect to express trauma in cultures all around the world but acknowledges that establishing this scientifically presents logistical and economical challenges. Likewise, a 2015 Cochrane review on dance therapy and depression concludes that there are limited studies available and that those in existence are mostly of low 'methodological quality' (Meekums, Karkou & Nelson, 2015: 3). Within the current ideological framework that dictates how and what we are meant to consider as viable research, this is perhaps unsurprising. It is argued that the 'neoliberal-methodology-machinery' (Koro-Ljungberg et al, 2017: 61) intentionally seeks to produce a certain type of knowledge and dictates exactly what qualifies as valuable data before the research even begins.

In light of Foucault's ideas about 'biopower' (Cisney & Morar, 2016) and the range of global institutions that seek to generate profit from mental health research, often termed 'biocapitalism' (Pykett, 2013; Fullagar, 2017), these criticisms draw attention to the difficulties of obtaining data from outside or beyond neoliberal agendas. They further highlight the struggles that DMP and embodied therapies face against the noise and force of dominant modes of knowledge production.

Prevalent Cartesian Western thought has been fruitfully challenged by postmodern feminist scholarship. Subsequently, a merging of feminist new materialism and posthuman ideas further extends this task. To no longer assume that humans are more important than any 'other' can reframe and open up new realms of enquiry (Cohn & Lynch, 2017) and, in so doing, highlight the inequalities that are maintained by binary thinking. The burgeoning field of ecopsychology (Roszak, 1995) specifically addresses this assumption by moving therapeutic interventions outdoors, where the natural world acts as co-facilitator within the therapeutic alliance.

In tandem with other-than-human and human entanglements, Braidotti (2007) discusses how our growing, technologically driven global economy is fuelled by the exploitation of bodies. This, she states, poses a specific threat to the lives of women and children in particular. She argues that, while feminism has always contested the master narratives, a re-visitation 'of the embodied and embedded kind, that moves progressively towards the posthuman' (Braidotti, 2007: 69) is essential. By de-centring the human, posthuman ideas create an emergent space within which the materiality of human and nonhuman bodies, systems, hierarchies, rules, concepts and inequalities may be exposed and reconsidered. This form of ecological thinking is very different to the mechanistic, alienating and usually male-dominated perspectives that are the norm.

The theoretical privileging of language over material experience serves to emphasise the similarities between the treatment of what is termed 'nature'[2] and human cultures that oppress, abuse or assault 'others' within society. For instance, the 'reduction of lively, emergent, intra-acting phenomena

---

2. There is an argument in ecological philosophy (see for example David Abrams' *The Spell of the Sensuous* (1997)) that, as biological beings, humans are nature. Even having a word for 'nature' creates a separation, an othering. This leads to a sense of being on the outside looking in, rather than being nature from within.

into passive, distinct resources for human use and control' (Alaimo, 2008: 249) can be seen in the raping of rainforests, the trafficking of women, the indiscriminate use of poisonous pesticides, refugee children drowning at sea, and too many other examples besides. MacLure (2017) writes that the very real likelihood of human extinction through global environmental destruction is due to ignoring the warnings of the material world. Despite lacking a voice because it does not use verbal language, nature is continually speaking and intra-acting through the material with human and nonhuman phenomena.

Barad's (2008: 120) key question, 'How did language come to be more trustworthy than matter?' resonates here. Many personal accounts of CSA (Bass & Davis, 2008; Ainscough & Toon, 2000) describe not being believed about the abuse they were suffering, how their cries for help were not heard, how they were lied to, coerced into keeping secrets and threatened to prevent them speaking about what was happening to them. Language, for some, is a zone of distrust, ineptitude or inconsequence.

Furthermore, for many women, the body also becomes a targeted site of disgust, mistrust and denial. It is recognised that the psychological effects of sexual violence often manifest in the body (Sanderson, 2006). This can lead to destructive behaviours including self-harm, substance abuse, eating distress, symptoms of post-traumatic stress such as numbing or a sense of disembodiment, depression, low self-worth and suicidal ideation (see, for example, *www.napac.org.uk*). Embodied therapies and practices like DMP invite participants to feel, care for and trust their bodies, perhaps for the first time. The entanglement of techniques and responses created by an embodied approach to trauma work will be examined in the next section.

Dance movement psychotherapy

This section is an autoethnographic account of my own training to be a dance movement psychotherapist while assimilating past sexual abuse. Alongside academic aspects, clinical placements, supervision and process groups, I covered a great deal of ground through experiential learning and personal therapy sessions with a body psychotherapist. Drawing on my reflective journals written throughout the three-year qualification, I will discuss how DMP and other somatic practices, including walking and poetry, can help to process trauma in an embodied way. Interwoven through the autoethnography is an edited version of my conversation with a fellow dance movement psychotherapist, Tina, whose history also contains sexual abuse, and with whom I trained.

More than a decade before I discovered DMP, I had three years of therapy with a clinical psychologist, which undoubtedly helped me to deal with the pain. Although it was a relief to finally reveal what had happened, talking through my past experiences led me into a spiral of depression, where I became stuck and from which I didn't so much emerge as just grew bored. This is known in psychological terms as a 'plateau'. Having run out of words, I tried to let my body speak, using a range of harmful and destructive behaviours to express the emotional pain I was suffering.

Thus, initially I was reluctant to revisit the issues surrounding CSA during DMP training. However, an assemblage of somatic and nonverbal processes entangled with a developing understanding of Rogers' (2003) person-centred concept of 'congruence' meant that revisiting painful material was both inevitable and essential. For Rogers, congruence means integrating both 'a world of visceral and physiological experience, and a world of recognition "in consciousness"' (Tudor & Worrall, 2008: 197). As a trainee dance therapist using the body as my main tool, I realised I needed to openly and honestly work towards a place of mind-body connection.

DMP recognises the expressive, communicative potential of the body moving, and works with the assumption that the connection between body, mind and spirit is such that a shift in the body – that is, moving through Laban's efforts (Newlove & Dalby, 2004) of space, time, weight and flow – necessitates a shift in thinking/emotions, and vice versa. According to the Association of Dance Movement Psychotherapy UK (see *www.admp.org.uk*), the combination of movement and nonverbal communication means that DMP can be accessible to a wide range of people, including those who cannot access more orthodox talking treatments, such as people with late-stage dementia or complex learning disabilities. For those who have experienced CSA, DMP can offer a space within which to express or explore memories, early sensations and experiences that may have been 'pre-verbal in their origin, or too complex to readily express in words' (Meekums, Karkou & Nelson, 2015: 10). It invites a potentiality within which to play, make noise or create a mess, build trust, connect with others, examine boundaries and, as I discovered, face the effects of CSA on my life until this point.

Journal entries from my early months of training are scattered with references to feeling '*empty and numb*' (9 October, 2012), alongside a reluctance to acknowledge the past again. The result of this was a return to old habits, including a restriction of food: '*If I can only show the pain with my body, I will feel less frustrated about not being able to communicate or be confident*' (6 November, 2012). I pursued the feelings of emptiness with my therapist, which I embodied as moving like a cat with extended claws. Together we explored this feline protective mechanism until I was able to retract the claws into paws and recognise my difficulty in experiencing sensual pleasures from food, touch and warmth. In experiential DMP sessions, I began to admit '*I am scared of the use of my body, it is more comfortable and natural, but much more challenging than verbal contact*' (18 November, 2012). I realised that '*the entire experience [of sexual violence] is held within me – in my body and cells, in my thoughts and feelings, and memories, so my 'story' is huge and enveloping*' (19 January, 2013).

My journals helped me to remember how profound these revelations were for me in the early days of accessing the DMP space, and I was curious to hear how my conversation partner, Tina, had also been challenged.

Conversation 1 with Tina Johnson

Millie (Amanda): During training when working with the whole peer group, I noticed that you became stuck quite often and sometimes seemed to feel unable to enter the movement space at all. Can you can say anything about your experiences in relation to acknowledging your past abuse while encountering DMP?

Tina: I didn't expect the training to bring up memories that belonged to the past and that I thought were no longer part of me. I had received counselling before,[3] after I found a faith and, through a connection with spirituality and prayer, had convinced myself that I had received healing. I was therefore taken by surprise by the very strong and powerful feelings that arose in my body. I became quite resistant to the process, as I felt I was there to learn and did not want to face again the shame of my past. I no longer identified as a 'survivor', mainly due to having been told to 'move on', and felt that I had talked the matter out through verbal therapy. I hadn't realised how much the trauma of CSA had embedded itself in my body.

In movement-based sessions, I often disassociated from my body, which was also something I did as a child; it was an automatic reflex and I felt I had no control over it. I regularly felt awkward and uncomfortable, with feelings of shame, insecurity and rejection constantly coming to the surface. I felt exposed, out of control and embarrassed by what was happening to me and not sure how to connect with others during this experience. My public self – an open, big smile, 'life and soul of the party'-type – disappeared and I was unable to access her. Instead I would often sit paralysed, feeling deep anger and resentment at being pulled back to the past and not wanting, but also wanting, to go there.

---

3. The use of 'received' by both Tina and I in relation to accessing talking therapy/counselling was highlighted as a point of interest by our co-editor, Deborah Lee.

While all these feelings were challenging and I was often resistant, on reflection I realise that, for the first time, I was actually able to access the deep and distant places in my body. At times this created fear and anxiety, but the DMP space was also a safe place to let the stories of my body find a form of expression – even if it was through resistance. It was acceptable to be with this and I became more aware of the triggers and more able to notice the process.

Millie: It's interesting that we both grappled with this pull towards embodiment in physical ways. You, by stillness or resisting the dance space, while I reduced food and suffered subsequent headaches or migraines. It's also notable that both you and I refer to having previously 'received' counselling. It seems very passive in comparison with the challenge of immersing one's whole self as an agentic, active being in a therapeutic and explorative environment.

Embodiment

Case studies from group therapy work with adults who have lived through CSA reveal the 'dilemma of embodiment' (Meekums, 2000: 88). In the process of embodying trauma, the material effects of surviving become an integral part of the story. Identifying and acknowledging a range of fallouts that had affected my past opportunities in employment and relationships and influenced my decision not to have children stirred up depression throughout Year One of the training, developed into anger and increased migraines by Year Two and initiated a process of grieving during Year Three. Yet creative movement explorations offered an insight that had not been grasped before.

> I identified depression. Rather than seeing it as a black cloud that comes upon me, I went into it in my body. And I realised it was like a black rectangle, dense and heavy with packed emotions and feelings that have no room to move [...] And inside I knew it was a familiar place, when life becomes 'too much'. A place to rest, almost dead. (10 November, 2012)

The significance of this lies in the realisation that at times the black rectangle was a place I was seeking out as refuge, rather than an external force that seemed to unwittingly descend. In previous bouts of depression, I had felt powerless to resist the all-consuming darkness, but the metaphor of the rectangular block helped me realise I was no longer stuck. I later write of the block being disturbed '*like bubbles, because my emotions were expressed*' (13 November, 2012); another time, the wall of the dance studio resembled the wall of '*my black box of depression, but it was outside of me, and brown rather than black'* (4 December, 2012). My therapist helped me to see that unravelling depression was like *'teasing different colour threads out of the block, and labelling them: self-critical, hurt child...'* (29 March, 2013).

During an exploration of internal rhythm, I found myself enclosed in the block, unable to breathe and feeling nauseous and dizzy. I noticed across the studio that another student had tapped into my rhythm and was mirroring my rocking movement.[4] She recorded her experience, writing: '*I felt tense and dark, introverted and scared; I felt like I couldn't breathe and I felt really, really sick.*' Our eyes were fixed on one another and she began to sob loudly while I remained trapped and unfeeling. In response to the tutor's concern, she replied, *'It's Millie's. It's not mine. It doesn't belong to me.'* Later we privately discussed the connection we had made through shared rhythm. The following is from my peer's journal reflections:

> I told [Millie] that I felt that once I had started crying, that I thought I was scared that I was never going to stop. She told me that she had said the exact same thing to her therapist that week. She said, 'I think you have just cried for me.' I replied, 'But I did stop.'

I learned that I needed to express the pain relating to CSA both physically and through utterances of sound, using a whole range of objects and creative expressions. It wasn't enough to just talk about it; I needed to cry, scream, hit cushions, stamp my feet and outwardly express the horrors that had been held, secretly, in my body for many years.

A combination of rhythmic movement, the somatic empathy of my peer and the safe space held by our DMP tutor supported these early, tentative steps towards embodiment. A way of theorising this entanglement of matter and meaning can be found through the Baradian notion of the 'material-discursive' (Barad, 2008: 136), which acknowledges that discourse 'is not what is said; it is that which constrains and enables what can be said' (Barad, 2008: 137). Barad's ideas give emphasis to material intra-actions, understood as a composite evolved through a whole range of processes, objects, utterances of sound and creative expressions, as being crucial to the production of embodied knowledge.

The symbolic journey of the block culminated in an activity where I used a large rectangular block made of sponge that I explored by lying underneath it and climbing on it. I was considering the concept that depression was no longer within me. I asked a number of my peers to sit on top of the block while I lay underneath, feeling that '*I needed to push out the past depression and*

---

4. My peer has agreed to be mentioned in this chapter and has willingly shared her own reflective journal notes from this time for the purposes of this publication.

migraines' (17 June, 2013). I endured the weight for as long as possible and followed this with a sequence of sit-ups and chin-ups, as testimony perhaps to my physical strength and re-connection with my body. In 'survivor' terms, it was reclaiming the body, acknowledging its boundaries, strengths and limitations. Nothing was verbalised and nor did I cognitively understand the intra-actions taking place between my body, the bodies of others and the material object.

Conversation 2 with Tina Johnson

Millie: I have discussed how identifying the rectangular block of depression created a breakthrough for me. Is there anything material/embodied or symbolic that has made a lasting impression on you?

Tina: I was often intrigued about your rectangular block, perhaps not always understanding it, but I was curious and at times envious that you were able to connect or seemed to know what your needs were and to go with them. I became aware that I might have needs and that it was OK to have those needs met.

I experienced this understanding of my needs and the beginning to accept and meet them during an authentic movement session. I initiated the exercise by automatically going into 'child pose' on the floor. I felt I was there for a long time, feeling the usual disconnected self, but a small movement began in my fingers. It felt like a small electrical impulse and the fingers were the origins of connecting to my body. My arms started to reach out and explore the space while my body remained curled. This felt a very safe place of exploration. You [Millie] had witnessed my movement and your feedback was of tentacles exploring the boundaries. This offered me a sense of substance and form; as my arms twisted and turned, making connections with the floor, I was testing and feeling the weight of the floor that might in the future support more of who I was.

Although I have danced for many years, mainly within a spiritual context in church, and while I had connected to some extent with my body, there was always a dark place that I would never go to as I didn't want to experience the messy blackness of the past. I was too afraid to get lost again. But after I was able to explore this part during seminars, and you witnessed it and offered this embodiment a name – 'the pterodactyl' – it became an alter-ego that felt OK. I was able to be curious without feeling inhibited or embarrassed. I could explore the shame and the critical voices. So began the journey of reclaiming my body – a journey I feel I'm still on. I discovered more of my body and the strength and power within it, the feeling of my muscles as they moved in my shoulders, the feeling of my skin as it touched and connected with the floor. I also began to explore this deeper connection as I danced in church, playfully developing the pterodactyl as it spread its wings and sensed and felt the space; I began to enjoy the physicality of this.

Millie: I love your pterodactyl… sometimes I 'borrow' the shape when I know I'm feeling vulnerable but can't understand why. It is such a safe, exploratory way of moving and I feel it like an unfolding until I can stand and face the world again.

For both Tina and me, the device of symbolism enabled a narrative to form, which did not begin in language but rather found a 'non-languaged' (Panhofer, 2011: 455) way of being. This phenomenon was firmly situated in the materiality of both human and nonhuman forms.

Poetry and the other-than-human

DMP training initiated a process of grieving that would lead towards integration and healing. In darker moments, I found great comfort from the syntactical disruption of language and themes discovered within ecological poetry. I began to research how poetry could be combined with DMP practices to support mind-body connectivity. Specific interests lay in the potential value of using the shared devices of rhythm, symbolism and metaphor that are prevalent throughout both art forms. A journal entry describes how David Whyte's poem 'Sweet Darkness' (2011) helped me to move through a range of feelings:

> I felt curled and small and could have stayed in a foetal position for a
> long time until I cried or climbed into my rectangular block, but the
> lines juxtaposing the darkness with the vastness of the horizon drew me
> out, enabling me to rise again from the floor and continue my journey.
> (11 April, 2015)

In the final stanzas, the poem speaks of how the darkness teaches you to let go of anyone or anything that closes you down:

> At this point I turned and pushed my hand to say, 'No – go all you who
> are too small for me.' But I didn't want to be running away; I wanted to
> press and advance and push those people away, out of my space, and
> even when I retreated occasionally, it was with a sense of choosing where
> I wanted to be […] I was asserting myself. (11 April, 2015)

Concurrently, poetry also led towards a re-communication with the natural world. David Wagoner's poem 'Lost' (2007), offered complexities regarding the other-than-human and its intra-actions with and without human beings. The sense I gleaned from this poem is that, no matter how lost you regard yourself to be, the trees surrounding you know where you are; from their standpoint, you are not lost. A journal entry records my realisation that *'it's not all from my perspective. Down below, the waves are crashing onto rocks [...] there is a relationship between the sea and the land that would continue even if all of humanity dies out'* (18 October, 2014).

Evidence of healing through connections with the other-than-human abound through my journals, moving away from the repetitive feelings of emptiness or numbing towards realisations that I could now:

> ... sense my presence in the world [...] Why wait until you're dead to become part of the earth again? I want to feel my rightful place now, in communion with plants and animals, with the elements. (12 February, 2015)

Neuroscientific research on trauma suggests that being traumatised is 'just as much a problem of not being fully alive in the present' (van der Kolk, 2014: 221) as it is about being stuck in the past. Mary Oliver's poem, 'Wild Geese' (2004), is a final, notable poem that marked my sense of being alive and present. Each end-stopped line resonated on a somatic level. At times when I felt hatred towards my body and wished to hurt or punish it in some way, I would recite the poem from memory. A line that likens the human body to a soft animal reminded me to nurture my healing self, like my previous cat exploration in personal therapy. The ending of the poem draws attention to the ecology of life and how there is a place for each of us among it – that people, environments, animals and things are all part of one big family.

It is suggested that bodies and environment 'co-create each other through mutual influence and interactional shaping' (Reeve, 2011: 48). Research on the ecological body states that:

> ... by moving in natural environments, ecological movement helps people to expand their embodied awareness to include the broader context from a position of 'being among', rather than 'being central to'. (Reeve, 2011: 50)

A broadening of my world view afforded me space to breathe and to grow. There was a shift in my newly felt embodiment that was supported and more positively experienced through my sense of connections with and among forests, cliff paths, birds, waves and animal kin. The somatic practices of dance, movement and mindful absorption in the natural environment have been primary factors in my journey towards embodiment and wellbeing. Cognitive understanding and reflections through writing or verbalisations have played an important but secondary role.

Conversation 3 with Tina Johnson

Millie: An assemblage of movement, poetry and nature connections enabled me to reach a place of integration, a word I use in preference to 'recovery'. The terms 'survivor' or 'victim' can also be contentious,[5] so I suppose what I am asking is, alongside the pterodactyl, what is in the assemblage of your process towards healing and embodiment?

Tina: I struggle with the term 'survivor' as I see it as an unwanted label that was forced on me, a stigma. I have had years of living with trauma, suffering with anxiety and depression. As a survivor, I feel robbed in so many ways. I have come to prefer being an 'overcomer' – one who has taken back my body and my life. For me, surviving meant living on high alert waiting for the next attack to come in. When a challenge came, my body would immediately become defensive, my muscles rigid and tense, and I would often feel pain in my limbs or stomach, or I suffered migraines. This was all very exhausting, but as a survivor I hadn't learnt how to notice my triggers or regulate my responses. As an overcomer, I'm more aware of my body's responses in challenging or uncomfortable situations, and I'm able to respond and manage this without becoming defensive or shutting down. As an overcomer, I'm far more self-aware and have a greater sense of peace and inner strength.

While I was studying, my father passed away. This was particularly difficult as it brought up old feelings of abandonment and rejection. I had always wanted my father to rescue me from the painful situation I was in, but he never came, and now he never could. I had to accept that this had not been possible in his life, although strangely, through his death, I was able to regain another part of me, a stronger, accepting part. It was helpful to be in a place (the DMP space) where I was able to explore the pain of loss and grief, to explore the feelings of being unseen or unheard, and to allow myself to experience and be with the depth of trauma in my body as this complex grief materialised.

I started to find my voice. Initially this came about because I felt I was being given permission by tutors and peers, but it was also about self-

---

5. Along with medicalised language, I am reluctant to use terms that are deductive or diagnostic. 'Recovery' assumes a linear and thus measurable process, which is problematic and potentially moralistic. 'Victim' and 'survivor' are terms that both Tina and I agree should be claimed or discarded by individuals in tandem with their own process, rather than being labels that somehow become fixed.

acceptance and empowerment, allowing myself to be with the scary and sometimes out-of-control responses that would trigger a shut-down. I began to feel an inner confidence and became a little more assertive in having my needs met. I became more self-aware during this time, noticing more and more how my body responded in situations where I didn't feel safe, where I felt controlled or unheard, and I began to speak out. Sometimes I spoke clumsily and what I said was not always received well, but the pterodactyl had been given life and she became more and more able to access her space.

The noticing of more and more of myself began a process of integration that enabled my body to feel more intact, more connected to the world. I'm also now more aware of nature and part of my self-care is to connect with this; I spend time in my garden listening to the sounds of birds and noticing how nourishing this is, feeling the grass with my bare feet, often dancing and connecting with the feel of the wind or sun on my skin. I never take any of this for granted and I'm continuously curious about what else I can discover, as I am becoming more and more whole.

Millie: I recall when I came to stay with you and how we danced barefoot in your garden. I'm not sure we had ever laughed and smiled so much as when we combined dancing, friendship, sunshine and soft grass. But even early on in the training, when we were in a lot of (verbally) unspoken emotional pain and didn't know each other very well, I felt a visceral connection with you. Thank you so much for your openness and honesty throughout this conversation.

Revisiting this period through reading our reflective journals and speaking and moving together has added another layer to both our processes of embodiment. Once again, Barad's (2008) concept of the material-discursive can be seen to redress the balance by communicating embodied knowledge while avoiding the hierarchical structures found in current dominant modes of thinking.

My autoethnographic material, and specifically the idea of the rectangular block of depression, and Tina's development of the pterodactyl are examples of the way in which the material-discursive can be seen to produce a merging of movement, poetry, objects, other-than-human actors, humans, thoughts, journal reflections, memories, body sensations, oceans, weather systems, buildings, floors, feelings, electric lights, music and digital filming – all of which are contributors to the assemblage that has co-created the narrative. Within this, language is appreciated as one of many factors that add to the assemblage. However, it can only ever be a representation of the material experiences, just like the black rectangles or winged creatures drawn throughout the pages of my and Tina's journals.

Conclusion

This chapter has aimed to advocate the use of DMP and other embodied practices to address the symptoms of trauma associated with CSA. By considering selected, pertinent ideas from feminist new materialism and posthumanism, I have argued that typical therapeutic approaches that privilege language over material experience are problematic. Sexual trauma is understood to be held in the body. Therefore, in order to work towards a place of mind-body integration, it is necessary to approach the problem in an embodied way. To accept that the body is important and agentic entails a refutation of the dichotomies that feed the binary privileging of minds and language over bodies and matter.

My narrative of embodiment also exemplifies the extension of the work of postmodern feminists in order to challenge the human/nonhuman binary. Removing the all-powerful and often threatening human from centre stage offers a new and safe sphere from which to access healing cultures that exist independently of human intention. By recognising the intra-actions between other-than-human, human and nonhuman actors, normative assumptions that currently inform research, policies and practices can be reconsidered.

Although it is difficult to articulate the knowledge held within our bodies, by legitimising the felt, active experiences of matter, feminist new materialism may, paradoxically, contribute a theoretical language with which to do so. The emergent process of DMP, which, as discussed, is difficult to measure within our current systems and typical onto-epistemological frameworks, could be supported by a new understanding of and respect for the agency of matter. Thus, a synthesis of ecological thinking, embodied practices and critical posthumanism can collectively present a challenge to existing modes of thought.

Within the context of current dominant models of thinking, it is easy to doubt the significance of felt knowledge or ignore the interdependency of humans and other-than-humans. Likewise, it is easy to forget that language is only a representation of material experience. In order to think and act holistically, it is necessary to challenge anthropocentric hierarchies. DMP is subtly powerful in its ability to integrate mind-body, human-nonhuman and material-discursive practices. Dance enables bodies to move, acknowledge, feel and release their experiences. All this leads me to argue that DMP is ideally situated to help integrate the fractured parts of people traumatised by the lived reality and legacy of CSA.

References

Abrams D (1997). *The Spell of the Sensuous: perception and language in a more-than-human world*. London: Vintage Books.

Ainscough C, Toon K (2000). *Breaking Free*. London: Sheldon Press.

Alaimo S (2008). Trans-corporeal feminisms and the ethical space of nature. In: Alaimo S, Hekman S (eds). *Material Feminisms*. Bloomington, IN: Indiana University Press (pp237–264).

Alaimo S, Hekman S (eds) (2008). *Material Feminisms*. Bloomington, IN: Indiana University Press.

Barad KM (2008). Posthumanist performativity: towards an understanding of how matter comes to matter. In: Alaimo S, Hekman S (eds) (2008). *Material Feminisms*. Bloomington, IN: Indiana University Press (pp120–154).

Barad KM (2007). *Meeting the Universe Halfway: quantum physics and the entanglement of matter and meaning*. Durham, NC: Duke University Press.

Bass E, Davis L (2008). *The Courage to Heal*. New York, NY: HarperCollins Publishers.

Braidotti R (2007). Feminist epistemology after postmodernism: critiquing science, technology and globalisation. *Interdisciplinary Science Reviews* 32(1): 65–74.

Cisney VW, Morar N (2016). *Biopower: Foucault and beyond*. Chicago, IL: University of Chicago Press.

Cohn S, Lynch R (2017). Posthuman perspectives: relevance for a global public health. *Critical Public Health* 27(3): 285–292.

Dieterich-Hartwell R (2017). Dance/movement therapy in the treatment of post-traumatic stress: a reference model. *The Arts in Psychotherapy* 54: 38–46.

Frost S (2011). The implications of the New Materialisms for feminist epistemology. In: Grasswick HE (ed). Feminist Epistemology and Philosophy of Science: power in knowledge. New York, NY: Springer (pp69–83).

Fullagar S (2017). Foucauldian theory. In: Cohen B (ed). *Routledge International Handbook of Critical Mental Health*. London: Routledge (pp39–45).

Hodge L, Simpson S (2016). Speaking the unspeakable: artistic expression in eating disorder research and schema therapy. *The Arts in Psychotherapy* 50: 1–8.

Hollin G, Forsyth I, Giraud I, Potts T (2017). (Dis)entangling Barad: materialisms and ethics. *Social Studies of Science* 47(6): 918–941.

Kelly L (1998). *Surviving Sexual Violence*. Cambridge: Polity Press.

Koro-Ljungberg M, Montana Cirell A, Gong BG, Tesar M (2017). The importance of small form: 'Minor' data and 'BIG' neoliberalism. In: Denzin NK, Giardina MD (eds). *Qualitative Inquiry in Neoliberal Times*. New York, NY: Routledge (pp59–72).

MacLure M (2017). Qualitative methodology and the new materialisms: a little of Dionysus's blood? In: Denzin NK, Giardina MD (eds). *Qualitative inquiry in Neoliberal Times*. New York: Routledge, Taylor and Francis Group (pp48–58).

Meekums B (2000). *Creative Group Therapy for Women Survivors of Child Sexual Abuse*. London: Jessica Kingsley Publishers.

Meekums B, Karkou V, Nelson EA (2015). Dance movement therapy for depression. *Cochrane Database of Systematic Reviews*. Issue 2. Art. No.: CD009895. DOI: 10.1002/14651858. CD009895.pub2 (accessed 20 June 2018).

Newlove J, Dalby J (2004). *Laban for All*. London: Nick Hern.

Oliver M (2004). Wild geese. In: Oliver M. *Wild Geese: selected poems*. Hexham: Bloodaxe Books (p21).

Panhofer H (2011). Languaged and non-languaged ways of knowing in counselling and psychotherapy. *British Journal of Guidance and Counselling* 39(5): 455–470.

Pykett J (2013). Neurocapitalism and the new neuros: using neuroeconomics, behavioural economics and picoeconomics for public policy. *Journal of Economic Geography* 13(5): 845–869.

Reeve S (2011). *Nine Ways of Seeing a Body*. Bridport: Triarchy Press.

Rogers CR (2003). *Client-Centred Therapy: its current practice, implications and theory*. London: Constable.

Roszak T (1995). *Ecopsychology: restoring the earth, healing the mind*. San Francisco, CA: Sierra Club Books.

Sanderson C (2006). *Counselling Adult Survivors of Child Sexual Abuse*. London: Jessica Kingsley Publishers.

Tudor K, Worrall M (2008). *Person-Centred Therapy: a clinical philosophy*. London: Routledge.

van der Kolk B (2014). *The Body Keeps the Score*. London: Penguin Books.

Wagoner D (2007). Lost. In: Astley N, Robertson-Pearce P (eds). *Soul Food: nourishing poems for starved minds*. Hexham: Bloodaxe Books (p45).

Whyte D (2011). Sweet darkness. In: Whyte D. *The House of Belonging*. Washington, DC: Many Rivers Press (p23).

Chapter 10

Shattering the sounds of silence

Reena Shah, with Clarinda Cuppage

Introduction

This chapter argues that the more contact the survivor-therapist has with their own wounds while working with their client, the greater the opportunity for client and therapist to *shatter the silences* of their childhoods.

The chapter begins with a brief discussion of my research, *Broken Mirror/ Survivors: an autoethnographic and narrative exploration of the intertwining of therapist and client stories of childhood sexual abuse.*[1] I then share my story.[2] In the remainder of the piece, I explore my research participants' experiences through the lens of language. I consider experiences of childhood sexual abuse (CSA) and the silence engulfing them (Mucci, 2014; Kitzinger, 2015). I also reflect on the ways in which language supports and limits shared understanding between therapist and client when both have a history of CSA, and particularly when the language used in therapy is different from the client's mother tongue. This adds to a relatively unexplored area of research on therapy in a language different from the mother tongue (Alonso, 2007; Guilfoyle, 2002).

---

1. In this chapter, any language in italics draws directly from my autoethnography or represents the participants' actual words.
2. I use 'story' in this chapter to describe the researcher's or participant's narrative. In this chapter, this includes both the abuse narrative and the narrative of the work as a therapist working with clients who have been abused.

Through the narratives, I explore the experience of other-ness, separation and enmeshment in the therapeutic dyad when both therapist and client have a history of CSA. I also consider how we navigate the 'unlanguaged'[3] experience of CSA and the further healing that can come from the symbolisation (making explicit feelings and experiences that have not previously been put into words) that occurs when both client and therapist are attending to their wounds.

I use the term 'survivor' to avoid the frame of 'victim', as I believe that the research participants and I have survived and worked through much of our history of abuse. Both participants self-identified as survivors.

Autoethnography and narrative inquiry

A brief note here about the two core components of my research methodology. I use the term 'autoethnography' to mean autobiography with an ethnographic dimension, using the following definition:

> Autoethnography is an autobiographical genre of writing and research that displays multiple layers of consciousness, connecting the personal to the cultural. (Ellis & Bochner, 2000: 739)

Consistent with autoethnography, I have written the chapter in the first person, in order to encourage the reader to enter and recall the stories emotionally and cognitively (Ellis & Rawicki, 2013) and to bring them closer to my experiences.

In my research, I also used narrative inquiry, focusing on the themes of silence and sameness. But, rather than *explain* my findings to readers, I believe that the most effective way for them to make sense through narrative inquiry is to 'think about' the stories (Polkinghorne, 1988) and 'think and feel with' the stories (Frank, 2013).

Consistent with this approach, the conversation at the end of this chapter with a fellow survivor-therapist offers some rich examples of Clarinda's experiences of thinking and feeling with the stories. In this conversation, Clarinda considers what could and couldn't be spoken about because of her religious upbringing, and how alternative ways of working may help overcome the barriers of language when working with CSA.

My research participants

My autoethnography includes my experience of CSA as a child brought up

---

3. When a child is sexually abused, there is rarely any language available to the child to describe what is happening to them – it becomes an 'unlanguaged' phenomenon (Mucci, 2014).

in a non-English family with Gujarati as my first language. In addition to my autoethnographic inquiry, my research included two research participants: both therapists and both survivors. Given the sensitive nature of our conversations, I required that the participants were in therapy and made it clear that they could withdraw their consent at any point before completion of the study. I have also gained consent from them for this publication.

Anna (a pseudonym) is bilingual, and language and verbal communication proved to be a complicated part of her experiences. Her abuser spoke to her in the language of her nation, and that of her father, while her mother's framing of the incident – of the man not being *'right in the head'* – was in English. One of the stories Anna shares is of the resonance she felt with a client who was also from her nation, who had an almost identical experience of sexual violence.

My second participant, Molly (also a pseudonym), was raised with a single language, but her abuse began before she had words. Art became a powerful vehicle for expressing what she had been through. Exploration of these accounts leads me to conclude that an awareness of the impact of language and its limitations is essential when working with survivors of childhood sexual abuse.

My story

Below are excerpts from my autoethnographic exploration of my experience of being sexually abused as a child. I have written in the first person and the present tense for different parts of my story to encourage the reader to enter and recall the stories both emotionally and cognitively (Ellis & Rawicki, 2013).

The early deprivation

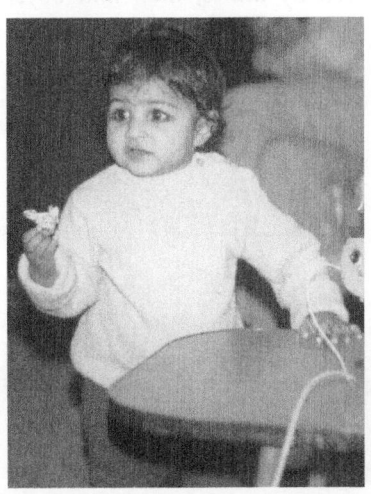

1972. Expulsion of Ugandan Asians. Idi Amin decrees that all Ugandan Asians are to leave the country with immediate effect, leaving behind all their possessions and taking with them no more than £50. My family flees to England. I am nine months old.

Although my mum speaks English fluently (she was a primary school teacher in East Africa), she decides to speak only in Gujarati, our mother tongue, with me. She believes that there will be ample time for me to learn English and wants me to retain some of my cultural heritage. My experiences growing up in the wider British community – shopping, school, doctors, hospitals, libraries – are always in sharp contrast to my home life, which is decidedly Indian. My mum's starting point in understanding any experience I describe to her is always to compare it with our Asian customs and traditions.

The origins of my shame

1975. I am three years old; he is a young adult. Within less than a year of him being in my family, the affection I felt in our relationship has become something much more shameful. I feel ashamed that I steal into his room in the middle of the night and that I want to do the things we do. I enjoy it. It is the absence of any sense of coercion that feels so shameful – I must want to engage in this behaviour, which I somehow know is wrong and illicit.

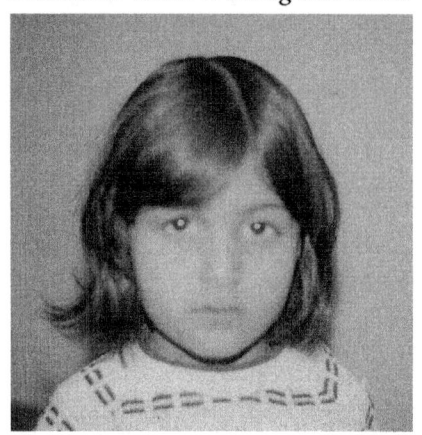

1978. I am five years old and I don't understand what it is I do in his bed, but I feel that my relationship with him is both bad and something to be enjoyed in secret. It is also something to be ashamed of in secret.

1977 – 1981. Living with the abuse, from age six to age nine. My home is dominated by males, men and boys, some of whom I am very close to, but not in this 'bad' way. My mum has brought me up to believe in reincarnation and the concept of karma – the lives we live now are predicated on the good and bad things we did in previous lives. I don't realise that he is 'violating' me or 'abusing' me – these are words I do not recognise. I feel I am doing this bad stuff with him because I am intrinsically bad (the legacy of my bad karma), and therefore I am acutely ashamed of this part of myself.

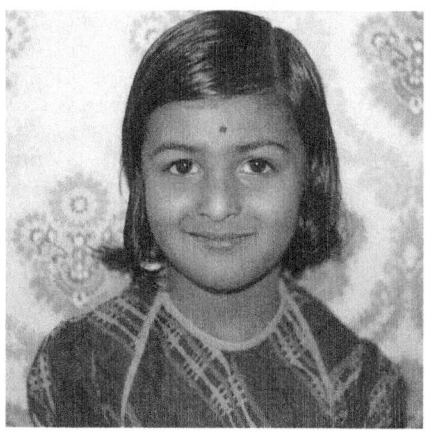

1982. We are doing a project about babies and I learn how babies are made. I am 10 years old. I feel sick, confused and terrified. As soon as I get home and for a month afterwards, when I go to the loo, I look down at my belly and fear that I am pregnant. I realise I have to put an end to it. The next time I am with him, I say no. He asks why. I don't explain, but this is it, it's finished.

I notice that my personality starts to change quite dramatically thereafter. I begin to shake off the shyness and start to enjoy being with other children my own age. The shame and the responsibility are now locked away within me, hidden. There is no ongoing reality of being found out. It is still a long time before I learn to walk tall, but it comes. Eventually.

What strikes me so profoundly as I reflect on my shifting sense of my experience of abuse is the level of responsibility I took for it, and, until very recently, have continued to take. Once I learned that it was 'sex,' and something to be performed between two adults, I assumed all culpability for it, and all the consequent shame. Part of my shame was that I believed I was precociously behaving as an adult; we were not taught about abuse, and I had not been taught that this wasn't 'sex'. I wonder if there was an additional layer to my shame where I felt inferior because I was not 'white'. As part of my rapid integration into English life, I internalised a sense of the white English as superior, something my family had also internalised in the colonies of the British Empire. When my mother contrasted English experiences with our own, it was usually with a sense that 'the English know better'. This only confirmed, on some unspoken level, that the internal badness I felt I had for what 'I did' at night-time was connected with my being brown – something in which 'good white children' would never indulge (Eddo-Lodge, 2018).

The experience of CSA and the sounds of silence

From the moment I could speak, I loved language, yet I had no vocabulary for what I was experiencing with my abuser until I was 10 years old. I devoured Enid Blyton books, and none of her characters did what I did. I now understand that I had split off that part of my experience (Stern, 2010) and it had become something that was mostly 'not-me'. I wonder if my mastery over, and delight with, the English language and words was my way of creating and shaping my identity. It enabled me to construct a self to those that knew me in the English language that was different to the girls and women in my home, and far away from the child that saw herself as choosing to participate in the illicit night-time encounters. There was a 'me' I was constructing in the English language, and a 'not-me' (Bromberg, 1996), or a 'night-time me', when the abuse occurred, which was entirely in Gujarati.

Childhood trauma and abuse is often described as 'un-languaged' (Mucci, 2014); the wrong-ness of it means there is no language. What added to my confusion and responsibility-taking was that the vernacular of my language, Gujarati, was considerably more limited than the English language I would come to learn and love. The language of emotions, love, sadness and compassion was unknown to me, perhaps reflecting the very practical, functional way in which my community had lived for generations (Oonk, 2007).

The word 'sharam' is Gujarati for shame, and it is a word I don't remember ever not knowing. In describing the survival value of particular affects we experience, Babette Rothschild offers that 'shame, at least through evolution, has served to keep an individual's behaviour in line with cultural norms that further "survival of the tribe"' (Rothschild, 2000: 63). Perhaps 'sharam' was more important than 'abuse', as it kept the collective together. I adopted my family's binary way of thinking – what we experienced outside our home was 'other' and, to my child-like way of thinking, the shame I felt about the abuse (DeYoung, 2015) was part of the wider shame I felt as 'other' – a 'brown' person in a white country.

Language and choice

I read *Lolita* (Nabokov, 1955) when I was 16 and recognised in myself the 'seductress' figure Nabokov describes. I was quite thrown when my therapist, who I started working with at the age of 37, named my experience as 'abuse'. Although I was familiar with the idea of CSA from the media and wider discourse, I did not recognise it as my experience, because of what I believed to be an absence of coercion. This is something one of my participants, Molly, also experienced:

> I still find, even though I've had therapy, and even though I know that this is true, I still find the word abuse, even though I know it was abuse, I still find it very hard to use.

When a child is abused, their developmental journey becomes fractured, particularly when the abuse is chronic and perpetrated by someone who is, on some level, a protective figure (Davies & Frawley, 1994). For my participants and me, the abuser(s) were not our parents. But for Molly and me, the abuser was known, lived as part of the family, and had some role as a protector within the family. Such abuse, therefore, has an 'incest' quality (even when the abuser is not the birth parent), as the person who is supposed to protect you is also abusing you. For a child who is not fully grown, it is usually impossible to hold an ambivalent position where the abuser can be both kind, gentle, loving and also a perpetrator of sexual violence. For this reason, the 'badness' becomes fully introjected; the child believes that they are the bad one, that they have caused it to happen (Miller, 1984).

For Molly, an additional dimension to her internalised sense of badness was that she believed the abuse began before she had language. Finding words for what happened to her, being able to symbolise the experience using language, took a long time. Molly spent the first year of therapy not speaking, and it was through her art that she consciously realised how far back the abuse went. In one session she drew the bars of her cot.

Choice takes on a different meaning for the child being abused. Molly, like many adult survivors, could not tolerate the idea of being 'abused', as it implies a vulnerability, a being 'done-to' that is almost worse than believing that she made it happen. At least there is some sense of agency if *we* caused it to happen. Molly's abuser capitalised on this confusion by suggesting that she did have choice. For her fourth or fifth birthday, her abuser took her to his car and said, 'Because it's your birthday, you can choose' (meaning choose how she wanted to be 'fucked'). She couldn't choose, and his response was, 'Because you didn't choose, I'll give you a bit of everything.' She still feels tormented by the guilt:

> ... knowing that actually that all happened because I didn't choose one.

In my work with clients, I am in deep contact with wounds from my abuse, because I let myself get close to my shame and don't bracket off my experience. I am also aware of the relational deficit that came before it, with my mother unable to be consistently available for me. I discover that, in spite of each person's experiences being unique and heartrendingly individual, the quality of understanding through having myself experienced something of their experience feels deeper. As we unfurl layer after layer of experience, early relational deficits, the chronic nature of the abuse, the paradox of being seen and not-being seen, and the horrific ongoing silence, I am confounded by the delving that my clients are prepared to undertake. We work painstakingly to find a shared language to understand and find compassion for the child within us who was abused.

Language and shared understanding between client and therapist

The dynamics of working with survivors of abuse mean that the positions of the drama triangle (Karpman, 1968) can change very quickly between client and therapist. In the triangle, Karpman suggests that we adopt the positions of victim, persecutor or rescuer. The frame that I use is that there is usually a dynamic of three in the room: the perpetrator, the victim and either the idealised rescuer or the unseeing observer (Davies & Frawley, 1994). In my work as a therapist with survivors of abuse, I bear witness and, by bearing witness, I dislodge, for both of us, the sense that there will always be an 'unseeing' observer. I have consistently found that, rather than being prone to vicarious traumatisation (Pearlman & Mac Ian, 1995), I have experienced a recognition that has been mutually healing. I have found that, by having done the deep work on my personal abuse history, and by being in close contact with it when with my clients, I have a resilience that supports positive transformation (Benatar, 2000) rather than vicarious traumatisation.

It was with a male client who described CSA as a 'mind-fuck' that Molly had the strongest experience of feeling like a victim. On one occasion, the client smoked a cigarette in the middle of the session. During another, he ate a banana. Both times he sat looking at Molly in a way that made her feel 'horrible'. Molly showed me how he would sit, with his legs splayed out in front of her. At the end of the session, he would dramatically lift his arm up in the air and look at his watch, ostentatiously checking that he'd been given his full-time allocation. In supervision, Molly and her supervisor considered the parallels with prostitution – getting his money's worth and having a cigarette after sex. As Molly reflected on her own feelings of humiliation and shame, she understood that the feelings she was experiencing in the work were in fact her client's feelings of humiliation and shame that he was projecting onto her (Klein, 1946).

I am struck by the absence of spoken language in this enactment, and how both client and therapist were caught up in the energetic field of the abuse enactment (Davies & Frawley, 1994). Molly's abuse history itself was mostly wordless, and occasionally papered over with euphemisms that served only to minimise an experience that was shattering to her psyche. It felt as though she was dissociatively frozen in this enactment with her client, just as she had to be when she endured the abuse as a child, with no rescuer in her field of vision.

The paralysis that Molly experienced when she felt like a victim with her client is mirrored in Anna's story of abuse, and that of her client's. Anna's childhood experience was of a single incident: she was molested as an eight-year old by a stranger in a lift in her apartment block. One of Anna's clients, now in her 50s and from the same country of origin, related that she was molested every day, aged eight, in an underground carriage on her way to school. The stranger would stand behind her and put his hand up her skirt. The girl would always go to the same compartment and the stranger would perform the same act each morning, for what felt to her like months. It came to an end when another passenger noticed and put a stop to it. Anna recognised the extent of the client's compliance with the stranger's behaviour:

> ... that reminded me, that compliance, really, you know I really thought about getting in the lift, you know, and I could imagine, strangely, I could completely understand why she did that. Why she kept doing, you know like, like a kind of paralysis.

For Anna, her own experience of being abused felt almost like she was hypnotised, under the control of an adult stranger who spoke with a firm but gentle voice, the sound giving authority to his instruction.

Language and verbal communication proved to be a complicated part of Anna's experience. Anna had always had a sense, perhaps because of her mother's original way of framing the abuser as '*someone not right in the head*', that any rational communication with a predator would be futile. She wondered if this was why, when her clients tried to take their abusers to court and failed, she had not felt enraged at the injustice on their behalf. In addition, Anna had a sense of sexual relations being more non-verbal in nature. She had a long and intermittent sexual liaison with an older male relative from when she was a young adolescent, and wondered if the early sexualisation, as a consequence of the assault in the lift, contributed to this '*relationship*' (Anna's word). She recollected that there were hardly any words spoken between her and her relative, and she also reflected that the relationship seemed to have more emotional meaning for him than for her.

In contrast to her clients who chose to take action, Anna was aware of a passivity within her, highlighting the difference between herself and these clients. However, linked to this passivity was a deep sense of shame – an effect that she knew, in her shared communion with her clients, was deeply helpful in enabling her to meet them with deep relational empathy. During our conversation, Anna tried to locate the feeling of shame in her body. While she experienced it as a whole-body sensation, she felt it most strongly in her genital area. The shame of obeying her abuser's instruction, '*pull your knickers down*', was having profound reverberations. Anna told me of how triggered she felt on hearing a nun in the film *Philomena* (Frears, 2013) ask 'Did you pull your knickers down?' She felt shock as her own childhood incident flashed back to her, and I, in turn, felt a shiver run through me as she told me this, as I resonated with the shame of being judged to have transgressed.

Shame is a powerfully physiological affect (Rothschild, 2000), and when we are in it, it's hard to have any language for it. Stevens, who uses a pseudonym when writing about her clinical work as a survivor-therapist, says of one client: 'When I don't ask, the shame remains unexplored and grows bigger' (Stevens, 1996: 195). What Anna hints at, and I recognise, is that when I make deeper contact with my own intimate relationship with shame, it supports me in feeling my client's shame in the countertransference. I find that when I am with my own shame and find some compassion towards my shame as I sit with my client, we don't always need words. My embodied presence, where we can be with the shame and we can be kind towards the shame without words, can be immensely healing.

Working without words

Below, I present a vignette illustrating my work. It describes a composite client, to respect the anonymity of my individual clients. It demonstrates the way in which words are not always enough in finding a shared understanding.

> Today Francesca decided she wanted to play with the doll's house. In previous sessions, we had drawn together and worked with stones, usually when Francesca was struggling to access her emotions. Today she wanted to revisit the scenes of the abuse.
>
> As we sat on the floor, I became aware that a younger version of my client was also in the room. While I remained the responsible adult, I felt that my own 'inner child' was resonating with hers. As Francesca set up the room of the doll's house, I looked at photographs she had brought of herself before the abuse began and afterwards. I am struck by how her eyes have lost some of their gleam after she was abused. Francesca was puzzled – why were my eyes moist? We sat in silence reflecting on the tragedy of the beautiful, vulnerable little girl who was violated.
>
> We found objects to represent people in the playroom and Francesca lined up all the vile adults from her childhood, some of whom had abused her sexually and/or physically and others who had failed to protect her. Moulding her hands into a mock gun, she fired at each of them and knocked them over. We looked at each other, and I felt she could see the depth of my understanding. I joined her in her bursts of

exhilaration, waves of unfathomable sadness and peals of laughter. It seemed to me that the laughter reflected the impossibility of justice and the revelling in the violence of the fantasy.

As we looked at the bedroom of the playhouse, Francesca talked about how she was groomed by her abusers, how she was so dissociated from the abuse (she was as young as I was when it began) that she doesn't know which body orifice her first abuser penetrated. I reflected how painful it seemed to not fully remember, to feel that memory cannot be fully trusted. She flushed at her recollection that she couldn't say no. It seems we are both in touch with the shame of not saying no. I looked at the picture again and told her that I saw a beautiful, innocent little girl – and wonder how it could have been her responsibility to say no, and am reminded of how long it took me to accept that it wasn't my responsibility.

Other-ness, separation and enmeshment in the therapeutic dyad

Much of this chapter has focused on how, as therapists, we can 'lean in' by tuning into the shared resonance with clients. Now I will explore difference and its importance. The language I have used in my personal therapy, and as a therapist, is English. A huge component of my healing has been finding a symbolic language to make sense of my story. It has helped me to grow my sense of agency – it is *my* story, and my understanding of what happened. As a client, within the transference, my experience has always been one of being one layer removed from the abuse, as the language I speak with my therapist is not the one I spoke during my formative years. I believe that the difference the client experiences when working in another language from that in which the abuse occurred can often be minimised if the therapist focuses on the universal, the shared humanity, in an attempt to shake the innate power imbalance of the therapeutic dyad (Totton, 2018). When therapist and client are both survivors, I believe there is a risk that both can be invested in finding the similarities and minimising the 'other-ness' of the other. After all, it was this 'other-ness' of the other that contributed to the abuse taking place in the first instance.

With my abuser, I believe I was seeking care and nurturing, but what I experienced through the sexual abuse was a form of 'unmarked mirroring' (Target, 2007). This is when the caregiver does not show sufficient differentiation between the child's feelings and their own, implying a psychic equivalence. This can manifest in the caregiver becoming equally overwhelmed or not showing how they are able, as the responsible adult, to hold and tolerate the child's feelings. I believed my abuser was not 'other', and that, in wanting to be with him, I was seeking to *be* him, or at least be like him. His failure to honour my desire to be close to him while not abusing me was how his 'otherness', his separateness from me, became dangerous.

What I fear can be circumvented is recognition in the transference *and* countertransference that the other is an 'other', which can lead to enmeshment and over-identification. Molly spoke of worrying about transference and enmeshment. She explained that, having recognised so much of her client's experiences in her own story, when she saw photos of her client as a child that the client brought to a session, it was *'almost like scissors cutting our story'*. Molly felt that this concrete recognition of their difference enabled her to more fully see her client as a separate individual, and therefore to serve her client better.

I believe that, when both therapist and client are survivors, the quest in the work is for the therapist to be able to tolerate and bear the anguish we may feel in the role of therapist. In holding this position, and in acknowledging our separateness from the client, we offer an opportunity of experiencing 'the third in the one' (Benjamin, 2004: 11):

> The experience of surviving breakdown into complementarity, or twoness, and subsequently of communicating and restoring dialogue – each person surviving for the other – is crucial to therapeutic action. From it emerges a more advanced form of third-ness, based on what we might call the symbolic or interpersonal third.

I feel that the most reparative moments in my own journey in the therapeutic dyad, and in many of my survivor-clients' journeys, have been when we recognise that we are different and that we survive being different. Our healing comes through being fully seen as different and separate. I believe that, because the child's natural development has been interrupted by the abuse (whether it is a single incident or chronic), the survivor may often struggle to accept their difference and separateness from the other, but that when this occurs, it can be remarkably healing.

Response from Clarinda Cuppage

I welcomed the opportunity to meet Reena and talk about her chapter. The conversation made me question why so little space currently exists for discussions between therapists who are also survivors. That's why this book is so important.

Reading 'Shattering the sounds of silence' highlighted for me that, although our histories differ, many survivor-therapists share significant commonality and understanding of the impact of CSA as well as considerations and concerns when working with survivor-clients.

The comments below are some of the themes that emerged from our rich discussion.

Central to childhoods of sexual abuse is the lack of language in which to speak of it, especially when children mostly do not know they are being abused and when the trauma response often renders them frozen, leading to confusion, sometimes compounding their sense of shame and culpability. Children, and sometimes adult survivors, need language to convey their experiences and this language is not available to them unless another facilitates this.

My voicelessness as a child was compounded by Roman Catholicism, from which my younger self inferred she was dammed, adding to my sense of self-alienation. Only when I came to see that my younger self was not responsible for what happened could I begin to let go of my shame. It is the meaning our clients make of their experiences of sexual abuse that, as therapists, we need also to attend to.

In my childhood, Catholicism also contributed to the idea of the limited value of girls in comparison with boys, which becomes internalised at a familial and societal level. Reena also comments on the absence of women's voices, and, despite the different socio-cultural backgrounds, there are echoes of patriarchal attitudes privileging the male voice, attitudes and opinions and excluding or minimising those of women. Such attitudes feed into women's shame, keeping them silent about sexual abuse for years. Even when they speak out, survivors continually have to navigate an external world dominated by male attitudes, often keeping these life-changing, life-shaping experiences hidden or suppressed. It can be in the presence of another, who wordlessly knows the challenges of navigating life with such an experience, that a survivor feels safer.

Supporting clients to put into language what happened to them and how they feel can be done by the therapist offering the use of symbolic or representational objects. I find using a range of small toys and stones introduces some creativity and playfulness into the clinical space. The objects can support a gentle exploration of a client's experience and their internal traumatised parts, or sub-states, which can be dialogued with, enabling the client and therapist together to gain a greater insight of the client's experiences. These can be photographed on a smartphone, so clients can carry with them a visual representation of their inner parts as an *aide memoire*, if triggered.

Regardless of whether a survivor was able to say no to their abuser, I observe many find the ability to hold strong boundaries permeating all areas of their lives. With clients who present with an invasive, almost penetrating presence, I particularly need to hold my self-boundary and consciously ground myself, while listening in the countertransference to what is being conveyed about the client's own experience.

In developing the Survivors' Voices project on behalf of the charity One in Four,[4] I have used my voice to increase understanding of the longer-term impact of childhood sexual abuse. The project supports survivors to find their voice through writing their own stories, highlighting how the abuse affected their lives. Feedback from participants highlights the invaluable and empowering experience of writing and externalising their experiences.

However, a key challenge for the project is how to ensure professionals and non-professionals hear and engage with these painful narratives. This challenge parallels the challenges survivors experience in processing their trauma before they are supported, which can lead to harmful coping mechanisms to manage the pain and shame of sexual abuse.

Survivors tread the line between not wanting to be seen because of searing feelings of shame, yet wanting or needing to be seen to be rescued and heal. Sometimes I think survivors' shame in not wanting to be seen is mirrored by society not wanting to know – not wanting to acknowledge the true scale and impact of childhood sexual abuse. Too often disclosures have been missed or dismissed, which, although unwitting, protects society from a fuller understanding. This limited understanding compounds survivors' feelings of isolation, shame and hopelessness, unnecessarily lengthening the time before they receive appropriate support.

#MeToo provides an important platform for greater public awareness and for frank discussions around consent, boundaries, sexual harassment and abuse. However, I am concerned that the voices of people sexually abused in childhood, most commonly within the family, may not be heard or acknowledged and become further marginalised. We, as a society, need to recognise these traumatic experiences as significant underlying contributors to major societal issues, including homelessness, substance abuse, addiction, prostitution and domestic violence, to name a few.

Concluding thoughts

My conversation with Clarinda confirmed for me the power of shared dialogue. What we have here is just a taste of a much longer conversation. #MeToo has helped survivors of sexual violence communicate with one another, as I did with my research participants, and I found the experience of talking with Clarinda,

---

4. www.oneinfour.org.uk/survivorsvoices

a fellow survivor-therapist, a rich and illuminating experience. Clarinda's experience of being raised a Roman Catholic added another cultural dimension, and we both recognised dominant themes of patriarchy, which were present in my participants' narratives too. I believe this shared communion has been, and will continue to be, an important part of the journey.

References

Alonso MA (2007). *Understanding the Role of Language in the Psychotherapeutic Process: exploring the bilingual clinician's linguistic experience*. Doctoral dissertation. New Brunswick, NJ: The State University of New Jersey.

Benatar M (2000). A qualitative study of the effect of a history of childhood sexual abuse on therapists who treat survivors of sexual abuse. *Journal of Trauma & Dissociation* 1(3): 9–28.

Benjamin J (2004). Beyond doer and done to: an intersubjective view of thirdness. *Psychoanalytic Quarterly* 73(1): 5–46.

Bromberg P (1996). Standing in the spaces: the multiplicity of self and the psychoanalytic relationship. *Contemporary Psychoanalysis* 32: 509–535.

Davies JM, Frawley MG (1994). *Treating the Adult Survivor of Childhood Sexual Abuse – a psychoanalytic perspective*. New York, NY: Basic Books.

DeYoung PA (2015). *Understanding and Treating Chronic Shame: a relational/neurobiological approach*. New York, NY: Routledge.

Eddo-Lodge R (2018). *Why I'm No Longer Talking to White People about Race*. London: Bloomsbury Publishing.

Ellis C, Bochner AP (2000). Autoethnography, personal narrative, reflexivity: researcher as subject. In: Denzin N, Lincoln Y. *Handbook of Qualitative Research* (2nd ed). Thousand Oaks, CA: Sage (pp736–768).

Ellis C, Rawicki J (2013). Collaborative witnessing of survival during the holocaust: an exemplar of relational autoethnography. *Qualitative Inquiry* 19(5): 366–380.

Frank AW (2013). *The Wounded Storyteller: body, illness, and ethics*. Chicago, IL: University of Chicago Press.

Frears S (dir) (2013). *Philomena*. [Film.] New York, NY: The Weinstein Company.

Guilfoyle M (2002). Power, knowledge and resistance in therapy: exploring links between discourse and materiality. *International Journal of Psychotherapy* 7(1): 83–98.

Karpman S (1968). Fairy tales and script drama analysis. *Transactional Analysis Bulletin* 7(26): 39–43.

Kitzinger J (2015). Who are you kidding? Children, power and the struggle against sexual abuse. In James A, Prout A (eds). *Constructing and Reconstructing Childhood: contemporary issues in the sociological study of childhood*. London: Routledge (pp163–184).

Klein M (1946). Notes on some schizoid mechanisms. *The International Journal of Psycho-Analysis 27*: 99–110.

Miller A (1984). *Thou Shalt Not Be Aware: society's betrayal of the child*. New York, NY: Meridian.

Mucci C (2014). Trauma, healing and the reconstruction of truth. *The American Journal of Psychoanalysis 74*: 31–47.

Nabokov V (1955). *Lolita*. New York, NY: Vintage.

Oonk G (2007). *Global Indian Diasporas: exploring trajectories of migration and theory*. Amsterdam: Amsterdam University Press.

Pearlman LA, Mac Ian PS (1995). Vicarious traumatization: an empirical study of the effects of trauma work on trauma therapists. *Professional Psychology: Research and Practice 26*(6): 558–565.

Polkinghorne DE (1988). *Narrative Knowing and the Human Sciences*. New York, NY: State University of New York Press.

Rothschild B (2000). *The Body Remembers: the psychophysiology of trauma and trauma treatment*. New York, NY: WW Norton & Company.

Stern DB (2010). *Partners in Thought: working with unformulated experience, dissociation and enactment*. London: Routledge.

Stevens BF (1996). The effects of sexual trauma on the self in clinical work. In: Gerson B (ed). *The Therapist as a Person: life crises, life choices, life experiences and their effects on treatment*. New York, NY: The Analytic Press (pp183–206).

Target M (2007). Is our sexuality our own? A developmental model of sexuality based on early affect mirroring. *British Journal of Psychotherapy 23*(4): 517–530.

Totton N (2018). Power in the therapeutic relationship. In: Tweedy R (ed). *The Political Self: understanding the social context for mental illness*. London: Routledge (pp29–42).

Chapter 11

While I was sleeping

Andrew Pari, with Katy Woodger

I sit in my office, hesitant to write as I've never told this part of my life before, except to my own therapists and the people in my life I care about most: my now ex-wife, my romantic partners and a very few close friends. On a few occasions, when I believe disclosure would serve the progress of my clients, I'll share. I don't hide it; nor do I share unless asked. I know that my experience can have power, but it can also serve as a distraction. We live in a world where more than 90% of all sexualised violence is inflicted on women, by men. I choose to keep my focus there, while privately acknowledging my own history.

Another reason for my hesitancy is to protect my former abuser. Some may say perpetrators deserve no consideration for what they've done. However, my perpetrator and I have long ago worked this through to a place where we can live with it and I have no interest in disrupting their life. It's unusual for abusers to do the personal reflection necessary to understand the pain and harm they caused. I respect that, out of their love for me, they did. While what they did will be with me for the rest of my life, I've learned that painful experiences can mark a path to empowerment when our eyes are fully open.

I'm a psychotherapist and speaker on challenging and taboo topics in sexualised violence. I train other mental health and law enforcement professionals around the world to understand and address the sensitive issues raised by arousal during sexual assault and repetition compulsion for women who re-enact their sexual trauma. I've developed a reputation as someone who is unafraid to challenge the myths and stereotypes that affect survivors and keep them hiding in shame. I've worked for more than 20 years to free female sexual assault survivors from trauma.

I'm often asked at conferences, 'How did you get into this? Why do you do the work you do on behalf of female survivors?' I'll talk about a documentary on what we now call child sexual exploitation that I saw as a teenager, and how seeing girls of my age being exploited woke me up to how the world treats women. I'll talk about my realisation at age 19 that this world has historically discriminated against one entire half of the population –more than seven billion humans – and that, as a man, I had some power to shift that. Or my very first therapy client who disclosed to me for the first time her adolescent rape, and our working through her trauma to the end when she told me I had a gift and should consider this as my path. Or my ongoing discovery of my ability to help women talk and heal from their trauma, or my willingness to tackle aspects of sexual assault that my profession still won't talk openly about. I've had numerous experiences that have led me towards the work I do now.

What I don't talk about is my own personal awakening. What I don't mention is my own experience of being sexually harmed as a teenager by someone close to me, for years. This book gives me another opportunity to help others through my journey from slumber into daylight.

It feels strange and awkward to review that time in my life and put it in writing after so many years – years of keeping it all in from my teens, through college, and into adulthood and marriage; years of therapy before I could first painfully admit, then begin to speak about what happened to me. How it affected me; how for much of my life I played a role, a persona, which was only parts of me. Years of pain and anguish lived because of what someone I loved did to me. Nearly 10 years of clouding reality with cocaine and alcohol and choosing a dream of a life instead of full immersion. Finally, years of understanding, of learning, of loving myself, of making sometimes painful decisions towards healthier outcomes, to turn years of hurt into decades now of helping others who hurt the same. Sleeping through life while awake and living.

This is also a story of silent violence – a quiet sort of abuse added to the original. This wasn't by my perpetrator but later, by my wife, my parents and others, when I disclosed as an adult.

But let's back up. To the beginning. To the darkness. At night, asleep.

Excerpt from an exercise my therapist assigned me to write about 'Hurt':

> Why don't you care about me?
> Why are you hurting me?
> Why are you doing this?
> Why are you touching me?
> Why are you making me feel this way?
> Why are you putting your mouth there?
> Why don't you leave me alone at night?
> I used to like you.
> I want to like you.
> But I'm scared.
> You scare(d) me.

From the time I was about 14 to 17, I had a night-time visitor. I've pored through letters and journal entries to put together what happened nearly 40 years ago. My memories now are the same as they were then, despite all the years I suppressed them, never forgetting what they did. The sliding down of the blanket when they thought I was asleep. Grasping my penis, feeling its hardness. Stroking. And, sickening as it is even now to write it, feeling their mouth on me.

They were my daytime friend and my night-time horror. Learning how to navigate and separate those parts of them and me led to shame, secrecy, alienation, bullying, isolation, two suicide attempts at 17, months in a psychiatric hospital, more years of denial, cocaine and alcohol abuse, and finally realising, as a beginning therapist, that I must resolve this if I was to do the work I loved.

My parents were loving, caring people. They raised me with the social consciousness that later developed into becoming a psychotherapist and social activist, caring for and standing up for others. Yet they had no clue what was happening in our home.

I always pretended to be asleep. In sleep, I could act as though it wasn't happening. I could protect both myself and my assailant from discovery. My greatest defence was 'the rollover'. Rolling away from them, their touch, scaring them into thinking I was waking up, hearing them scurry away, and finally knowing they wouldn't return, at least for that night, and only then being able to really sleep.

The days weren't much different. I 'slept' during the day as well, pretending things were fine. We spoke and played, continuing a life that crumbled in the darkness, pulling metaphorical blankets over my head to protect myself from the memory of the ones that were pulled down the night before.

At 17, I made two attempts at permanent sleep. My family still only knows about one. I bought a bottle of sleeping pills and a packet of Oreo biscuits, and sat in front of the television watching *General Hospital* (don't judge, that soap opera was really popular then!).

The first time, I got sick, fell asleep and woke up the next morning, groggy, with a pounding headache. I told my parents I was sick and stayed home from school. I figured that 30 pills weren't enough, and a week or two later I stood in front of the bathroom mirror swallowing handful after handful of pills until I emptied the bottle. To this day, I can't take more than one pill at a time without thinking of that day. I sat again on the couch to watch *General Hospital* and die. The therapist in me finds it fitting and ironic that I wanted sleep to be the way that I rescued myself from the daily forced awareness of my sexual abuse. As I felt my consciousness descend into oblivion, I began to seize and tremor. My mother found me on the couch, writhing and hyperventilating. She called 911 while I stumbled to the bathroom to begin vomiting up black sludge – blood mixed with the pills. I'm realising only now, as I'm writing this, that this was probably the cause of ulcers a few years later – another painful reminder of what was done to me.

I still remember sitting on the big orange chair, my father's chair, with the paramedic taking my pulse and stammering to his partner, 'Jesus, this kid's running like a racehorse!' I was taken to the hospital, given charcoal and ipecac, and made to vomit for the next several hours, my terrified family at my side. Everyone quickly found out it was a suicide attempt, although they had no clue as to why. I had an outgoing, comedic nature. I was always more social than academic; the budding actor and performer, caring more about a play I was in than my grades. In fact, that was a major piece of confusion for them. Why did I try to kill myself when I was enjoying acting in a play? Perhaps because realising that doing what I loved could not ever be enough to counter the painful lie I lived. My tortured adolescent brain made the decision I couldn't comprehend.

I spent the next three months in an adolescent psychiatric ward. In a strange twist of fate, during my psychology programme a few years later, I worked at that same hospital under the woman who had been my therapist during my time there. Dr M not only remembered me but took me under her wing and remains one of my first true mentors in the field. After my discharge, my father quit his job to stay at home and spent a lot of time with me; his not working prompted clashes between him and my mother. In conversations as an adult years later, I found out that he did this because he was scared that I would try to kill myself again and desperately needed to watch over me.

I graduated from high school with grades far lower than my academic potential indicated. 'Potential'. That was the word my mom always berated me with: 'I know you can do better. You have so much potential.' I hated that word.

It's still a trigger for me now as I constantly fight between ambition and self-acceptance.

I floated for several years, attempting to be an actor and stand-up comic, hanging out in Los Angeles comedy clubs, staying up late writing bits with partners while snorting gram after gram of cocaine. I had a short, sexy and coke-fuelled relationship with a wealthy South Bay woman, who cheated on me constantly but who I credit with prompting my decision to go back to school to earn my bachelor's and later my master's degree in social work. I met my wife-to-be in comedy improvisation classes. And over the years I never talked about what had happened, although I never forgot.

During the hospitalisation and outpatient therapy afterwards, I never spoke about what happened – not until I was in my 30s, an established psychotherapist and in therapy myself. It was with my second therapist that I found the emotional distance from the abuse to disclose and process. Less than a year into my marriage, in our one-bedroom apartment. Looking back, the marriage was a mistake. I knew it but lacked the confidence to say it. I needed to wake up to who I was because of my abuse. I was still sleeping.

Weeks after my very first disclosure to my therapist, to anyone, my wife found and read my journal. She was dealing with her father's health problems and, in her grief, became fearful that I was cheating on her. She later admitted to projecting her own desires to cheat onto me, so she did what she needed to regain a sense of control. Her guilt led to her tearfully admitting she had read my private thoughts. Her shame turned to certainty that my abuser must be reported.

My wife forced me to confront my offender, telling me that unless my abuser dealt with this in therapy, we had an obligation to report what was done to me. I knew the work ahead would be difficult and I wanted time in therapy to figure things out before telling my wife. I wasn't allowed that. My choice on how to move forward on my own sexual abuse was being dictated by someone else. My anger and betrayal were tied together in one thought: once again, my consent was being taken from me. It was to be one of the factors that later led to our divorce.

I confronted my abuser before I was ready. They told my parents before I was ready. It was out of my control and I wasn't ready to wake up yet. My parents' support was caring yet ambivalent. They added to my pain by questioning me, in the way many survivors experience. 'Why didn't you say something? Why didn't you do something? Push, hit, kick? Why didn't you come to us?' This was about how bad *they* felt, with the implication that it was my fault they felt that way, that it was somehow my responsibility because I had not told them what was going on, so they could do... something.

The repeated theme I see in much of my writing back then is betrayal. Anger, hurt, betrayal. An excerpt from my journal after confronting my abuser: 'Anger, fear, doubt, sadness… just another typical molestation in America!'

That dark, sardonic, gallows humour that served me on stage was born from my abuse. I still use it now, to help my clients and audiences understand deeper points about power and sex. My abuser agreed to go to therapy. I met with that therapist once, so they could hear my side. I was confronted by someone in my own field who didn't know the difference between sexual abuse and childhood sex play. I had to explain to this man, licensed and in practice for far longer than me, that consent wasn't possible when I didn't agree, when I didn't want it, when my abuser thought *I was fucking asleep*! I have anger and pride to this day that I was able to hold my own in that meeting, and terrible sadness that it was necessary.

Three years of no contact with my abuser. Three years of family gatherings where we wouldn't speak or acknowledge one another. Three years of intense therapy with two different therapists. Then years more of letters, emails and phone calls with my abuser on how to move forward. I was invested in doing so.

Yet, when we finally began talking, after three years of silence, *they* were angry! Letters and talks recriminating me for not responding to their abuse differently. 'Did you just pretend to like me? Was that all a charade? Why didn't you stop me?' Yes? No? I wish I knew. I loved you and you hurt me. And beneath it all: *How dare you question me?! You created this!*

Yes, I was so incredibly angry and hurt at what was done. For the first time, my eyes were opening to my anger and I was able to express it, to fully feel it. I was waking up.

And yet, there was my friend, my playmate growing up, the parts of them that I believed to truly be caring and to care about me. I didn't want to lose that.

There was a lot of soul-searching on my part as to whether reconciliation could happen; if it would be worth it. What they said was different from my memories, but they were sorry. There were apologies, expressions of genuine remorse, self-recrimination that it had ever happened, and admission that they knew it was wrong. That was enough for me to try. How often the touching happened, how many times, and how far it went mattered less than my wish to understand the relationship.

My focus was on having them hear my pain of betrayal, my experience of what they did. Theirs was on details and minutiae; why I acted like everything was OK all those years. Intellectualising versus emotional truth.

I was no longer asleep, but now I was in the position of having to wake them up. Staying awake for me became about holding onto my truth, my process, my need to move through this in a way that centred my healing. I had ignored my own voice. Now I needed to ignore the voices, and insistence, of others. The silent violence of being pressured to do this in ways to make others comfortable. It's all part of rape culture, of sexualised violence. The cloud of silence around the abuse itself, the insistence of silence later, to not make a 'big deal' of what happened; the desire from others to make it go away so they don't have to look at it. There is even a violence in the insistence for forgiveness. Well-meaning violence. Who is forgiveness for? If it fails to centre the survivor, then it fails.

Not giving in to silent violence was one of the most difficult parts of my healing. Even now, my anger at my wife's betrayal for revealing my abuse before I was ready, my father's anger and hurt that his son didn't fight back, my mother's push for me to reconcile with my perpetrator are all aspects I had to endure, learn to recognise and give voice to in order to remain awake to my truth. I can still hear my father's voice when I told my parents about what happened. 'Well, I feel like shit now,' as though it was his trauma, something I had done to them.

During this time, I faced the most horrific aspect of this silent violence, and one of the most difficult decisions of my life. The cancer my mother had beaten when I was a child returned. After several years of chemotherapy and operations, she was dying.

My own words from a letter I wrote to my abuser give insight into my struggle:

> When my mom was sick and at the end, I thought a lot about trying to put this aside, to put on a good face for them. My father put a lot of pressure on me to do this, as did my mother. It was painful for me, but I decided I had lived with this inside for so long that to pretend things were okay when they weren't was to go back to wearing the mask I had before. To make people think things were okay with me when they weren't. I am working hard not to do this. It's difficult, but I am getting better at it.

My healing continued as my abuser awoke. Outside of therapy and over the course of months, we met, just the two of us. We sat and talked about our lives together, what was real and not, what was my truth and theirs, talking and, most importantly, listening to each other about the self-deception we had both used to cover up what they did. The life-long patterns of denial and misdirection so others couldn't see our true selves, our waking selves.

And, gradually, over time, they heard me. They heard my pain, my confused horror at not knowing which version of them to believe and accept.

They cried, not for themselves, but for me, in understanding what they did. Admitting, both verbally and in writing, what they did and the damage it caused. They woke up.

From a letter they wrote to me:

> I am extremely sorry for what I had done to you. I know now that it was a horrible violation that should never have happened. I wish that I had the ability to travel back and stop my younger self from making your life so miserable. I am not saying this because it would make my life easier. I wish to undo what I did because of the damage I have done to your life.

I wish to be clear that this was not an easy path. Ironically, I had to force them to open their eyes to what they did, to *listen* to the effect their actions had on my life. In turn, I had to listen. To what led them to it. Their inadequacies, their fears. It was illuminating, if nauseating. I believed then, and still do all these years later, that we were both motivated by love. A desire to capture, maybe for the first time, the relationship we really wanted. Without the support and incredible compassion of my therapist, I wouldn't have had the strength.

I see this same profound desire in the women I work with. Greater than any need for punishment, for prosecution, is a need to understand, to hear from their perpetrator: *why?* Like in my 'Hurt' poem. Why did you put your needs before my safety?

When we, as a profession, discuss the need to focus on rehabilitation over punishment, it is the survivor's desire to understand why the assault happened that often drives the conversation. I am grateful to be one of the fortunate few who had an abuser willing to do the soul-searching to answer those questions for me. It doesn't make what they did go away. It does give it context and understanding, which was more powerful for me than retribution.

I don't write this lightly. I know this is not the experience most survivors have. I am privileged, strange as it may seem to the reader, to have my abuser apologise and take responsibility. In that privilege lies my own responsibility.

There is always more work to do. The 'work' is one theme in treatment that I convey to my clients. Healing is work done over time, in pieces. You don't just wake up one day with epiphanies and realisations. I struggled with that idea during my entire therapy. When will I have my 'Aha!' moment, that clarity that ties everything together? They do happen, but it's a revealing over time, in the way that our vision comes into focus in the morning, transitioning from dreams to the day.

We learn. We heal. We stumble. We start again and continue forward. I lost my marriage due to the secrecy; the alcohol and cocaine use that began with the abuse led to my choosing someone who provided the external control I lacked. Her inability to adjust to the woken man I worked so hard to become, even after years of sobriety, was something we couldn't overcome.

I regret my mother dying of cancer before she saw my reconciliation with my abuser. I regret my father's anger over that for years after. I regret not recognising the danger in a young woman who attempted to rape me when I invited her into my home, believing she had nowhere to go.

I'm more than 15 years clean now and with so much more insight into my relationships and my needs. However, my experience has given me great depth of understanding and compassion for the girls and women I treat and for the topics I am known for nationally.

I found a path post-divorce towards deepening my involvement in my work, finding passion and commitment to helping other survivors. I recently left a 20-year career in community mental health as a clinical supervisor and program director to fully immerse myself in my own agency, providing treatment, training and expert testimony to further recovery from sexualised violence.

My awakening, keeping truth centred, has become a focal point to help my clients through their own struggle. There is some irony in turning our secret shame and horror into light and love to wake others. How do I reconcile that? I don't. I accept it and move forward, with my focus on how I can try to make their lives liveable in a world in which there is so much more to do for them than my life will allow. I can tell you this much. I plan to be alive… and awake for all of it.

This next part of the chapter is Katy's reflections based on our conversations. She draws attention to how our experiences differ yet have poignant similarities. She focuses on particular issues raised in our discussions, exploring the implications of these in the recovery from sexual abuse. Katy's experience contrasts with mine, especially our search for healing. I like Katy's takes on what justice can look like, depending on person and context. I think, together, our perspectives encourage viewing the abuse experience as a continuum and understanding that sexual abuse does not have to be defined as one thing or another. It fits very well with how I work with my clients to define their experience and hold their truth.

Response from Katy Woodger

1. I'm not a survivor

When I read what Andrew had written, I was struck by the word 'survivor'. Arguably, 'survivor' has become the most widely-used and accepted term by both those who have experienced abuse and professionals working in the sexual violence field – seen as a more empowering term perhaps than 'victim.'

But 'survivor' is not, in fact, a term I use to describe myself, or would use to describe someone else unless they had already used it for themselves – and even then, I find it troubling. For it seems to me that 'survivor' has now become a blanket term for all who have experienced abuse: like we all identify, believe, or feel like 'survivors', or that we should do so; that somehow 'survivor' or 'victim' are my/our only options, and that 'survivor' is a 'better' choice of identification.

Surely, we should be able to decide for ourselves which words are most fitting to describe ourselves and our experiences? Here too, even after experiences where power has been taken away, power is taken away.

The term 'survivor,' I would argue, fits with society's desire to reconcile sexual violence and abuse with healing and recovery. Yet liberation from positivity, comfort and even hope has been an important part of my recovering. Six and a half years of psychotherapy enabled me to acknowledge what happened to me without the positive reframing of others, freeing me to feel the pain and grieve my loss. It continues to hurt when I am referred to as a 'survivor'. It imprints positive spins on these, my most horrific and traumatic experiences.

I am drawn to the voice of Jean Amery, an Austrian Jewish philosopher who was tortured by the Gestapo before deportation to Auschwitz. His perspective on what happened to him and others at the hands of the Nazi official secret police is refreshingly liberated from positivity, comfort and hope. He writes: 'Anyone who has been tortured remains tortured… Anyone who has suffered torture never again will be able to be at ease in the world, the abomination of the annihilation is never extinguished' (cited in Levi, 1989: 17). Amery candidly captures how dehumanisation and depraved acts can continue to haunt people. I'm not ready to be called a survivor; I may never be.

2. Context of sexual violence and abuse

There isn't one set recovery path, for either the abuser or the abused. Indeed, there may not be a recovery path at all. Elie Godsi, a friend and a consultant clinical psychologist, helped me untangle and begin to build an understanding of my own experiences. Godsi makes clear in *Violence and Society: making sense of madness and badness* (2004) his view that some violent offenders should never be released back into society – the risk of them re-offending is too high and psychological therapies have limited rehabilitation effects (Godsi, 2004: 150). I think this is the territory my abuser falls somewhere within…

... Aged approximately between eight and 10, I was sexually abused and raped by a 19-year-old man. At first it was gentle grooming, offering sweets, playing in our dens, picking me to be on his side in football matches, helping to get the rope swing down from the willow tree by the stream, just 100 yards from where I lived... I too, like Andrew, had a bedtime visitor – my abuser was friends with my babysitter.

His abuse escalated into depraved acts of sexual violence when I began to resist his sweets and sexual requests. On one occasion, he tricked me into accompanying him to his house to put more air in a football. He locked the doors and hid my alphabet print trainers. He stripped, blindfolded and gagged me and tied me to a bed. I was annihilated by his sexual assaults, including oral penetration and rape. When he had finished with me, he stood me in a bath and washed the blood away down the drain with cold water. On another occasion, he struck me across the back with an air rifle and then used it to hold me down to anally rape me.

I agree with Amery; the tortured remain tortured.

3. Disclosure and reporting of abuse

My experiences are markedly different to Andrew's. I knew I wanted to disclose to the authorities one day, when I felt strong enough. I have never been faced with the dilemma that Andrew had, wanting to protect my abuser and their identity. I've never had any concern for my abuser other than for the danger and threat he poses to children and society. I'm free of the difficulty and conflict of caring for a loved one who is also my abuser. One of the first things I shared with Andrew was how it saddens me that people have frequently asked if it was a family member who abused me. I know it is so often the case, but for me it wasn't.

Andrew and I discussed the tension between responsibility and safeguarding and the pressure on individuals to report abuse. I felt responsibility rather than pressure, perhaps because I eventually wanted to report to the police. Andrew has felt betrayed and pressured by loved ones to disclose to the authorities what happened to him. I came to the point of reporting without this pressure. An acute dis-ease began to grow within me. At this point in time, I was a youth worker and safeguarding was an integral part of my role. I was training as a therapist and had also become a mother for the first time. The knowledge of a violent child sexual offender free in society, possibly harming other children, started to absolutely jar in me.

I had attempted to report some of the abuse to social services in the late 1990s when I was 16, but I wasn't ready to make a full disclosure. I didn't have all the memories clear enough or words to describe what had happened to me. I was scared and didn't want my parents to know; I wanted to protect them, feeling it would break them. I was suicidal, self-harming and taking cheap cider or spirits stolen from my parents' well-stocked cabinet to drink in school. Like Andrew, I took two overdoses in my late teens. I wasn't at all ready or able to make a disclosure of this magnitude; I couldn't have handled it (Woodger, 2016: 32–33). I certainly wouldn't have been considered a viable witness.

I was 29 when I called the police to make a full disclosure. I had been working with my therapist for more than two years before I was ready. If I had been forced to confront things in the way Andrew was, before I was ready, my interview evidence wouldn't have been as strong as it was and would subsequently have hampered the chances of my case going to trial. Both mine and Andrew's experiences highlight that disclosure and reporting needs to be handled with a great deal of thought and care, minimising the risk of causing further harm. My therapist describes this part of the therapy as 'a coming together, in a space with one another, no pressure, judgement or expectations'.

This is the level of thought and care I needed. It helped me get to a place where I was ready to disclose. This was no straightforward process, however; it was incredibly painful and painstakingly slow. I wrote a poem called 'Frozen Melt' during this part of my therapy. It is an attempt to articulate just how difficult it was to express and disclose the sexual violence and abuse I had suffered.

Frozen melt

I hold the tool in my hand
Encapsulated, embodied, frozen
So dense, so cold

The ice compounds me
The coldest water drowned me
So still now in my chilling case
So far away from life-giving warmth

I scrape my tool from inside my frozen capsule
Chip, chipping, scraping away at the ice, then.
I feel warmth touching the cold
Drip, drip melting so gently and slow

Andrew Pari, with Katy Woodger

What is this melting my ice?
Who is this who warms my side?
Oh, so gradually and carefully
Painstakingly slow

How is it you are managing to melt through this?
I'm held so deep within my black ice case
How did you cause the ice to thaw?
I was rigid, still, oh so encased

I feel the warmth drip, drip melting through
Drip, drip, and crack, cracking out towards you
The cracking grinding so loud it pulsates my chest
Gushing, crashing, screaming

Breakout screams from the freezing cold within
You hear the screams and gently warm the cold
The screams release the breath that was froze
Breathing the warm, soothing air

Still the body is thawing and warming
And my mind emerging from its hypothermic state
Chilblain pain, the coldest bite
I tremble and shake, in confusion I fight

The black ice gradually gives in to the warmth
My body feels its gentle healing heat
Chilling words whispered from once frozen breath
Is held in warm vapours, evaporating mist
A steady flow of thawing words
While you hold and warm my clenched tight fist

A blanket, so warm and safe
Heat radiating from you into me,
Your words continue speaking to my frozen inner core
Hot aches now rushing into my extremities
Alive with pain once more

Rocking and shaking,
You hold me steady in recovery
We breathe together. I find your pace
As we sit together on the edge of my cliff face

4. Justice

After four years of investigation, my case finally went to trial in July 2015. Mine was one of the first to proceed to trial through 'The victim's right to review', a process set up by the former Director of Public Prosecutions Sir Keir Starmer MP QC, in the wake of the Jimmy Savile revelations and the uncovering of many failings by the criminal justice system to prosecute sexual offenders. My case had been previously rejected, deemed by the Crown Prosecution Service not to be in the public's interest and to lack forensic evidence. The outcome of my case, and of others in this first wave, was watched with interest by media and legal professionals. These cases held the potential to demonstrate what was enough credible evidence to enable successful prosecution.

Weeks before the trial, I was asked to take part in a documentary for BBC One called *Abused: the untold story* (Lambert, 2016). I agreed, as the documentary focused, refreshingly, on the stories of those whose lives had been affected by childhood sexual abuse, and not on Savile. My part in the documentary reached its pinnacle when I faced the cross-examination of the defence barrister. She accused me repeatedly – over three-and-a-half-hours, before a judge, jury and public gallery – of making up allegations, of being an attention-seeker and being motivated by financial gain. I felt like I was on trial. It was profoundly traumatic and had an immense impact on my recovery (Greenwood, 2018: 97–103).

5. Retribution, rehabilitation and forgiveness – no thanks

More than 2.5 million people watching the first broadcast heard my piercing screams outside the courthouse following the verdict, when just five of the 11 charges were returned guilty by the jury. (To avoid the legal implications that sharing my account in this piece would cause, I haven't named my abuser, as the most serious allegations returned 'not guilty' verdicts.) The sentence turned out to be cruelly shorter than the investigation, although the judge delivered the most severe sentence he could: 36 months in prison and release on license after serving 18 months.

Retribution could never right this most dreadful wrong and neither, as I have already mentioned, do I believe that the rehabilitation of my abuser is a realistic option. Not all abuse is the same, and nor are all abusers. Prioritising rehabilitation over punishment is problematic, in the same way that forgiveness over retribution would be, and *vice versa*. A response that might be the most appropriate for some cases might not be for others. Approaching and responding to each case individually and promoting each client's autonomy to make these decisions for themselves avoids the pressure to take one direction over another. This was the approach of my therapist, and it was healing and empowering.

I believe, in many cases, that those who commit violent offences can be understood through the context of their own experiences of childhood trauma and distress (Godsi, 2004: 150). I'm not suggesting the extension of forgiveness here, or that it is inevitable for the abused to abuse – far from it. I am just saying that I have found it helpful to ask what my abuser's lived experience might have been that he carried out such sadistic, depraved acts against me. Through this lens, I have no desire for retribution; I wish no ill or harm upon him. Enough harm has been caused already.

For me, it is about facing the consequences of actions. My abuser is now on the sex offenders register and is denied access to children for life. He had been living with a female partner and her child when I reported him to the police. On learning of the investigation and his previous convictions of sexual assault against two boys of a similar age to her own son, pre-dating the allegations I had made, she left him. I'm sure it felt punishing for him to face those consequences. I have to live with the fact that, if he had been sent to prison for those offences that pre-dated what happened to me, rather than receiving a suspended sentence – presumably in pursuit of rehabilitation – then he wouldn't have been able to do what he did to me. That court's leniency, which incidentally is synonymous with forgiveness, had devastating consequences for me. My drive for conviction was born out of wanting to keep children safe and there is some peace knowing these safeguarding measures are now in place.

References

Godsi E (2004). *Violence and Society: making sense of madness and badness.* Ross-on-Wye: PCCS Books.

Greenwood D (2018). *Responding Badly: church and institutional cover-up of child sex abuse allegations.* David Greenwood.

Lambert O (dir) (2016). *Abused: the untold story.* [Documentary.] BBC One; 12 April. www.ollylambert.com/abused

Levi P (1989). *The Drowned and the Saved.* London: Abacus.

Woodger K (2016). Encouraging disclosure can harm. *Therapy Today* 27(1): 32–33.

Chapter 12

#WeToo: group work as an act of solidarity and resistance

Leah Salter, with Emily Jacob

> ... dominant knowledges which influence women in constructing their personal stories are patriarchal ideology... psychiatric ideology and classification. These are the linguistic and epistemological contexts in which incest has traditionally been located. (Durrant & White, 1990: 22)

I start with this quote to offer a backdrop to why I do the work I do. I work as a systemic psychotherapist and group facilitator, supporting women to come together in a community context, when they might otherwise remain hidden in 'patienthood', in a mental health system that not only largely ignores abuse but potentially maintains it. The system can too easily mirror the silencing practices evident in families and communities, and therefore condones sexual abuse.

This silencing is not just evident in the people working in our health and social care systems who directly abuse patients; it can be seen in those of us working in the systems who do not abuse but who also do not challenge the structures that silence, marginalise and pathologise. Durrant and White (1990) note how we are all influenced by the dominant discourses (Foucault, 1967) that are privileged in society. They draw particular attention to women within the mental health system, who are subjected to patriarchal societal discourses and discourses that medicalise distress (see also Chesler, 1972). They suggest, and I agree, that these contexts can at best silence and at worse legitimise and support abuse.

When relational experiences such as sexual abuse are individualised and pathologised, shame is sustained, and stories of resilience and resistance are quashed. This chapter offers my reflections on why I have developed group work with women who have been sexually abused as an intervention that challenges such pathologising, individualising and dividing practices; why I have found it important to operate within a frame of *solidarity*, and why I believe we can all take action in re-framing shame.

I have constructed the chapter with these contexts in mind, drawing on my personal and professional experiences in the spirit of solidarity. In the same spirit, my conversational partner Emily Jacob and I were in contact throughout the process of shaping and writing this chapter. Our comments on that dialoguing and connecting can be found at the end of the chapter.

Something about #Me

I have been working in economically disadvantaged towns and communities impacted by oppression, abuse and violence for the past 20 years. These communities (mostly mining and industrial) are not dissimilar (though usually smaller) than the community I grew up in – an industrial town in South Wales that was not particularly diverse. Like most of the other residents (and like many of the communities I have worked in), we were a white, working-class family. I hesitate to use this definition, as our socio-economic status fluctuated. My parents' separation when I was a young child was turbulent and emotionally charged, but it was their divorce in my teenage years that signalled change for us as a family, not just structurally and emotionally but financially too. We had some messy years in my teens, but this was usually contained within the family – kept *private*.

However, one of the stories of my childhood entered the *public* domain at about the same time that my family was going through this transition. A male music teacher who had taught me and some of my friends was arrested for sexual abuse of children – boys and girls. The police interviewed all of us who had been taught by him. I had previously been bold enough to tell my mother that I was uncomfortable in these private lessons and, although I was too embarrassed at that stage to tell her the details, she supported me to stop attending, thankfully. This was, perhaps, part of my own story of resistance. Some of my friends were less fortunate. The teacher was prosecuted at the age of 76 and spent some of the last years of his life in prison. I went on being a teenager. But one of my most prolonged experiences of shame is that I did not/could not tell the police all of what he had done. I minimised it, because of shame. My story remained partially private/invisible, and I have often asked myself how helpful that was. I have other stories, some in childhood, some later, that remain entirely private, also because of shame and a fear that I might somehow have been to blame. I am being careful how I word this because I am subject to the same silencing discourses as the women I talk with in therapy. I am, though, more comfortable with sharing my story than I have been in the past. I see this as part of my own move towards resistance that changes over time.

These stories from my life continue to resonate in my practice as a psychotherapist who works with women with their own, in my opinion, more traumatic stories of abuse, oppression and injustice; experiences that have affected their lives and health in multiple ways. I am not trying to minimise my own story here, but I *am* acknowledging that many women I work with have experienced enduring, shaming and traumatic experiences of abuse from a young age that have disrupted their ability to feel safe or make sense of their world in a way that my experience did not. I was not abused by a parent or a significant caregiver; I *was* believed, and the abuse was neither protracted nor enduringly traumatic for me. It is difficult, though, to talk about sexual abuse without entering into the territory of minimisation and/or discomfort, and I want to explore what happened to me here in a way that honours how I have felt about it. There's no requirement for all #MeToo testimonies to have the same character.

Embedded into women's stories, my own included, are stories not only of abuse but also of shame. Minimising, maintaining silence and staying hidden are part of that narrative. Nevertheless, also embedded into these stories are stories of resilience and resistance, but they are often unseen. These are the stories I believe need to be heard. If I, like other women with similar experiences, had been or *are* enabled to tell these stories, I/we would not have been and will *not be* so silenced by shame. This is why I have made my story public – to highlight the resistance and resilience that I, and others, have developed, in spite of the pressure to remain silent.

Hearing resistance

Systemic psychotherapist and activist Allan Wade (1997) inspired my curiosity about everyday acts of resistance in the face of privatising experiences, such as sexual abuse and everyday stories of resisting violence and shame. Wade's work and that of Linda Coates (Coates & Wade, 2007), Cathy Richardson (2012) and Vikki Reynolds (2012, 2013), for example, actively promote socially just and effective responses to violence and other forms of oppression and adversity.

Activist and narrative therapist Vikki Reynolds (2013: 53) uses the phrase 'leaning in' to describe her approach and writes of being an 'imperfect ally' of people(s) who have experienced oppression. Systemic psychotherapist Sheila McNamee (2015: 373) refers to this kind of work as 'radical presence'. These ways of seeing resonate for me as a practitioner who has been influenced by narrative practices throughout my career.

Narrative therapy offers 'double listening' as a way to listen actively for stories of resistance. Michael White (2004; White & Epston, 1990) suggests that therapists need be attuned to listening *to* stories of trauma or distress as well as listening *for* stories about the ways that people overcome and resist trauma, abuse and oppression.

This influence has especially shown itself in my practice of developing group work for women who have been sexually abused, initially when I was working in a British island community and now, having returned to Wales, in communities in South Wales. I am a strong advocate for group work, especially in challenging shame, isolation and silencing practices, and in promoting a focus on resilience, resourcefulness and resistance. As groups tend to be regarded as a more efficient use of limited resources and so more cost-effective than one-to-one therapy, they also tend to get the approval of management and commissioners. This is not my starting point, but it can be a useful one for gaining support to develop interventions that help people come together.

The groups I run are set in the context of statutory mental health provision and so they need to *survive* within that context. I think this means that my colleagues and I work especially hard to offer a service that is not drowned out by diagnoses such as borderline personality disorder (BPD). BPD is a contested and controversial diagnosis that is, in the context of mental health, associated with adverse childhood experiences, most especially that of childhood sexual abuse. Castillo (2000) found that 88% of people diagnosed with BPD had experienced some form of abuse – 80% childhood abuse and 70% early sexual abuse. The NHS Confederation (2008) also notes that 70% of women in mental health services have experienced abuse.

Poet and activist Clare Shaw and person-centred psychotherapist/psychologist Gillian Proctor (2005) argue that the diagnosis of borderline personality disorder is disproportionately given to women and pathologises survivors by failing to locate the experience within its social context, thereby deflecting attention from the origins of the distress. I could not agree more. In addition, Peter Breggin (1993), from the field of critical psychiatry, notes the toxicity of psychiatric diagnoses (including and emphasising the diagnosis of personality disorder) that dehumanise and pathologise human experience and ultimately view women as defective. I connect with this strongly. Although all the women who attend the groups I have facilitated have been involved in (and diagnosed by) secondary mental health services (so, arguably, by definition, pathologising is inevitable), we have refused to let this dominate or define our coming together. We privilege instead the stories that connect us and the relationships we develop. This is a purposeful act of resistance.

Relational perspectives

Sexual abuse and rape are relational and social experiences. Buchwald and colleagues remind us that rape is not an individual experience but a societal and cultural phenomenon (Buchwald, Roth & Fletcher, 1995) that oppresses those directly affected by the act and the wider community, who are part of the society that continues to condone it. They coined the term 'rape culture' to mark it clearly as a societal issue rather than an individual one. This in no way removes the responsibility from the abuser but goes some way to shift the responsibility from those who have been abused. As the quote I started this chapter with suggests, abuse thrives in environments where the structures and systems within/around it minimise, hide and ignore inequality, maintain oppression and condone abuse, overtly or otherwise blaming those who have been subjected to it. Our legal system is one of those systems – perhaps the most obvious one – but our health and social care systems are far from exempt (see, for example, Chesler, 1972; Proctor, 2010, 2014; Shaw & Proctor, 2005; Szasz, 1972; Ussher, 1991; Whitaker, 2002).

Shaw and Proctor (2005), quoting earlier research by Penfold and Walker (1983), highlight how services/therapies respond to individual symptomology rather than deal with systemic failings. Damage and dysfunction are seen to be located 'not within the system that produces [them] but within the individual who experiences [them]' (Penfold & Walker, 1983: 31). That so many people with diagnoses of borderline personality disorder have experienced sexual abuse is a sharp reminder of the limitations of an individualised approach to abuse (Castillo, 2000; NHS Confederation, 2008).

In my view, those of us who work in these systems need to be more active in *naming* abuse and violence *and* doing something about it – finding our own ways to *do* resistance. Creating space for women to be with (and validate) other women is part of that story of resistance, not just against the act of abuse but against the wider society that condones it. This is supported by facilitators (and, in this book, therapists) being transparent about their own experiences and including themselves/ourselves as 'us'.

Solidarity as an act of resistance

This way of thinking always leads me back to solidarity practices in my life and work.

Naming my personal experiences (my own #MeToo moment) has been an active choice of solidarity. It loops me back to activists like Vikki Reynolds and Allan Wade and connects me with Sheila McNamee's (2015: 373) advocacy for a 'radical presence', mentioned previously. In any therapeutic encounter, I am not just talking about abuse, I am positioning myself as 'anti-abuse'. This is purposeful, as is my decision to share my experiences with the academic community, and is based on my belief that women speaking out (at local and global levels) has a de-silencing, de-subjugating effect and moves the conversation (and subsequently the discourse) on from defining women who have experienced abuse in singular terms as 'disordered' or as 'victims' – as Shaw and Proctor's (2005) work suggests. The language of victimhood limits stories of collective resistance. I am not talking about victims in a legal sense, where, in my view, the word has credence, is contextual and makes sense. I am talking about how, at a societal level, we continue to victimise those who experience abuse by focusing on and 'problematising' their experience of abuse as an individual phenomenon, using either psychiatric diagnoses or behavioural labels. We focus on the *individual* impact of trauma and abuse and minimise (or contain) the wider *social* impact. In so doing, we also miss or 'invisibilise' stories of resistance by pathologising that resistance as (more historically) hysteria, madness or (in more contemporary terminology) dysfunction or disorder.

The language of victimhood, and especially 'patienthood', promotes this medicalisation of trauma, which, from this standpoint, could be seen as a defence that serves to divide 'us' from 'them'. It evokes difference rather than sameness, and makes people 'other', 'not like me'. Foucault (1967) might say we are seeking to protect ourselves from our 'feared parts' by labelling those who have experienced abuse as different/damaged. This is the same tactic that the media often use, demonising human behaviours in order to distance 'us' from 'them', whether with reference to the offender *or* the victim.

The #MeToo campaign has helped to break this down and to highlight (in my view) a wider narrative, beyond one of victimhood. It has brought into the light the often invisible stories of the one in four of us who have experienced some form of sexual abuse or assault and the one in two of us (Kelly, Regan & Burton, 1991, quoted in Shaw & Proctor, 2005) who will have experienced some form of unwanted sexual contact before the age of 18. In so doing, it has the opposite effect of marginalising people as victims, as broken and damaged 'others.' Abuse of women does not happen because *women* are flawed. Abuse happens and is kept silent because our *society*, based on outdated, adversarial and hierarchical power structures, is flawed. Since the #MeToo campaign, this is becoming more visible. It might evoke fear in some, but it is a necessary 'truth' to reveal. In addition, because of #MeToo, we are now also talking about the previously hidden women who do not feature in the statistics around sexual abuse – the countless women who have experienced some form of sexual harassment, or been subjected to misogynist comments – insidious, subtle forms of abuse that maintain an oppressive, patriarchal culture within which abuse can flourish.

In this book, therapists and counsellors are taking the step to speak out about *our* experiences. As we do so, we challenge the discourse of individualised pathology, of victimhood and the 'them and us' story of the 'healthy' therapist and the 'unhealthy' patient. We bring into focus instead a wider social narrative based on solidarity, from which new stories can emerge – stories that speak to collective resistance and challenge the idea that having experiences such as sexual abuse might preclude women from becoming therapists.

Storytelling as resistance

Stories are important. They help us make sense of our individual and collective experiences and our cultural contexts and legacies. Developing new stories is a 'future-forming' (Gergen, 2015: 287) activity that helps us go on and move forward. From this standpoint, this book is not *just* a collection of connected writing, it is an action. It is part of a movement that includes us all, in unique and interconnected ways, in a collective story of resistance.

In earlier writing (Salter, 2015, 2017a, 2017b), I explored the language of victimhood, sisterhood, survival and 'going on' (Wittgenstein, 1953). This deconstruction of language has been an important part of the group work I have been part of and can support the co-construction of new, potentially empowering narratives. In these groups, I do hear, of course, harrowing stories of abuse, but I also hear stories of connectivity, of competence and how women have resisted abuse and resisted the stories within families and communities that aim to lay the responsibility for that abuse on them. Double listening – listening for resistance as well as stories of trauma – and deconstructing stories of blame are how we uncover these accounts of resistance and solidarity. As Paula Boston (2005: 272) says, the 'practice of deconstruction has been imported into narrative therapy, as a means of offering alternatives to problem-saturated self-narratives and unhelpful dominant cultural discourses'. For me this has been a helpful import. It allows what might otherwise be seen as social 'norms' to be unpacked and challenged. For example, in our groups, gender stereotypes have been deconstructed and questioned, as have definitions of mental ill health.

The role of the facilitator

Family therapist Janine Roberts (2005) defines the relationship between therapist and client as an 'intimate' one; not a personal relationship per se, but one with 'many personal aspects' (Roberts, 2005: 61). This is my experience in a psychotherapy relationship and in therapy groups, where many aspects of intimacy can be played out. I think this has additional resonance in a group context. As a group practitioner, we might expect 'participants' to open up, to respond to others and to contribute by drawing on their own experiences, whether we make this explicit or not. But what do we expect of ourselves, and what do others expect of us? Kris Drumm (2006: 20) also raises the question of expectations, suggesting that 'practitioners are required to be able to be vulnerable and flexible and able to take and give up control in ways that benefit both the group and its individuals'. The expectation, then, is high, but does not include personal sharing on the part of the facilitator. I find this interesting. Group work participants are often matched with the group facilitator in terms of visible commonality such as gender and age, but this does not usually extend to other commonalities or life experience, such as experience of abuse.

Family therapist Elsa Jones (1991: xv) offers some reflections on this, highlighting both the pitfalls and potential benefits of female therapists working with what she has chosen to call 'survivors' of sexual abuse. One of the pitfalls she notes is the potential for 'ghettoisation' when therapist and client are matched by gender. This, she says, can lead to women with experiences of abuse being assigned to female therapists only, which can (in turn) lead to female therapists being overwhelmed by caseloads with a high proportion of clients bringing experiences of abuse. Jones (1991: 13) warns of the danger of 'burnout' in such situations. I would add (based on my own experience) that this can especially be the case for female therapists who have shared experiences of abuse. However, I can also see many benefits, the potential for women to experience a sense of connection and solidarity being one of them. I have experienced feelings both of paralysis and liberation in therapeutic encounters. There have been times when I feel my personal experiences – not just in relation to abuse – have held me back or frozen me and times when I have felt my experiences have enabled me to forge connections and co-construct meaning in ways that support transformation and speak to solidarity and to social justice.

Both Elsa Jones (1991) and Janine Roberts (2005) raise a concern about the potential negative impact a disclosure might have on the 'client' and I do not disagree with this either. However, I believe this too can be carefully managed by the reflexive therapist. It is part of the complexity of working in this field, which is why we make use of opportunities to reflect on our practices and our own experiences.

Resisting pathology

Challenging pathologising language in the context of mental health is not new (see, for example, Szasz, 1963; White & Epston, 1990; McNamee & Gergen, 1992). In particular, the critical psychiatry and post-psychiatry movements have been instrumental in challenging subjugating discourses in mental health (Whitaker, 2002; Timimi, 2010). It is important to unpack the language of victimhood and the associated language of 'patienthood,' both of which can perpetuate limiting, oppressive and unhelpful discourses. If we do not challenge pathologising language, we continue to limit the stories we can tell.

As a further act of resistance, when evaluating outcomes in therapy and group work, we need to widen the story of impact to include more focus on relationships rather than solely looking at symptom reduction. Feedback in the evaluation of the groups we have run so far suggests that women *do* indeed experience increased wellbeing through the intervention and a decrease in what might be viewed as negative symptoms, but they also consistently report that simply being in the group, with other women with similar experiences, is extremely helpful and important for them and helps them develop new stories of personhood, beyond 'patienthood'. The argument here is that coming together – the facilitator included – supports a sense of solidarity that breaks down 'them and us' boundaries that serve to divide. These stories rarely get heard because they do not fit neatly within a medical discourse, but we need to make room for them.

Creating space where all sorts of stories can be heard, shaped, deconstructed and re-constructed is important. Michael Durrant and Cheryl White (1990) highlight how dominant stories can prevent people from accessing stories of resourcefulness. They tell a story of Alice, who was sexually abused by her grandfather, physically abused by her parents, and subsequently influenced by family stories that she was 'emotionally disturbed'. This became the dominant narrative that she carried around with her. They offer this as a (local) example of practice that speaks to the (global) challenge of narratives that sustain power that maintain and 'invisibilise' abuse and the resistance to it. It is a familiar story. Working with women who have experienced abuse has taught me that these individualised, medicalised discourses continue to be dominant and can, at best, minimise abuse, and at worst, condone it. Coming together helps to construct new discourses that can re-shape the systems in which we work and re-frame stories of shame.

Elsa Jones (1991) explores how and why a victim-blaming, individualising discourse has developed to reframe childhood sexual abuse as an internalised experience, rather than a social phenomenon. She notes that this discourse has been transformed by the survivor movement, which, she says (as does Virginia Goldner in the foreword to the same book), has shifted the focus from individual therapy towards a social action frame. Virginia Goldner states succinctly that 'activism transforms victims into survivors' (pxii). This, to me, speaks of that same sense of solidarity to which I am referring. In my experience, though, very little is written about therapists being part of that movement as 'survivors' themselves. This is why *this* book is important: to disrupt what might otherwise be seen as a divide between survivor and supporter.

Without a frame of solidarity, women's stories of sexual abuse get individually rather than culturally problematised and can become fixed narratives that define us, get stuck to us and follow us life-long. When this happens, the story of why and how abuse happens slips into the shadows, along with the perpetrator, as the story of Alice demonstrates. Anne, one of the members of the group who participated in my research inquiry, told me why telling her story was important:

> I feel this kind of outrage when we realise that this is not our
> responsibility, this is someone else's responsibility and we have a right to feel angry and pissed off about what's happened to us, and angry about injustice, and angry about how some stuff *hasn't* happened, even though we've been telling people… Every time I was raped, everything I felt as a woman disappeared and all I was left with was fear and pain.

For Anne, her experience of mental health professionals compounded that sense of loss of womanhood and competence. She called them *'head doctors'*, but told me that she experienced me and my colleague as *'stepping out'* from that model. *'Cos you don't just see us as patients; you see us as people.'* It saddens me that Anne experienced it as exceptional that she should be regarded as a person, not a patient.

It is a constant challenge for me to work and live within a culture that sees the legacy of an experience such as sexual abuse as an illness and sees people as patients and, ultimately, as *problems*. As Michael White (1988/89) argues, there is a continued need to separate out the person from the problem. They are not one and the same.

Given that most statistics agree that one in five, maybe as many as one in four, women will have experienced sexual abuse, we are talking about vast numbers in the population who can too easily be seen as problems that require individual 'treatment' – treatment that may be used to silence or reframe as 'illness' expressions of distress. Within those treated by the mental health services, this 20% statistic rises to 70% – 70% of women that I/we work with in the mental health services will have experienced sexual abuse or assault (NHS Confederation, 2008). This is vast.

Allowing space for *new* stories to be told, heard, shaped, and shared then becomes a *political* act in the face of such numbers. As Kim Etherington (2004: 9) says: 'New selves form within us as we tell and re-tell our stories.' Group contexts, if supported appropriately and based on collaboration, invite that possibility and provoke transformation, beyond an individual or unilateral level.

De-individualising abuse

In my experience the impact of abuse is usually talked about, in both research and in the media, as a response to the (unilateral) *act* of sexual violence. However, often when people reflect on their experience, they are not focused solely on the sexual *act* but on the betrayal they experienced, the confusion they felt that someone they trusted/loved broke their trust, the anguish they experienced at not being believed, the *rage* when justice is not done and the pain they feel as women who have been ignored, forgotten and written out of history. This is a relational story and a cultural one, *not* an individual one. The problem does not exist *within* the women who tell it. It is a cultural and political story that impacts on us all, whether we see ourselves as having directly experienced abuse or not. As we reframe the myth that the responsibility for the abuse lies with the person who was abused, then we can also reframe, interrupt and potentially *redirect* the legacy of shame and that burden of responsibility.

When working with women in groups, my co-facilitator and I ensure we are clear that perpetrators of abuse are 100% responsible for the *act* of abuse. We do this using a pie chart diagram to visually represent how the responsibility shifts away from the 'victim'. We also explore the social backdrop of abuse so that we keep a connection between local and global discourses. One of the roles of the facilitator, as I see it, is to challenge limiting discourses, open up the space for new ones to emerge and encourage cohesion by making connections (and opportunities for solidarity) explicit.

For example, in the first week of the group we use a ball of string to physically represent connections between participants. This introduces a secondary component of physical movement. There is movement towards others as the string moves around – an almost-touching of hands, a physical sign of connection. The proximity also shifts. People move closer to reach out, to extend the amount of connections that can be made before the string runs out. We repeat this exercise at the end of the group as a way to mark the connections that were forged through being together. The proximity shifts again in the context of ending, and in one group resulted in participants holding hands, and in another a group hug. This speaks not only to movement, voice and visibility but also (I believe) to a reclamation of intimacy and a distancing from shame.

#WeToo

In this chapter I have presented a summary not so much of what I do as a psychotherapist and group facilitator but of why I do it. I have made explicit connections with my own stories of abuse, of shame and ultimately of resistance, ways that I have 'gone on', and how that might connect with other women's stories – women I consider myself to be in solidarity with; women like Anne; women whose stories too easily get hidden by stories of pathology and victimhood in contexts such as mental health services.

In this context, I have advocated for group work practices that position themselves, not as didactic, expert-led, skills groups, but as forums for coming together, for solidarity. I have also advocated for narrative practices that support the co-construction of new stories that can contribute to wider narratives that, in turn, can contribute to new cultural discourses. My hope is that this can go some way to evoke change that resists shame-inducing and shame-maintaining practices and promotes dignity and humanity.

I began this chapter by naming the shame I have felt that I did not tell what I feel I should have told. This, I recognise, is an old story – one that resides in the past. Viewed within a frame of resistance, I can see this differently. Instead of thinking about what I did *not* do, I see what I *did*, keeping myself safe through childhood and adolescence, successfully making it into adulthood and educating myself in order to work with/*be* with other women so that I can hear and respond to *their* stories of resistance. Shame covers up these stories and hides this competence. Solidarity brings competence to the fore and liberates us from the isolation of shame.

Anne described to me the significance of the group in helping her loosen the grip of shame and keep herself safe. She told me:

> The unique part was that I stopped seeing myself as an individual and started thinking wider… I set out to kill myself and sat out until daylight, but I was able to snap out of it… I have more strength to do that now… The group helped me to not fall in the hole… Before I couldn't think, but now I can… it's given me a lease of life, 'cos there are others who need help.

This is a story of resistance. Being with women in this group has also helped *me* to rethink my relationship to shame; by recalling and reframing my own stories of resistance.

Reflections on our collaboration

In the spirit of #WeToo, we would like to acknowledge that, although Leah wrote this chapter, she wrote it in collaboration and solidarity with Emily and this dialogue shaped the chapter. We each reflect on the process below.

Emily: In collaborating with Leah on this chapter, I was initially sceptical as to what might be gained and how I could contribute. After all, it was her chapter, her experience, her perspective, and who was I to comment or criticise? And yet, I have found the experience – our discussions, debates and dialogues – immensely rewarding: I think the chapter itself is stronger for our collaboration, and I feel that my work will be changed for the better from our collaboration.

I am a coach and neuro-linguistic programming master practitioner and I use my experience of recovery to guide others to their recovery, with an understanding that recovery means different things to us all. My #MeToo story is what attracts my clients to me, knowing that I understand beyond empathy. A solidarity and rapport is thus pre-created and there is an implicit trust that I can guide the client along the path that I have already walked.

Coaching in the recovery journey is not new; coaches have often helped trauma survivors become 'more than'. And yet it feels pioneering to be doing it so explicitly. Trauma coaching fills the gap that often exists after the counselling part of the journey, where the client can still feel uncertain of their place in the world: no longer broken, yet still fragile. Coaching empowers the client to craft the life that enables them to not merely bounce back from the trauma but bounce forward and embrace a new life that can be more than it was before.

I also manage a Facebook community for survivors of sexual trauma, called ReConnected Life Community.[1] The solidarity and sisterhood that I've observed from those who, despite their own pain, find the space to support others who are also hurt is more than heart-warming. Many have commented that membership

---

1. https://reconnected.life/community/

of the community has been a lifeline, and in some cases life-saving. #MeToo has become #WeToo, and it has changed and shifted, subtly sometimes, more obviously at other times, the shape of the individual experience. This was most obvious in the way the community members came together to create the ReConnected Life Community book, *To Report or Not to Report: survivor testimony of the (in)justice system* (Jacob, 2018), which is a profound example of the #WeToo solidarity that arises from sharing stories and experiences.

Until I spoke with Leah as we developed this chapter, I hadn't explicitly considered what was happening in the Facebook community, and now I see the power of #WeToo in all its beautiful action. For some, the solidarity of #WeToo is creating a bounce forward all by itself. #MeToo gave a rallying cry to many who had felt stifled and silenced by stigma; then, through our coming together in #WeToo, projects have emerged that create splits in the system that perpetuates rape culture. Thus, the individual's #MeToo story is changed as well. We are part of something bigger than our own experience and our perception of our experiences changes as a result.

Having worked with Leah, my focus is going to be more on how I can leverage the power of #WeToo to help empower the individual's #MeToo story. I'm considering story circles, where sisterhood and solidarity can be created by listening, acknowledging and validating. It's an embryo of an idea for now, but whatever happens, I know my work will be richer and even more profound for my clients in supporting them to craft their ReConnected Life and bounce forward.

Leah: When Emily and I first connected over this chapter, I was sitting with the same scepticism that Emily talks about. Even as a systemic psychotherapist who places significant weight on the importance of collaboration, I was unsure how all of this would hang together. When we talked, though, we began to notice the many themes that connected our practice, one of which was the very notion of connectivity and of solidarity. I see the relevance of this all the time in the group work that I facilitate – women connecting with women and feeling a sense of togetherness that positively impacts on their sense of self and the stories they tell themselves and others about their experiences and their lives. I also noticed how this sense of connection with Emily was having an impact on what I wrote and how I wrote it. I was being moved by the conversations I was part of, as I am in my practice. I was also beginning to feel less isolated in my thinking, writing and talking. Emily encouraged me to be bolder, which caused some tension but helped me to speak out in a less tentative way. I was part of a relational process, experiencing that sense of '#MeToo', (or what I am calling '#WeToo'), which lent me additional strength to write what I felt I needed to write.

This concept of #WeToo has been central to the development of the group work I have been part of. Being stronger (louder) together is a big part of that. This is why voices coming together makes sense in this book too, and why (together) we can un-privilege the stories that divide and shame us and promote the ones that connect us to each other and *re*-connect us to our own immense resourcefulness. In solidarity.

References

Boston P (2005). Doing deconstruction. *Journal of Family Therapy 27*(3): 272–275.

Breggin P (1993). *Toxic Psychiatry. Drugs and electroconvulsive therapy: the truth and the better alternatives*. London: HarperCollins.

Buchwald E, Roth M, Fletcher P (eds) (1995). *Transforming a Rape Culture* (revised ed). Minneapolis, MN: Milkweed Editions.

Castillo H (2000). You don't know what it's like. *Mental Health Care 4*(2): 42–23 and 53–58.

Chesler P (1972). *Women and Madness*. New York, NY: Doubleday.

Coates L, Wade A (2007). Langauge and violence: analysis of four discursive operations. *Journal of Family Violence 22*(7): 511–522.

Drumm K (2006). The essential power of group work. *Social Work with Groups 29*(2–3): 17–31.

Durrant M, White C (1990). *Ideas for Therapy with Sexual Abuse*. Adelaide: Dulwich Centre Publications.

Etherington K (2004). *Becoming a Reflexive Researcher: using our selves in research*. London: Jessica Kingsley.

Foucault M (1967). *Madness and Civilisation: a history of insanity in the age of reason*. London: Tavistock.

Gergen K (2015). From mirroring to world-making: research as future forming. *Journal for the Theory of Social Behaviour 45*(3): 287–310.

Goldner V (1991). Foreword. In: Jones E. *Working with Adult Survivors of Sexual Abuse*. London: Karnac.

Jacob E (2018). *To Report or not to Report: survivor testimony of the (in)justice system*. Resonance Press.

Jones E (1991). *Working with Adult Survivors of Childhood Sexual Abuse*. London: Karnac.

Kelly L, Regan L, Burton S (1991). *An Exploratory Study of the Prevalence of Sexual Abuse in a Sample of 1244 16–21-Year-Olds*. London: Child Abuse Studies Unit.

McNamee S (2015). Radical presence: alternatives to the therapeutic state. *European Journal of Psychotherapy & Counselling 17*(4): 373–383.

McNamee S, Gergen K (1992). *Therapy as Social Construction*. London: Sage.

NHS Confederation (2008). *Implementing National Policy on Violence and Abuse*. London: NHS Confederation.

Penfold P, Walker G (1983). *Women and the Psychiatric Paradox*. Montreal: Eden Press.

Proctor G (2014). *Values and Ethics in Counselling and Psychotherapy*. London: Sage.

Proctor G (2010). Working with women. In: Lago C, Smith B (eds). *Anti-Discriminatory Practice in Counselling & Psychotherapy*. London: Sage (pp53–62).

Reynolds V (2013). Leaning in as imperfect allies in community work: narrative and conflict. *Explorations in Theory and Practice 1*(1): 53–75.

Reynolds V, Polanco M (2012). An ethical stance for justice-doing in community work and therapy. *Journal of Systemic Therapies 31*(4): 18–33.

Richardson C, Reynolds V (2012). Here we are, amazingly alive in the work: holding ourselves together with an ethic of social justice in community work. *International Journal of Child, Youth and Family Studies 3*(1): 1–19.

Roberts J (2005). Transparency and self-disclosure in family therapy: dangers and possibilities. *Family Process 44*(1): 45–63.

Salter L (2017a). Research as resistance and solidarity: spinning transformative yarns – a narrative inquiry with women going on from abuse and oppression. *Journal of Family Therapy 39*(3): 285–494.

Salter L (2017b). From victimhood to sisterhood part II: exploring the possibilities of transformation and solidarity in qualitative research. *European Journal of Psychotherapy and Counselling 19*(1): 73–86.

Salter L (2015). From victimhood to sisterhood: a practice-based reflexive inquiry into narrative informed group work with women who have experienced sexual abuse. *European Journal of Psychotherapy & Counselling 17*(2): 402–417.

Shaw C, Proctor G (2005). Women on the margins: a critique of the diagnosis of Borderline Personality Disorder. *Feminism & Psychology 15*(4): 483–490.

Szasz T (1972). *The Myth of Mental Illness*. London: Paladin.

Szasz T (1963). *Law, Liberty and Psychiatry: an inquiry into the social uses of mental health practices*. New York, NY: Macmillan.

Timimi S (2010). The McDonaldization of childhood: children's mental health in neo-liberal market cultures. *Transcultural Psychiatry 47*(5): 686–706.

Ussher J (1991). *Women's Madness: misogyny or mental illness?* Hemel Hempstead: Harvester Wheatsheaf.

Wade A (1997). Small acts of living: everyday resistance to violence and other forms of oppression. *Journal of Contemporary Family Therapy 19*(1): 23–40.

Whitaker R (2002). *Mad in America: bad science, bad medicine, and the enduring mistreatment of the mentally ill*. New York, NY: Perseus Publications. White M (1988/89). The externalizing of the problem and the re-authoring of lives and relationships. *Dulwich Centre Newsletter* (Summer issue). Adelaide: Dulwich Centre.

White M (2004). *Narrative Practice and Exotic Lives: resurrecting diversity in everyday life*. Adelaide: Dulwich Centre Publications.

White M (2000). *Reflections on Narrative Practice*. Adelaide: Dulwich Centre Publications.

White M, Epston D (1990). *Narrative Means to Therapeutic Ends*. New York, NY: WW Norton & Co.

Wittgenstein L (1953). *Philosophical Investigations*. Oxford: Blackwell.

Chapter 13

Pushing, pulling and parts coming together

Joy Farrimond, with Emma Palmer

Introduction

First, I'd like to give some context to my writing this chapter. I was originally paired to be the 'conversation partner' with another author, who decided not to continue to the publishing stage. I felt a mixture of disappointment and relief. Part of me wanted what we planned to say to be heard; another part was happy to step back and let it go. I felt a sense of loss at not having completed the task, alongside a feeling that it didn't matter – 'Put it behind you and move on.' The sharing and writing had in itself been a very valuable experience in my healing journey, and that could have been enough in itself. For me there has always been a process of engaging with what happened to me, and then a pulling away again. So I felt this familiar push and pull in different directions.

The editors then invited me to write the chapter, to continue to share my experiences, and to engage in a conversation with Emma Palmer, one of the book's editors and a friend of mine. I needed to think deeply about whether I really wanted to do that. Part of me felt an allegiance to the person I had originally been paired with – a part that said, if we were not going to publish what we had written together, then that was the end of my involvement in the process too. Another part of me pushed strongly against that. I looked back at why I wanted to be involved in the writing in the first instance. What was the pull towards a book about sexual violence, when it would undoubtedly lead to some degree of discomfort, possibly even considerable inner pain? But then why does anyone want to write anything on this topic? I believe that it is because I/we have something we need to say – either privately or publicly. I realised that sharing my experiences was serving an important function in relation to the silencing that had happened in my childhood. The part of me that had been silenced wanted to be heard, and I also hoped that sharing my experience of survival and growth might help someone else in some small way.

To begin with, I was not sure I wanted to write under my own name. There was a feeling of safety in staying anonymous. I decided to write and leave the decision about anonymity until later. Right up to the point of submitting the chapter, I still felt unsure about putting my name to it. I think that this was the last remnant for me of a lifelong pattern of keeping silent. It feels good to have broken that.

* * *

I was young when my great-uncle used me for his sexual gratification. I cannot say exactly when it started, although I remember clearly the day it stopped, the day I ran away, the day my dad saw my distress. I was eight or nine years old. I was with my uncle in his shed on the allotment. He was trying to kiss me, and I could not breathe. He was holding me tight and it was hurting me. I was afraid, and I don't remember having been afraid of him before then. I don't know how I got free, but I did, and I bolted out of the door. I remember my dad digging further up the allotment and he stopped and turned towards me – my dad in his black donkey jacket and cap, with a look of surprise on his face. I remember thinking 'He knows what I've been doing!' I turned and ran, but I have no clear memories of where I ran to or what happened next. Sometimes, during times when I have felt emotionally overwhelmed, images have come into my mind of hiding in bushes and keeping very, very still. I do not know for certain if this is what I did. When these images have arisen, I have felt afraid and have tried to get very small and hide. Sometime later I overheard a conversation between my dad and my great-uncle Jack's wife. She said I was not to be left alone with him again.

All other memories are scattered across a period of time, and I cannot say this happened and then that. Apart from that final day, memories are mixed up together and in snippets. This is something I found distressing when I first started to talk about it, because I thought I should be able to remember more and kept trying to put memories into a linear timescale, but I couldn't. It made me doubt myself and I accused myself of making it all up and thought that it was a symptom of mental illness. It all felt so unreal; it couldn't have happened. Yet I had always known that 'things' happened in Uncle Jack's shed.

I did not see what happened as abuse for a long time. Uncle Jack was like the grandfather I did not have. He seemed to care about me and was kind. He kept racing pigeons, canaries and lovebirds. He showed me the chicks and I helped him put the rings on their legs when they were old enough. I could cuddle the rabbits he kept in a hutch at the allotment. I loved that, because we did not have pets at home. He gave me an appreciation of nature and gardening, which I have never lost.

But there were the other games we had to play that had a bad feeling around them, although there was an element of pleasure, too. It has been a long journey for me to accept that the person who showed me so much care also abused me. I can see how confusing this must have been. Uncle Jack was a kind person, but he did things that didn't feel right. I now have a greater understanding of how we stereotype people as 'good' or 'bad' as a shortcut to deciding who is safe and who isn't. The reality is that 'nice' people can do bad things and 'bad' people can do good things. Nothing is simply black and white.

I have no memory of my parents talking to me about what had been happening. I do not know if my dad ever said anything to my mum, but I know it affected him deeply, as he developed stress-related alopecia around that time. In my family, unpleasant things of all sorts were 'brushed under the carpet'. I think this was more common in the 1950s and 1960s and I believe my parents would have thought I would just forget it happened – not talking about it would have been seen as the best thing to do. The event must have been distressing for my parents, but not being able to talk about it and helped to understand that it was not my fault was very unhelpful and led to a deep sense of shame. I feel I was silenced as a child and developed a strong belief that what had happened was nothing to make a fuss about – no big deal. I took this same attitude towards other traumatic events in my life, always telling myself to stop making such a fuss about nothing. I felt so ashamed of being me – I felt like I had this bad core inside, and if people really knew what I was like, it would shock them.

I broke the silence of 40 years during an occupational health counselling session. I sought help because I was struggling to cope with work and my psychology degree course. A project on attachment theory was causing me a lot of distress and my mind was going round in circles. I felt I was going crazy as I tried to work out aspects of my childhood in relation to what I was studying.

After saying 'I was sexually abused,' I immediately wanted to take the words back. I felt dirty and even more distressed. So many things triggered attacks of anxiety, when I would want to curl up small and hide in corners and up against walls in order to feel safe. The mental pain was a stabbing at my core and at times I could not bear it. It felt like I had shattered into a thousand pieces. On the outside, I seemed able to function, but my inner world was full of pain and confusion. It was only through self-harming and drinking alcohol that I was able to keep a sense of control.

I sought further therapy when sessions with the occupational health therapist ended fairly abruptly. For nine years, I worked with a very skilled counsellor, who helped me to process the conditions of my childhood. She helped me to take steps towards seeing that what had happened was not my fault. I could see that the abuse by my uncle was the coming together of a host of conditions, rather than a one-off event. There was the man who acted out of his pain; the difficult family backgrounds of both my parents; the social conditions of the age; the mental difficulties of my mum, which made it difficult for her to show her love, and me, a child desperate for love and approval.

The journey was slow and painful. I believe now that we worked very much on the edge between re-traumatisation and healing. My therapist shared almost no personal information with me in the years we worked together, which I think was in my best interests. It might have felt invasive to me if she had shared her experience; the boundaries of our relationship could have been breached. I have great respect for how my therapist held us both in the 50-minute sessions.

Particularly difficult was coming to terms with the fact that my body was aroused and felt pleasure during some of the sexual activity. I found this horrifying and I hated my body for that. I could not understand how that could happen. If what had happened to me was abuse, then surely it would not have given me pleasure? In my mind, the fact that I felt pleasure meant I was a willing partner in what was happening. I can also remember feeling a sense of power in it all. I was pleasing him and making him happy. It was both a surprise and very helpful to find out that a child can feel pleasant feelings while being abused, because it frequently takes place without overt violence (Parks, 1990). The genitals are designed to be responsive to gentle touch, so it simply meant my body was working normally.

During the first years of talking about what happened to me as a child, I very much identified with being a victim of childhood abuse. This identity filled my life and built up a sense of myself that was painful. I very much identified with a medical model of healing and I tried to fit the distressing symptoms I was experiencing in my body and mind into a diagnostic 'box'. I felt that, if I could put a name to what was happening, then I would be able to make some sense of it all and it could be fixed by medicine or therapy. My dependence on a medical model was reinforced by the fact that I had worked in the medical profession from the age of 18.

In 2005, I went to a drop-in meditation class at the Bristol Buddhist centre and came into contact with the teachings of the Buddha. Gradually, I moved away from a medical model of thinking into one that was more accepting of the way things are: there is nothing to be 'fixed'. Suffering is an inevitable part of being human and how we react is the key. I believe that it is the moving towards painful experience that opens the way to healing. Learning a meditation called the 'mindfulness of breathing' allowed me to start connecting more fully with both pleasant and unpleasant body sensations. At the same time, it gave me a tool to calm my body and mind when I faced difficulties. This led me to see that I had a choice in how I reacted to physical sensations and their associated emotions. I learned the 'metta bhavana' meditation, which is a practice of developing loving kindness and compassion towards both ourselves and others. I really struggled to find loving feelings towards myself and tended to focus on the breath in my practice. I continued to struggle with low mood but was not as anxious as I had been.

Following another period of depression in 2015, I was offered 12 weeks of cognitive behavioural therapy (CBT) through the NHS talking therapy service. By good fortune the therapist I was allocated had some experience of compassion-focused therapy (Gilbert, 2010). This therapy has its roots in evolutionary psychology, attachment theory, and neuroscience. Paul Gilbert also drew a lot on the Buddhist teachings about cultivating compassion towards suffering. My therapist explained to me about the three types of affect regulation system: threat, incentive and resource seeking, and soothing and contentment (Gilbert, 2010). I was able to understand more clearly why I had difficulty feeling love towards myself. A part of me still felt I was to blame for what happened with my uncle, although a part of me knew that this belief was illogical.

I could see that the threat and self-protection system was very dominant and the self-critical voice was still strong, although not so loud. On the other hand, the soothing and contentment system was underactive within me. It was still difficult for me to find positive and pleasurable experiences and to self-soothe. However, I also started to understand that the threat system was simply protecting me – it was how I had survived, and therefore not to be demonised, as I had been doing. Compassion-focused therapy is where science meets Buddhism, for me, and in the last three years I have achieved a greater integration of my cognitive thinking and my emotions.

My practice now is to be with what arises in my body and mind without over-identifying with it and offer kindness and acceptance to the part of me that is suffering. I actively look for pleasurable feelings both in and outside of meditation and have come a long way in learning to spot old, unhelpful patterns of thinking and behaviour. Developing love for myself has allowed my whole being to open up more and I feel a greater connection to the world.

I appreciate this opportunity I have been given to allow the silenced part of me a voice. Being a conversation partner and sharing another's process in healing was a privilege and I feel sad that the original shared writing will not be read by a wider audience. Through that shared process, I have been able to integrate even more of the fragmented bits of childhood experience. The fact that I have been able to hear and engage with both our experiences shows how much healing has taken place.

Conversation with Emma Palmer

Emma: I was struck by you referring early on in your chapter to the 'familiar push and pull in different directions'. I remember vividly when I first told you that I was co-editing the book – we were meeting up for a cuppa – and your spontaneous question 'Can I write?' felt like a strong pull! Can you say more about that?

Joy: I remember that clearly, too. We were sitting in the cafe at the garden centre. I immediately felt I wanted to be involved in writing something in relation to the book you were talking about. I can't say why that strong pull came at that particular time. Maybe I saw an opportunity to write and grasped it. When you replied that the chapter contributors to the book were therapists who had experienced sexual violence and abuse, I felt a slight disappointment because I am not a therapist. I then put it out of my mind. When you later invited me to be a conversation person, the enormity of how that might affect me hit home. I spent some time reflecting on whether I was emotionally robust enough to engage with what the chapter author might write. At this point, I did not expect to be writing about my own experience in great detail, although I knew it would very much flavour how I engaged in the conversation with the author. It took about a week for me to make the decision and, throughout that time, I remember a very strong pull to contribute in this way. I knew it could be a painful process for me, but I had faith that it could also have positive outcomes both for me and others.

Emma: If it's OK to ask, what has been most painful and most positive in this process so far?

Joy: Most painful has been the effort it has taken to bring in the parts of me that were ambivalent about writing. The swing between wanting to engage and then not. A part of me was pulled towards sharing and writing but other parts wanted to push away. At times I had feelings of wanting to run away because it felt too painful and difficult. Even as I write this, I can feel the visceral pain of it deep inside: a gnawing, burrowing, pit-of-the-stomach sensation. My jaw is so tense it feels like it could shatter. I have noticed the draw to want to numb this pain through alcohol, which has been a coping mechanism for most of my life. Controlling the urge to do this has been very challenging.

The most positive outcome so far has been finding a voice. Through the process of writing, I have heard a part of me that has been kept silent through fear and shame. I have been able to face the fear that what I have to say is unacceptable and speak out. I am also seeing that it is OK to be 'me' with my needs and longings. I have realised that I have kept silent about many things in my life through fear of hurting others. Coming face to face with this silenced part of me has been very empowering and I am finding courage to make changes in my life that I have needed to make for a long time. I feel more comfortable in my own skin.

However, as I am responding to your questions, I am noticing what feels like a drive to get what I say 'right'. It feels like I am trying too hard with this!

Emma: Oh, do you know what that's about?

Joy: Like there's a right or wrong way to respond. It feels like I have to get the words right and sometimes the words are a struggle. Words have always been a struggle for me, especially if I have to say something about how I feel. I don't rightly know how I feel at times, at least not in words. I can explain in images or colour, but not words. I have to find the 'right' words from somewhere so that I can explain what's going on inside. It feels like such a battle, and when I can't find them, I feel less than adequate and start apologising for my stupidity.

As I am writing this, I feel agitated inside, like there's a bag of spiky nails in the bottom of my stomach. A memory has popped up of me as a little girl – eight or nine years old. Standing in our kitchen, up against the kitchen door. I am crying. I don't want to go to school but I can't say why. Very distressed… I have tummy ache; I'm saying, 'Please don't make me go.' My mum seems distressed too, but in an angry way. She says the problem is my long hair. It is sapping my strength. My hair gets cut short. I don't understand!

I censor what I say. It isn't safe to speak. I have to keep what I think and feel pushed right down inside so it won't cause any harm.

Emma: Such powerful images and memories, Joy… I can feel how finding your voice, what you think and feel being brought up rather than 'pushed right down', is transformative and incredibly challenging – and I feel honoured to be alongside you witnessing this.

Joy: Thank you for acknowledging this. I am finding it incredibly challenging and have at times felt it was too much and that I would have to retreat back into silence. There has been a pull to stop writing and close down. Feeling that you are right alongside me in this shared exploration has helped me to continue. This is something I have acknowledged in our private email exchanges. However, when I first replied to this comment in the conversation, I totally pushed away what you said about feeling honoured to be alongside me and witness the emerging process. I think there is something here around me not wanting my process to impact on you – the fear of the intimacy that brings. To not affect or be affected by others feels safer because I can stay in my self-contained bubble. Fear of intimacy has affected, and continues to affect, my life in a significant way. I feel afraid and threatened by closeness to another…

Emma: Yes, I can resonate with that very much.

Joy: … At the same time there is a relief in the honesty of moving from hiding to being seen. I am hiding from parts of myself as well as keeping things concealed from others. The lifelong habit of pushing feelings down is a hard one to break. The small child part of me tells me speaking out is dangerous, better to keep quiet. This is often justified as 'letting go of hurtful things'. I want to question this – throw some light on it. Am I really letting go of pain in a positive way or is it being pushed down in order to avoid conflict?

There is a part of me that will avoid conflict at any cost. Time after time I have realised that I have colluded with others due to lack of confidence in speaking the truth of what I feel. A lot of my difficulty arises because I don't know what I am feeling, so I agree with others or stay silent. This strategy works for a while but ultimately leads to confusion on all sides and unhelpful and painful communication.

I am learning the importance of listening to my body and taking time to do this rather than thinking I should know straight away. I am learning that, if I feel I am being 'pushed' and notice that I am fearful, then it is OK for me to say 'No, I need time' and give myself a chance to feel into what is going on. In the last few months, I have been using focusing (Gendlin, 2003) in order to get in touch with what Gendlin calls the 'felt sense'. This is technique is proving transformative as I start to listen to what I have pushed down and allow it to emerge in a gentler way than previously. I believe it is helping me to feel more comfortable in my own skin.

Emma: I can imagine focusing being useful as you learn the importance of listening to your body. What does it *feel* like being more comfortable in your own skin?

Joy: Yes, learning to focus has been very positive for me. I am sometimes in awe of what can emerge during a 25-minute shared session.

What does it feel like being more comfortable in my own skin? Oh, that's a big question! My first response is, 'I don't know!' I don't even know if I do *feel* more comfortable. I *think* I do, but do I really feel that way? I need to focus in and try and feel...

What comes to mind as I sit reflecting on this are the lyrics from the Dido song 'Honestly, OK', about being safe in our own skins. This song was one that really spoke to me for many years because I simply did not feel safe in my own body. I remember feeling that I did not know where my body boundaries were; where I ended and where others began, and that felt very frightening. I do not feel that way any more. I feel 'at home' in the body form I have. Yes, it's ageing; yes, it has pain, but I do not feel I want to cut open my skin and crawl out of it. I realise that the deep shame that I used to feel about being me has mostly gone. There is an inner knowing and strength, and confidence that I am basically OK. I also feel more resilient to the ups and downs of life. I can feel pleasure and pain and it doesn't overwhelm me. These are the things that make me feel comfortable in my own skin.

Emma: That's amazing to hear – that the deep shame you used to feel about being you has mostly gone… I also find that song, and quite a few of Dido's lyrics, evocative. The reason I asked that question – yes, it does look big in the written word! – was because I was struck by you saying, 'I *believe* it is helping me to feel more comfortable in my own skin' and I wondered how that belief *felt*. Thank you – I really sense it now. That image of cutting open your skin and crawling out is so vivid and feels familiar to me, too.

Joy: Oh, to know that image resonates with you is so good to hear! I can also see that using the word 'believe' was deflecting from being with my felt sense. Thank you for drawing out what my felt sense was. Talking about cutting open my skin and crawling out isn't something I have shared very much because it feels too graphic and there is a fear that people won't understand. The Dido lyrics helped me to put words to what I was feeling – that I simply wanted to get out of a place where I did not feel safe.

Emma: Yes, that makes sense. Thank you Joy, I've really appreciated having this email conversation and I'm so glad we're friends. Over the years, I've found it precious when we've talked about both having experienced sexual abuse and living through the aftermath. I can sense an unspoken resonance, which has made me feel less 'wrong'. Thanks for finding your voice even more here.

Joy: Our continuing friendship is very important to me, too. We don't meet that often but when we do there is a heartfelt connection and depth of honesty between us that has endured over the years. The effect of this email conversation is rippling out in a way I could never have envisioned. I have never done anything like this before and the power of it is awesome! I have felt very held and heard throughout this week of intense conversation together. I am in awe of what we have both put into this process. Thank you, Emma.

References

Dido (1999). Honestly, OK. In: Dido (2008). *No Angel*. London: Sony BMG Music UK.

Gendlin ET (2003). *Focusing: how to gain direct access to your body's knowledge; how to open up your deeper feelings and intuition*. London: Rider Books.

Gilbert P (2010). *The Compassionate Mind: a new approach to life's challenges*. London: Constable.

Parks P (1990). *Rescuing the Inner Child: therapy for adults sexually abused as children*. London: Souvenir Press.

Chapter 14

Dirty secrets, ecocide and the specialness of the world all around

Emma Palmer, with Charleen Agostini

My engagement with #MeToo started with this Facebook post, which I wrote in October 2017 as the current wave of the #MeToo movement began to go viral on social media:

#MeToo

Content warning: impassioned rant with swear words
And the crisis of 'masculinity' is just one symptom of the mess we're in: the inevitable consequences of capitalism (commoditise everything, including bodies and their worth), ecocide and the extinction crisis (we fuck with the planet and we fuck with one another), and structural inequalities from genocides (partition, the wiping out of First Nation people, ethnic cleansing), to institutionalised racism which goes unquestioned. Why am I saying this? Because I don't want this to focus only on gender as understood in consensus reality. It's totally part of the harm we're causing the biosphere and other-than-human and more-than-human life – we act as if we're the only species here – and if we don't start addressing this soon we won't be here for much longer (that's according to the world's leading scientists, not just my opinion!).
(Palmer, 2017)

This ranting energy is not where I am starting today. Today I feel the softness of survival; the open vulnerability of knowing, in my bones, the harm caused by repeated acts of sexual violence and abuse. I feel soft sadness towards this ageing, middle-aged body, roaming slowly south, its wrinkles mainly a welcomed comfort. I feel gladness, too – we made it. It is no small miracle. Many don't, remembered as suicide statistics in this post-truth, over-clinical, (un) brave new world. To those beings I bow deeply, for it could have been me.

I feel sadness towards the perpetrating men – and it is men, in this case – who didn't have a chance to dwell with their soft, open vulnerability (maybe brutalised, too?). I look them in the eyes. I feel a sudden, quiet compassion towards them today as my heart beats deafeningly. Often, it's not just compassion, granted. I'm no saint. As a client, working in somatic experiencing therapy sessions years ago, I strung up one man from a tree as I thrashed the living daylights out of him. I have spat fire where words won't do, and I have cut one of them slowly and deliciously down his midline, relishing the emergence of blood – rich, red, velvet, ribbon-like lines. I'm not proud of those imaginings ('Can I *really* write that?' Good Girl, quaking), but it beats wanting to score my lower arms with a knitting needle before I even realise what I'm doing, in a faint attempt to let out the pain – even after years of work in therapy.

Inflicting pain – in my mind's eye, at least – has served me by helping me to feel, to feel *anything*, as well as show them what they've done. 'Don't you see?' I've screamed, silently, and bellowed loudly. They don't. Well, one does, but he's dead. Gone but not forgotten and sometimes I feel fragments of forgiveness towards him. He hugged me in my waking Boxing Day dream, and I sensed he did see, he does see, somewhere, somehow. My screaming has subsided these days; for now, anyway. Now it's broken sleep and gentle, middle-of-the-night soothing with tea and films when the screams re-emerge as bouts of insomnia.

Personally, I don't resonate with being a survivor of sexual violence or abuse. I'm too proud to see myself as either a survivor or a victim, even though I know others who feel the opposite, finding these terms empowering. I'm done with war imagery, sick to the bone, so familiar am I with a war raging in this body; this immune system thinking this body is the enemy. All this swirling, underworld confusion. I'm too stubborn and bloody-minded, too, to be either victim or survivor. I won't be beaten, not until the last breath – and, of course, I've still got denial going on. I am not much into building an identity around being a survivor, even though I've seen friends and clients do it, finding it an important and useful healing phase.

Meditating from early adulthood blew a hole in identity-building. Not that Buddhist meditators can't be terrific at building identities – quite the opposite, in fact. But sitting here, bum on cushion, day after day, did blow my (misplaced) faith in solidity and sameness and nothing ever changing, especially as I started meditating at my lowest ebb, holding onto life by my already tired, just turning 24-year-old fingertips. My strategy has been to bolt from identity; to remain hidden, to lurk in the shadows where creativity and destructiveness dance – and sometimes fight. It's true, though, that in a factual sense I am a survivor, many times over. Sylvia Fraser sums it up better than I am able to in this spine-tingling quote:

> I feel about my life the way some people feel about war. If you survive, then it becomes a good war. Danger makes you active, it makes you alert, it forces you to experience and thus to learn. I now know the cost of my life, the real prize that has been paid. Contact with inner pain has immunized me against most petty hurts. Hopes I still have in abundance, but very few needs. My pride of intellect has been shattered. If I didn't know about half my own life, what other knowledge can I trust? Yet even here I see a gift, for in place of my narrow, pragmatic world of cause and effect and matter moving to immutable laws, I have burst into an infinite world full of wonder. The whole mystery of the universe has my reverence. Nothing is sure but nothing can be dismissed. I pay attention. (Fraser, 1987: 252)

'I pay attention.' Paying attention and offering reverence to the whole mystery of the universe is how I am able, and good enough, to offer therapy, a therapeutic space, for other 'survivors' and survivors of all sorts of things that do not necessarily include sexual abuse and violence. I thought this subject would floor me – it does – and yet the words are ready to flow out of my typing fingers. The strategy of lurking in the shadows, remaining hidden, worked up until the point when I started writing books on hot subjects. Truthfully, they didn't seem hot to me, until I noticed the response from others. I've always written; word-weaving is my sanity but going public with the words is a whole other thing. I have written about meditation, embodiment and developmental trauma (which is how I see post-Reichian character structure, explored in my first book *Meditating with Character* (Kamalamani, 2012)), and about the choice not to have children and the charged backdrop to the parenthood decision (explored in *Other than Mother: choosing childlessness with life in mind* (Kamalamani, 2016)). Then, later, a collection of articles I wrote for a somatic psychotherapy journal, *Bodywise* (Kamalamani, 2017).

It hasn't occurred to me until now that the common theme with my books is that they concern the body, the body's creativity and the body in relationship to the bigger body of the earth, this beautiful planet and all of life. While I was in the shadows – sometimes playing, sometimes hiding – my body was always weaving words. The thought of launching a second book is what took me back into therapy and another round of work.

'I pay attention.' In today's waking dream I search for burglars. But the treasure is long stolen. There's the resonance with clients of knowing about the lost treasure – lost, and something deep down feeling broken. Is it my body? Is it trust? Is it all of me? The disintegrating lets in the great shame – the word 'great' never doing justice to this bottomless well – of 'It must've been my fault.' Repeatedly remembering that the shame isn't mine. It was never mine – except my body still struggles to believe that. I coach myself: 'Not my shame,' 'Not my shame,' 'Not my shame.' Sitting with clients in their heavy shame cloud, its chill touching their bones, too. The sadness of deadened eyes, defeated shoulders. The ability to cover up that shame, whipping on a cloak of pleasing charm or entertainment rather than staying with the unthinkables (a sensible strategy, because the unthinkables are, indeed, unthinkable). In time, with kind effort, the disintegrating lets in light and love, too.

'I pay attention' to the clients in front of me and know this is a long-haul thing. I don't judge the 'weird' fantasies; they seem pretty normal to me. I don't judge the desire to be special – 'I came to like the attention – am I warped?' Nope, an adult acting sexually with a child is warped, your genitalia were doing what genitalia do – they respond sensually; pleasure sometimes happens (not always, of course, especially not when it's been messed with too many times, when a state of freeze is far safer). There are no quick fixes for bodies that have been brutalised; the bodies that believe they were the brute, rather than the perpetrator of violence – even the softly spoken gentlemen and the 'pillars of the community'; the bodies that, however healed, fall through the air, fearing they will never again feel earth beneath their feet; too broken, too wrong, too damaged, too much, not enough, 'if only I'd….' Enough, already!

'I pay attention.' No one on my qualifying training prepared me – how could they? – for the moment when clients would – albeit briefly – see me as the perpetrator. Despite the rapport building – in fact, it is not despite, it's precisely *because* of the care-ful rapport building, the building of understanding, respect, safety, knowing they have choice, knowing this is a consensual space. When the client hurts, touching the agony of the original wound, I'm the only other human in the room, tenderly, lovingly inviting the healing of that wound, so the pain *must* somehow be my fault. It's obvious, right? The countertransferential moment passes, as all moments pass, and I-thou (Buber, 1996) is restored; the eye of the storm passes. It's a hard and sometimes necessary role, being turned into the 'baddie', as we may be dreamed up by our clients with their histories, with all the characters, in the pursuit of wholeness. It's a scary place, therapy, for all concerned; as Bion said, 'In every consulting room, there ought to be two rather frightened people' (Bion, 1976/2005: 104).

'I pay attention.' I witness clients coming back to life, returning to their skins, returning to earth. Everyone's healing journey is different. Within that truth, I've witnessed turn-around phases when the pain is so acute, so debilitating, often despite the victim's ability to whip on the cloak of coping. It's too painful to stay in the present, even though there's nowhere else to go. It's too hard to move forward; they know there are things to reclaim, left in the past – except they're in the present. Time isn't linear or chronological here. We're seven and 70 all at once, ricocheting back and forth through the generations, piecing together fragments, ancestral detectives rebuilding broken hearts. My own coming back to life process began most markedly the day after my eldest niece's birthday party. My body reeled again, dizzy and confused and in a new round of sifting through, spiralling and sleepless nights.

There is a second half to Fraser's quote – the one I included above. It is too apt not to include:

> All of us are haunted by the failed hopes and undigested needs of our forebears. I was lucky to find my family's dinosaur intact in one deep grave. My main regret is excessive self-involvement. Too often I was sleepwalking through other people's lives, eyes turned inward while I washed the blood off my hands. My toughest lesson was to renounce my own sense of specialness, to let the princess die along with the guilt-ridden child in my closet, to see instead the specialness of the world around me. (Fraser, 1987: 252)

'The specialness of the world around me.' I survived. In today's post, a stunning painting arrives: 'Young Man's Requiem', by a talented artist friend, Val Hudson.[1] The painting – I first typed that as 'paining', which seems about right – is for Private Albert Tattersall,[2] who fought in the 20th Battalion of the Manchester Regiment and was injured on the first day of the Battle of the Somme on 3rd July 1916. He died two days later. It is a picture of the trenches: washed colours, earthy through to blues, eerie yet comforting, the main detail being barbed wire. The first time I saw it, I fell into its grief, hope and remembrance for the souls lost during and in the aftermath of war.

---

1. For information about Val Hudson, visit www.valhudson.co.uk
2. For information about Albert Tattersall, visit https://livesofthefirstworldwar.org/lifestory/4359973

I'm reminded again of the words of Sylvia Fraser, above, when she says 'I feel about my life the way some people feel about war. If you survive, then it becomes a good war.' I have the war painting to my left and, in front of me, a photograph of my grandfather, Cyril, who died in World War Two. It is there when I'm writing *War Torn* (still a work in progress), the story of his death. It spirals back to his father-in-law, out for his afternoon stroll, killed by shrapnel during the first day raid on Bristol. It spirals back even further to the death of my great-great uncle Alf on the last day of World War One in Belgium. These fine men, forefathers, killed in action – whether out strolling or fighting. Their loss, their plight and what broke in our family after their bodies were broken: smashing to earth, burnt and torn, thrown to the ground, shot in a ditch. Stolen lives. All this enshrined in my body's DNA, for the first few decades itself 'missing presumed dead' until I inched back to life. I survived and will remember them and the futile carnage of war – will you join me?

'The specialness of the world around me.' I can't build an identity around survival, because I know how fragile identity – sanity – is and I don't want to create something that will inevitably be shattered one day, even if it's at the point of my final breath, when whoever on earth Emma is returns to earth, solid and comforting. I pay attention to the specialness around me, realising that talking about the abuse I have experienced only makes sense when I talk about the violence we inflict minute by minute upon the biosphere and all of other-than-human and more-than-human life. It is the same violence and abuse.

Violence and abuse is a continuous wave: through history, through human supremacy, through white supremacy, through patriarchy, to name a few of the more prominent waves. The eco-feminism and women in development literature I read as a young undergraduate made common sense to me, even though it was still seen as a bit 'far out'. It made even more sense when I was reading about eco-feminism in the context of international development and it was my first taste of intersectionality, although it wasn't called that, then: sexism, racism, capitalism, classism, caste, ableism, anthropocentrism, ecocide, among others. Maybe it made sense to me because roaming the common and the bridleways, staring at the sky and talking horse and dog were my childhood sanity. I was nature more than human – not that they're separate. It's where I was at home – 'eco'. The earth and all the other elements were simply an extension of this thing I call my body.

I was lost and found in nature, too. I could feel the damage being done, even then. I feel so vehemently about it because of this. I do ecopsychology work because I long for this reconnection of human with other-than-human and mother-than-human, to right a relationship going and gone badly wrong and threatening our very survival. I pay attention and am able to be in the horror, dread and abject terror with dear clients, whether it's horror that they've experienced or horror at what's happening in this anthropocentric age of the sixth extinction crisis, unprecedented climate chaos and yawning gulfs in wealth and wellbeing. I don't always flinch then, though tears may fill my eyes and anger may catch my voice. It's after the session and in supervision and therapy that I do my main flinching. Paying attention and seeing the specialness of the world around me ensures I practise and think systemically. Violence and abuse – sexual, or not – is complex and messy.

'The specialness of the world around me.' I count my intimacy with other-than-human and more-than-human life as the silver lining of being a 'survivor'. When I didn't get humans and they got too much of me, nature understood, with no expectations. I am her and she is me: wind, grass, dog, sky, horse, all of them. I admit I am a survivor in as much as 'nature', as we call her, enabled me to survive, offering me a lifeline rooted to the core. It was a lifeline filled with awe and wonder, not just a route for escape. In Sylvia Fraser's words, I sensed 'I have burst into an infinite world full of wonder' (Fraser, 1987: 252). I am glad to be, in the words of the excellent Jerome Bernstein, a 'borderlander', someone 'whose transrational experience is nothing short of sacred…. who would not be able to function in our society without their deep personal connection to that domain' (Bernstein, 2005: xvi).

'The specialness of the world around me.' Just stop and look; it's everywhere – the specialness, I mean. I used to think about meaning a lot. I'm a recovering thinking addict and a recovering looking-for-meaning addict, too. Imagine my delight when I came across the notion of 'meaningfreeness', coined by my friend and mentor, David Loy (2000: xvi). If we can accept meaninglessness, in yielding to what can seem like the dreaded nothingness of life – nothing fixed, everything always changing – we might attain the playful state of meaningfreeness. I might step out of my own way – thoughts, feelings, fixed-ness – to play, dance, let life show me the meaning, rather than constantly thinking and managing. To feel the wind on my cheeks, the sun on my back, strands of wet hair sticking to my neck, a mighty storm approaching, with the barely discernible rumbling of thunder. Words flow, sometimes tears.

'The specialness of the world around me.' The princess is taking her last breaths. The guilt-ridden child has opened the closet door and is stepping out. For me, #MeToo is, in part, a unique, exciting, rabble-rousing (Rise hags! Crones! Feisty princesses!), scary moment of history in the making: raising awareness of how widespread sexual violence and sexual abuse are. It is a special time and one that is long overdue. It is a chance for we therapists to create space for us and others to be heard; to stand together, telling stories, fighting injustice, creating new dialogues, finding ways to join together and campaign for change. Can the telling of these stories, the healing of these wounds, re-connect with ancient stories of healing, helping us to heal our relationship with the world? Dare we see that individual sufferings spiral backwards and forward to all of suffering? Can the healing be healing for all that lives, not just the human ones, in this age of intersectionality and in this head-spinning vast web of interconnection?

Conversation with Charleen Agostini

Charleen: This is a very passionate and strong piece of work. Reading your words had quite an impact on me. It feels that it's right that it has this impact because sexual abuse had such an impact on you, so we, the reader, also need to feel deeply affected.

I'm interested in the part fairly early on where you say that you don't resonate with being a self-identified survivor of sexual violence or abuse. In the paragraphs before that, you describe and show very clearly how you are a survivor. So I was interested in that contradiction. Maybe I'm a little confused that you say you don't resonate with being a survivor, having just shared some strong experiences – for example, some of the somatic experiencing therapy work you did as a client.

Emma: I think it's the sense of being utterly, utterly sick and tired of sexual abuse being part of my experience and my history – something like that. So maybe I don't *want* to resonate with being a survivor, maybe, more than I don't resonate with it. Maybe that's closer to the truth.

Charleen: Oh, OK.

Emma: … and a really strong sense of, 'No, I don't want to be limited or reduced to a label!' Because being a survivor of childhood sexual abuse is or has become a big label.

Charleen: Yes, that makes sense.

Emma: I'm not keen on labels, even though I know they can be helpful some of the time for some people. For me, it feels like a secondary blow to then be reduced to being a 'survivor', when I'm so many things besides. It's a nub of an important conflict here for me (laughs). In my mind's eye, I'm holding a placard high in the air in my right hand. It says, 'I'm more than that!' A survivor – I mean.

Charleen: (Laughs too). Yes, yes. So what you've said is really helpful and now

I understand. You are communicating the heart of this conflict about being a survivor but not wanting to be reduced to just being seen as a survivor above all other things…

Emma: Yes… So you started out by saying how this piece impacted you. Which aspects or which parts most affected you? Because I think I said, when we first talked about this writing and I read it to you, that I couldn't sense its impactfulness. I remember you said you could feel the fiery nature of the piece and I was a bit surprised.

Charleen: It is something about your style of writing here. It's very no-messing-around: 'I'm not going to mess around with you, here it comes, straight at you; a feeling of 'Get this!' And a question, 'Are you going to get this?' And those understandable feelings when you were working as a client in those somatic experiencing sessions that you refer to early in the chapter – spitting fire, thrashing and cutting. At the same time, I could really appreciate the work you did in those sessions and how right it was and, almost, how *delicious* it was…

Emma: It was terrifying – *is* terrifying – to include those accounts from the somatic experiencing sessions, because it's letting my insides out onto the page.

Charleen: So, in fact, what you did there is a very – oh, what's the word that I want here? – a very *responsible* – no, not just responsible… Being able to connect to the rage in yourself from these imaginings and processing is very responsible, because you're not acting it out, you're not perpetrating something on somebody else…

Emma: … in real life…

Charleen: … in real life, yeah. You're actually taking care of yourself and taking care of the 'field' at the same time.

Emma: Yes.

Charleen: You're taking responsibility for that intense reaction in yourself; it's the ethics of it, and you are discovering the power in yourself. Even though it's shocking to read, it's also informative about how you take care, how you are being responsible, actually. Not acting out either on yourself or on other people.

Emma: And my experience was that it was a way for the pain to actually start to come out more, rather than to stay inside, stagnating or turned inwards on myself. Not just stagnating, either – pulsing, or…

Charleen: ... amplifying...

Emma: ... Yes, amplifying. Yes, and destroying and dis-easing. And it led to – it's funny, I forgot this bit – the somatic experiencing work led to a fascination back then, around the time of my 40th birthday, with lions and lionesses. The energy and the strength of the lion, the energy of the lioness. Especially that image in the piece I've written of cutting one of those men. I think I say something like 'slowly and deliciously down his midline'.

Charleen: Yes, and how congruent a lion is when it it's after its prey.

Emma: Yes! That simple, clear action of 'I'm going to eat this –' I don't know what – 'this gazelle', and the clarity of the ripping of the skin. I mean, I'm not a lion and I'm a long-term vegetarian, but it put me in touch with that feeling. I can't put it into words easily. It strikes me that the immediacy, that clarity and spontaneity, contrasts very much with the slow grooming I experienced with this man, the man I cut – in this therapy work, in my mind's eye – down his midline. Maybe this feeling is regaining pride, in a good sense of the word? Starting to re-gain my own skin, too. He was over there, I'm here.

Charleen: Yes, for sure.

Emma: Not through hurting, not in real life through wanting to hurt someone else, 'cos that won't work; that isn't a solution, but through being able to fight back when, in reality, I wasn't of an age when I could fight back. I wasn't even able to have a voice, let alone defend myself.

Charleen: And it was empowering, I bet, to carry this through. That's what you didn't have at the time; that's what you were seeking – some power to stand up for yourself and to stop something from happening...

Emma: Exactly... to right something that was very wrong. Put it right. And just to be able to do anything, not to be immobilised. It was incredible after those sessions, very 'lightening'. I felt lighter, freer, and could start to let go of something.

Charleen: Because you found the resources in yourself, empowered yourself, found the power that would stop something.

Emma: Yeah. You'd need lion power to stop a man against a child.

Charleen: What child could have that power? Children don't have that.

Emma: Children can't and shouldn't have to defend themselves, should they…

Charleen: … shouldn't have to, no.

Emma: That part, as soon as I wrote it, I thought, 'Oh God, I don't want to write that, I don't anyone to know that.' But actually, when a few people have read this piece, that's the bit they say, 'God that's awful, and you have to include it.' I can see it's disturbing. It's a major disturbance in my body. It's a major disturbance in all of our bodies when sexual abuse and violence happen.

Charleen: And it's part of the healing, what you're saying. It's part of the healing of connecting to that power. That lion in you can just say 'no' to that and can retaliate and will not accept. So that's really important.

Emma: Will not accept – I love those words! 'That is not acceptable.'

Charleen: Not acceptable. Absolutely not. And 'I'll show you'.

Emma: Yes. That makes me laugh, it's quite releasing. (Pause.)

Charleen: That somatic experiencing work you did seems so important, the ethics of it, in a way, because you are discovering the power in yourself…

Emma: … for the first time, possibly…

Charleen: … for the first time. And taking yourself out of the victim role, which is so important for the healing. Finding and discovering some power in yourself. But keeping it within the framework of your inner work.

Emma: Yes, and it's in relationship, the therapeutic relationship; I'm not alone.

Charleen: And not having to act this out against somebody, injure somebody else, which is what creates conflict and war, ultimately, and retaliation all the time.

Emma: And creates a cycle of violence and more abuse.

Charleen: Yes. So even though it's a shocking thing to read, it's actually very responsible and very ethical to access that in yourself.

Emma: It's useful to see it framed like that, because when I feel it come out, it's very easy to fall straight into shame again.

Charleen: Oh?

Emma: I don't think I did. Fall into shame this time – talking about it, I mean.

Charleen: What would the shame be?

Emma: Oh, well, how would a nice girl think things like that? It's back to that conversation we had earlier today about girls being groomed to be good, compliant, never angry. The message of 'It's a man's world'…

Charleen: … but you're not only a nice girl… No! You're a powerful lion. A powerful woman, thank God, we all need to discover that.

Emma: But it's the shame of knowing that, reading it myself, and feeling slightly shocked and thinking 'I can't write that.' For fear of others judging me and my thoughts.

Charleen: They'll judge you because they won't understand?

Emma: Yes, maybe. Because you've really spelled it out so that I understand it more. Because they don't understand why your – my – body would be so enraged.

Charleen: That energy, also like you say, could mean you hurt yourself, it can disease your body…

Emma: It has, with chronic illness.

Charleen: Yes, so that's why it's so important to access that energy and know it, and the possibility of that is healing for you. And it takes care that you're not going to act it out.

Emma: Yes, it's in the safety of the therapy room.

Charleen: And the dreaming level is very, very important. At the dreaming level, you are standing up and stopping this person and retaliating, but it stays at the dreaming level. And it works at the dreaming level for this whole field around sexual violence. Yes, it's contributing to this field.

Emma: That's good to hear. And hearing that, I feel more OK to include these accounts of these somatic experiencing sessions. (Pause.)

Charleen: Thanks for the work you're doing.

Emma: Thanks for joining in and being part of it, too.

References[3]

Bernstein JS (2005). *Living in the Borderland: the evolution of consciousness and the challenge of healing trauma*. London: Routledge.

Bion WR (1976/2005). Interview by Anthony G Banet, Jr. In: Bion WR. *The Tavistock Seminars*. London: Karnac Books.

Buber M (1996). *I and Thou* (Kaufmann W, trans). New York, NY: Touchstone.

Fraser S (1987). *My Father's House: a memoir of incest and healing*. London: Virago Press.

Kamalamani (2017). *Bodywise: weaving somatic psychotherapy, ecodharma and the Buddha in everyday life*. Somatic Psychotherapy Today.

Kamalamani (2016). *Other than Mother: choosing childlessness with life in mind*. Alresford: Earth Books.

Kamalamani (2012). *Meditating with Character*. Alresford: Mantra Books.

Loy D (2000). *Lack and Transcendence: the problem of death and life in psychotherapy, existentialism, and Buddhism*. New York, NY: Humanity Books.

Palmer E (2017). *#MeToo*. Facebook; 16 October. www.facebook.com/kamalamani.palmer/posts/10155934040997932 (accessed 16 February 2020).

---

3. Until 2018 I was known as Kamalamani, which is why my books are published under this name in the references.

#MeToo

Clare Shaw
For Deborah Lee

It will be difficult,
just as Helen Keller's world was difficult,
or the act of taking to flight.

There was water
for which she had no word
until it poured on her

and a good woman held her hand
and believed in her.
And a *wonderful cool*

Something[1] woke in her.
Then there was a light
she had always remembered

and everything that day
was altered.
There are categories of impossibility –

change is not one of them.

---
1. The italicised phrase is taken from: Keller H (1903). *The Story of My Life*. New York, NY: Bantam Classic.

*

And instantly she spelled
I want to talk with my mouth too.
That seemed impossible. [2]

But – placing her hands in this position –
a thumb resting on the throat, on the larynx –
her first finger on the lips, the second on the nose,

we found she could feel the vibrations
of the spoken word.
The throat – she felt the hard g.

On the lips, the b, the p,
and with the second finger,
the nasal, the m, the n –

and the first word was learned –
it.
After the seventh lesson,

she was able to speak the sentence
word-by-word –
I am not dumb now.

*

You are not dumb now. It was as if
somewhere nearby was a shore
you had never forgotten
where waves were breaking
and gulls were crying, as if it were grief,
as if it was not your fault.

---

2. The text in the second part of this poem is a verbatim excerpt from the words spoken by Anne Sullivan and Helen Keller in *Deaf, Blind and Mighty: how Helen Keller learned to speak.* [Video.] *The Guardian*; 18 June, 2018. www.theguardian.com/society/video/2018/jun/01/helen-keller-deaf-blind-and-mighty-video (accessed 10 June 2019).

There were wolves out there
and the river was calling you
to it, as if the rain surrounded you
as if you were held,
as if there are millions of us
and you didn't need to ask

am I broken, as if the house creaked
under the weight of it,
as if the building was awake
as you wrote it, as if nobody thought
you were mad, as if
you were never alone.

as if your voice cracked when you spoke it
as if it mattered, as if there were two of you
in the room, as if everyone was listening,
as if you were singing,
as if you burned with it.
As if your life depended on it,

as if you could change the world.

Contributors

Charleen Agostini
Researching and personally exploring the relationship between our inner experiences and outer everyday reality has been, and is, an ongoing life path. Charleen has recently retired from a private psychotherapeutic practice and from teaching in Europe. Trained in process-oriented psychology, she has been on the faculty of this training in both London and Slovakia from 1999. Previously she trained as a Montessori teacher and set up and ran a nursery and primary school in West Wales in the 1980s.

Taylor Broughton
Taylor Broughton is a psychotherapist-in-training who lives in Edinburgh, Scotland. She trained in psychodynamic and person-centred approaches. Originally from Phoenix in Arizona, she spent years studying psychology in Denver, Colorado, at MSU. Her current research interests include young women's formation of sexuality under the Trump administration and the psychology of gender. For the future, she hopes to build her private practice and become a sexuality educator, perhaps to stay in school forever. She spends her time stubbornly drinking iced coffees in the Scottish winter and debating with her partner which walls to paint colourfully in their new home.

Haley Clifford
Haley Clifford has a master's in counselling (interpersonal dialogue) from the University of Edinburgh. She has a private practice, Cairn Counselling, in Edinburgh, and also works with The Spark as a counsellor for school children in North Lanarkshire. Haley has published research with Maria Dempsey at University College Cork around the dual diagnosis of substance abuse and mental health disorders.

Clarinda Cuppage

Clarinda Cuppage is an integrative counsellor, studying for an MA in psychotherapy. She developed an awareness project with the charity One in Four, giving survivors the opportunity to write about the impact of sexual abuse on them, to educate and inform others. The first *Survivors' Voices* report, published in 2015, focused on sexual abuse in the family context; *Numbing the Pain*, published in 2019, highlights childhood sexual abuse as a common underlying trauma in people with addiction. Clarinda draws on this work in teaching mental health nursing and social work students. She volunteered on the National Association for People Abused in Childhood (NAPAC) national helpline and is a counsellor at One in Four.

Fionnuala Dempsey

Fionnuala Dempsey is a community worker and sexual assault survivor from Northern Ireland. She is currently living, studying and working in Melbourne, Australia. Fionnuala is passionate about depathologising abuse and trauma related mental health issues and developing community working practices that support recovery and increase community connection, support and safety.

Joy Farrimond

Joy Farrimond trained as a general and paediatric nurse after leaving school and worked as a paediatric nurse until 2005. She graduated with a BSc in Psychology and Health in 2004 and had a career as a researcher in mental health at the University of Bristol until her retirement. She trained as a reflexologist in 2006 and still treats a small number of clients. She enjoys volunteering in a local care home and on a community composting project. She follows the teachings of the Buddha and is training for ordination in the Triratna Buddhist community.

Emily Jacob

Emily Jacob is the founder of ReConnected Life. A survivor, coach and NLP master practitioner, Emily uses her skills, knowledge and experience to help women move forward from living one day at a time, to live their own ReConnected Life. She is the author of *Desperately Hopeful*, and editor of *To Report or Not to Report: survivor testimony of the (in)justice system*, with contributions from the members of the ReConnected Life community. Emily has spoken on behalf of survivors at Reclaim the Night and Who Will Hear My Cry, among others. She has been featured widely in the media. She is most proud of her involvement in the BAFTA-nominated Channel 5 documentary *RAPED: my story*. Emily's other career has spanned more than 20 years in marketing strategy and capability. She lives alone in Oxford.

Tina Johnson
Tina Johnson initially trained as a counsellor but soon discovered that words were not always a way of connecting with the body. Training in dance movement psychotherapy linked her personal spiritual beliefs with the experiences of healing through dance and movement. Tina has worked with people in recovery from drug and alcohol abuse and with women involved in the criminal justice system dealing with childhood and adult trauma. She is currently working with people who have suffered loss due to infertility, miscarriage or still-birth.

Kaur
Kaur is a pseudonym.

Deborah A. Lee (co-editor)
Deborah A. Lee is senior lecturer in sociology at Nottingham Trent University and a person-centred psychotherapist. Deborah's current research interests include arts-based approaches to psychotherapy case studies, critical psychopathology, psychotherapy training, therapists and creativity and auto/biographical explorations of sexual violence and its aftermath. She has publications forthcoming and recent in journals such as *Psychotherapy and Politics International*, *The British Journal of Guidance and Counselling*, *Self & Society* and *The Journal of Gender-Based Violence*. Previously a steering group member of Psychotherapists and Counsellors for Social Responsibility (PCSR) and editor of its *Transformations* journal, she is an associate editor and co-editor for reviews at *Psychotherapy and Politics International* and a member of the ethics committee of the UKCP.

Amanda (Millie) Light
Amanda (Millie) Light is a PhD researcher at Ulster University looking at critical feminist epistemologies in relation to precariousness and embodied mental health. As a dance movement psychotherapist, Millie has been privileged to work with people in the fields of learning disability, dementia, substance abuse and women's groups. She has a love of poetry and border collies, and often combines the two while walking coastal cliff paths.

Sara Teresa Mollis
Sara Teresa Mollis is in the first year of an MA in psychotherapy and counselling at the University of Leeds. She also works as a peer support worker in a crisis service, alongside her 'other life' as a freelance photographer. Sara's interests lie in somatic therapy, trauma and the female self, and the potential healing power

of self-portraiture. She enjoys excessive coffee drinking, long-distance running and having hilarious chats with her four-year-old child.

Emma Palmer (co-editor)
Emma Palmer is a BACP-accredited counsellor, relational body psychotherapist, facilitator, supervisor and ecopsychologist, and a Buddhist since 1995. She was previously a steering group member of Psychotherapists and Counsellors for Social Responsibility (PCSR) and editor of its *Transformations* journal. She has worked extensively as an educator, including teaching postgraduate international development studies at Bristol University, working with NGOs in Africa, offering ecopsychology public talks and workshops and leading retreats. She has published several books under her former name, Kamalamani, on topics including meditation, childlessness and somatic psychotherapy.

Andrew Pari
Andrew Pari is founder and director of Sexual Assault Awareness, LLC and a psychotherapist with more than 20 years' experience of treating survivors, including specialised populations in the sex trade and victims of trafficking. He is an online moderator for forums on rape and recovery, consults and trains forensic and mental health professionals nationally and internationally. He provides expert testimony and was selected as a national expert by his professional organisation to respond to media inquiries/interviews on trauma, sexualised violence and disaster response. In 2018, Andrew led the campaign to have Antelope Valley, California, declared the largest 'Start by Believing' region in the state, as part of a national programme dedicated to believing sexual assault survivors. www.saawareness.com.

Peggy
Peggy is a pseudonym.

Concetta Perôt
Concetta Perôt is an integrative counsellor and psychotherapist. She has more than 20 years' experience as a social worker with children in care and prisons and of running peer-led groups with adult survivors of abuse through Survivors' Voices, the organisation she co-founded. She has an MSc with distinction in mental health studies from the Institute of Psychiatry at King's College London. Her dissertation was on the assessment and treatment of trauma and PTSD when it co-occurs with psychosis. She is an associate

researcher with the University of Bristol and King's College London, where she is involved in studies investigating peer-support for survivors and the mental health needs of people using Sexual Assault Referral Centres and is lead researcher on the Charter for Engaging Abuse Survivors, a survivor-led project exploring safe, effective and meaningful engagement of survivors. She has also worked on the National Association for People Abused in Childhood (NAPAC) national helpline providing support for adult survivors of abuse.

Phoenix
Phoenix is a pseudonym.

Seb Randall
Seb Randall started work in London as a labourer, followed by employment in Essex as a ship's carpenter, joiner, windsurfing instructor, draughtsman, and house builder. He has studied at King's College in London, the Open University and the University of Essex. He has worked as a psychotherapist in private practice as well as in NHS settings for more than 25 years and has taught on, and directed, a number of psychotherapy courses. His research and political activities include an exploration of the impact of authoritarian instrumentalism within prevailing representations of psychotherapy and counselling.

Leah Salter
Leah Salter is a family and systemic psychotherapist and supervisor working in the NHS in Wales within secondary care adult mental health services. Alongside working with individuals, couples and families, Leah also facilitates creative groups with women involved in mental health services and therapeutic groups for women who have experienced abuse. Leah's research interests are in parental mental health, women's mental health, the impact of abuse, practitioner reflexivity, solidarity practices and working with groups and communities. She completed a professional doctorate in systemic practice at the University of Bedfordshire, researching group work with women who have experienced abuse and oppression, weaving in her own stories, poetry and creative writing. Leah has continued working with the University of Bedfordshire as a supervisor and visiting lecturer and has also taught at The Family Institute in Wales. She lives on the coast, in South Wales.

Sam
Sam is a pseudonym.

Reena Shah

Reena Shah is a British Asian woman who works as an integrative psychotherapist in London. She works in private practice, specialising in working with childhood trauma, in particular with childhood sexual abuse. She has had a long association with One in Four, a charity providing long-term counselling for survivors of childhood sexual abuse, as a volunteer. She set up the North London branch of the charity and is on its Board of Trustees. She also teaches counselling and psychotherapy at the Minster Centre in London, and at the College of Haringey, Enfield and North East London.

Clare Shaw

Clare Shaw has three poetry collections published by Bloodaxe: *Straight Ahead* (2006), *Head On* (2012), and *Flood* (2018). Clare won a Northern Writer's Award 2018 for her fourth collection, which is currently in progress. Often addressing political and personal conflict, her poetry is fuelled by a strong conviction in the transformative and redemptive power of language. Clare is an Associate Fellow with the Royal Literary Fund, and a regular tutor for a range of literary organisations, including the Poetry School, the Wordsworth Trust and the Arvon Foundation. She is also a mental health trainer, activist and author with a particular interest in self-injury, borderline personality and alternative/critical mental health narratives. She is passionate about the meeting ground between poetry and mental wellbeing and is the facilitator of the Poetry School's international online course 'Poetry as Survival'.

Tara Shennan

Tara Shennan is a qualified, integrative therapist specialising in trauma and a psychology undergraduate at University of Lincoln. Tara's dissertation subject is the validity and comprehension of depression and anxiety scales and she is also researching disenfranchisement in counsellors for a UK organisation. She guest-lectures on the University of Essex's clinical psychology doctorate programme on topics such as diagnosis and ethics in the therapeutic relationship.

Liz Smith

Liz Smith is just completing her master's in psychotherapy and counselling at the University of Leeds. She currently works in Bradford's My Wellbeing College service and also has experience in non-clinical peer-led crisis work. She has a particular interest in feminist therapy and trauma work with women and girls and is currently a volunteer therapist at Sheffield Women's Counselling and Therapy service. Liz is a keen runner and loves being outdoors with her naughty but cute Patterdale terrier, Alfie.

Jemma Tosh

Jemma Tosh is a chartered psychologist with the British Psychological Society (BPS) and Director of Psygentra, an organisation that specialises in the psychology of gender and trauma. She is the author of *Perverse Psychology: the pathologization of sexual violence and transgenderism* (2015), *Psychology and Gender Dysphoria: feminist and transgender perspectives* (2016), and *The Body and Consent in Medical Settings* (2019). Jemma's paper on the medicalisation of rape was awarded the Psychology of Women Section's Postgraduate Prize in 2011 and her first book was shortlisted for the BPS Book Award in 2016.

Sarah J. Wilson

Sarah J. Wilson works as a counsellor, psychotherapist and supervisor. She began her counsellor training in Australia in her 20s, working on a telephone helpline, and she has continued training ever since. Originally trained as a social worker in addictions, Sarah qualified as an integrative counsellor and was then drawn to the physical therapy of Shiatsu and trained as an embodied relational therapist. She has since undertaken specialist trainings in sensorimotor psychotherapy and internal family systems to support her work with trauma. For the past 20 years, Sarah has worked for organisations specialising in addictions, abuse and trauma and has managed a counselling service and counselling organisation. When she's not working, Sarah loves wild swimming, yoga and dog walking. www.sarahjwilsoncounselling.co.uk

Katy Woodger

Katy Woodger is a psychotherapist, supervisor, trainer and writer. Her MA in Trauma Studies at the University of Nottingham explores witnesses' experiences of cross-examination in non-recent child sexual abuse cases. She is a member of the independent advisory board of LimeCulture, a sexual violence training and development organisation. The board of seven is chaired by Sir Keir Starmer QC, MP. She is one of the contributors to *Counselling, Class and Politics: undeclared influences in therapy*, by Anne Kearney, republished July 2018 in a new edition by PCCS Books. Katy is currently working towards a PhD at the Open University through the Grand Union doctoral training partnership between the Open University, Brunel University London and the University of Oxford.

Celia Urbach

Celia Urbach is an integrative transpersonal counsellor and therapist in private practice. She grew up in North London and graduated in history and politics at Warwick University in 1983. She spent the first 10 years of her working life as an advice and rights worker in voluntary agencies and for the London Borough of Islington. She later qualified as a lawyer and spent 10 years mainly in legal aid private practice. In 2005, she gave up her legal career and became a befriender of people with terminal illness and a bereavement counsellor at City and East London Bereavement Service, and later at St Joseph's Hospice in Hackney. In 2009 she qualified in integrative transpersonal counselling and psychotherapy at Re.Vision, established a private practice in 2010, took a diploma in couples counselling in 2012, and now specialises increasingly in working with couples. She lives in Hackney, East London, with her husband. They have a 20-year old daughter.

Name index

A
Abrams, D 143
Abramson, K 70
Acosta, F 71
Adams, M xi
Affixxius Films 139
After Silence 137
Agnew Davies, R 44
Ainscough, C 144
Alaimo, S 142, 144
Alcoff, L 118
All Party Parliamentary Group (APPG) on Adult Survivors of Child Sexual Abuse 44
Alma, D 2
Alonso, MA 157
Alter, A 106, 121
American Psychiatric Association (APA) 71, 120
Amery, J 182, 183
Anda, RF 49
Association of American Universities 56
Atkins, D 103
Atkinson, M 135

B
Baird, K 44
Baker, C x
Baker, S 86
Ball, L 87
Bancroft, J 71
Barad, KM 142, 144, 148, 153

Barker-Collo, S 42
Bass, E 73, 144
Bass, TM 57
Basset, F 105
Bazzano, M 100, 107, 120
Beaulieu, S 87
Bekker, M 59
Benatar M 164
Benjamin, J 168
Bennell, B 87
Bennetts, C 119
Bentley, H 133
Ben-Yehuda, N 129
Beres, MA 58
Berliner, T 120
Bernstein, JS 220
Bieber, I 71
Bieber, T 71
Biley, F x
Bion, WR 218
Black, M 1
Blanchard, R 71
Blasey Ford, C 86–88, 90
Blyton, E 10
Bochner, AP 158
Bond, E 44
Boston, P 194
Bowcott, O 66
Boyle, M 45
Bradley, M 68
Braidotti, R 142, 143
Brantley, J 73

Breggin, P 191
Brennan, M 103, 105, 109
Brisola, E 103, 105
Brison S 1, 59
British Association for Counselling & Psychotherapy (BACP) 41, 46, 105, 109
Brodsky, A 118
Bromberg, P 162
Brown, S 94
Buchwald, E 192
Buncombe, A 92
Burke, T 1, 97–98
Burrows, A 133
Burt, M 86, 87
Burton, M 87
Burton, S 193
Butler, J 142
Byrd, D 71

C

Campbell, F 74
Carlin, L 66
Carlisle, B 103
Carson, K 71
Castillo, H 191, 192
Charmaz, K 101
Chesler, P 188, 192
Chevous, J 43
Cisney, VW 143
Clark, AE 2
Clarke, L 133
Cliffe, G 87
Coates, L 190
Cohn, S 143
Coleman, S 66
Cook, K 110, 119
Cooke, M 110, 119
Cooper, M 119
Corrigan, P 104
Creswell, J 101
Cuddy, A 66
Curtis, C 104
Curtis, L 69
Cury, V 103, 105

D

Dain, H 71
Dalby, J 145
Davey, M 70
Davidson, J 131
Davies, JM 163, 164
Davis, L 73, 144
De Guzmán, V 87
DeYoung, PA 162
Dick, K 102
Dido 212
Dieterich-Hartwell, R 141
Dogaru, C 42
Donaghy, G 68
Douglas, RM 1
Downes, J 109
Drumm, K 195
Duffy, N 66, 70
Duggan, M 68, 70
Dunn, A 87
Durrant, M 188, 196
Dye E 117

E

Eaton, J 131
Eddo-Lodge, R 161
Eichler, M 104
Elliott, R 119
Elliott-Cooper, A 68
Ellis, C 158, 159
Ellis, F 42, 44
Epston 191, 196
Erikson 120
Erikson 120
Etherington, K 198

F

Fahs, B 55
Farrell, S 68
Farwell, N 68
Feder, G 44
Feldman, M 71
Felitti, VJ 49
Ferman, D 68
Fine, M 67
Fitzgerald, LF 86, 87
Flanagan, S 101

Fletcher, P 192
Folkes-Skinner, J 119
Fonda, J 107
Forsyth, I 142
Foucault, M 188, 192
Frank, AW 158
Fraser, S 216, 218–219, 220
Frawley, MG 163, 164
Frears, S 165
Freedman, KL 1, 105
Freeman, H 67
Freud, S 71
Friedman, J 67
Fromm, MG 107
Frost, S 142
Fullagar, S 143

G

Gabbard, W 68
Gavey, N 119
Gay, R 1, 2
Gendlin, ET 211
Geoghegan P 69
Gergen, K 194, 196
Ghaill, MM 69
Gibson, N 119
Gilbert, P 208
Giraud, I 142
Glick, E 53
Godsi, E 182, 187
Goldenberg, H 109, 119
Goldner, V 197
Golightly, S 65
Gong, BG 143
Gottschalk, P 131
Grant, A x
Green, W 1
Greenwood, D 186
Grey, L 118
Guilfoyle, M 157

H

Hadden, S 71
Haire, J x
Halliday, J 44
Hallsworth, S 68
Halpin, H 66

Hammersley, P 42
Harden, KP 53, 58
Harding, K 56, 60, 119
Harper, D 42
Harrison, R 42
Hawkins, J 120
Hekman, S 142
Herman, JL 45
Hernandez, A 70
Herwig, CE 110, 119
Hickman, M 75
Higgins, P vi
Hodge, L 141
Hollin, G 142
Hudson, V 218
Hughes, J 100
Hume, I 101
Hunt, C 119

I

International Centre for Missing & Exploited Children 128

J

Jacob, E 201
James, S 71
Johns, H 108
Johnstone, L 45
Jones, E 195–195
Jones, H 110, 119
Joseph, S 101, 197
Joy, S 102
July, M 100, 105, 106, 121

K

Kamalamani xi, 216
Kaplan, M 54, 58
Karkou, V 142, 145
Karpman, S 164
Kelland, L 105
Keller, H 12, 227–229
Kelly, J 66
Kelly, L 106–107, 109, 120, 141, 193
Kennedy, A 42, 69
Keren R, 86
Kirschenbaum, H 107
Kitzinger, J 157

Klein, M 164
Koro-Ljungberg, M 143
Kramer, E 68

L

Lambert, O 186
Lamoureux, M 87
Lawrence, A 71
Leberg, E 129
Lee, DA x, 27, 29, 84, 100, 101, 103, 104, 105, 106
Lees, S 57
Leigh-Phippard, H x
Lenning, A 59
Leonard, M 68
Letherby, G 103, 105, 109
Levi, P 182
Leys, R 69
Li, WM 2
Liang, Y 104
Lockhart, E 72
Loewenthall, D 103
Lonsway, KA 86, 87
Louis, E 2
Loy, D 220
Lynch, MN 57, 59
Lynch, R 143

M

MacCulloch, M 71
Mace, R 68
Mac Ian, PS 164
MacLure, M 144
Mann, T 66
Marks, I 71
May, J 68
McAlinden, A-M 129
McBean, S 107
McClelland, S 67
McDonald, H 66
McKay, M 73
McKusker, J 44
McLeod, J 103, 110, 121
McLeod, R 87
McNamee, S 191, 193, 196
McNaughton Nicholls, C 42
Meaney, G 68

Mearns, D 119
Meekums, B 103, 142, 145, 147
Melvin, K 46
Metler, S 110
Miller, A 163
Miller, C 92
Montana Cirell, A 143
Morar, N 143
Moulton, E 2
Moustakas, C 101, 103, 105, 108, 110, 119
Mucci, C 157, 158, 162
Mumford, EA 56

N

Nabokov, V 162
National Association for People Abused in Childhood (NAPAC) 38
Nelson, EA 142, 145
Newlove, J 145
NHS Confereration 192, 198
NHS England 44, 50
Nicolosi, N 71
NI Direct 66
Nordenberg, D 49
Northern Ireland Statistics & Research Agency 67
Novey, I 2

O

Ó Dochartaigh, N 69
Office for National Statistics (ONS) 46, 67
Oldale, M 110, 119
Oliver, M 151
One in Four 50
Oonk, G 162
Ovenden, G 120

P

Palmer, C 71
Palmer, E 214
Pandora's Aquarium 137
Panhofer, H 150
Parks, P 207
Pascual-Leone, A 110
Patterson, T 101
Payne, H 119
Peachey, L 110, 119

Pearlman, LA 164
Penfold, P 192
Perlin, M 74
Perôt, C 43, 46
Phillips, J 118
Piercey, M 8, 101, 104, 107, 120, 121
Pino, AL 2
Polkinghorne, DE 158
Porges, S 44
Potts, T 142
Prock, K 69
Proctor, G 85, 91, 191, 192, 193
Pykett, J 143
Pyne, J 75

Q
Query, M 70

R
Rae, L 72
Randomsky, N 72
Rawicki, J 158, 159
Read, J 42
Reeve, S 151
Regan, L 193
Reich, W 58
Reider, J 103
Reynolds, V 190–191, 193
Richardson, C 190
Richardson, L ix
Richman, S 107, 120
Roberts, J 195–196
Robson, J 119
Robson, M 119
Rodriguez-Rubio, B 110
Rogers, CR 8, 85, 86, 91, 92, 94, 95, 97, 105, 107, 119, 145
Rose, C 104, 109
Rose, N 75
Roszak, T 143
Roth, M 192
Roth, S 117
Rothschild, B 162, 166
Rowley, L 97
Rudegeair, T 42
Ryan, L 68

S
Salter, L 194
Sanderson, T 144
Savile, J 38, 186
Saward, J 1
Schmid, PF 104, 119, 120
Schmidt, J 119
Schriver, L 87
Schwartz, R 73
Scott, S 42
Sebold, A 1
Sedgwick, E 75
Seikkula, J 45
Sembi, R 109–110, 119
Sen, D 102, 104, 120
Shah, R 120
Shapiro, F 73
Sharkey, S 68
Shaw, C x, 91, 191, 192, 193
Silva, A 68
Simpson, S 141
Sloat, A 66
Smith, K 120
Smith, N 42
Snyder, G 68
Stanley, L 109
Staples, L 70
Starmer, Sir K 186
St Clair, K 117, 118
Stein, ND 56
Stephenson, S 103
Stern, DB 161
Stevens, BF 166
Stone, B x
Sullivan, MM 119
Szasz, T 75, 192, 196

T
Target, M 167
Tattersall, A 218
Taylor, BG 56
Taylor, D 87
Taylor, S x
Tesar, M 143
Thapar-Björkert, S 68
Thompson, ZB 102, 119

Thornhill, R 71
Timimi, S 196
Tolman, DL 54, 55
Toon, K 144
Tosh, J 65, 66, 68, 71
Totton, N 167
Trainor, K 104
Truell, R 110
Trump, D 6, 55, 88
Tucker, I 42
Tuder, K 145
Turner, B 9
Turner, D 106
Turner, S 119

U
Ullman, S 118
Unsworth, C 87
Ussher, J 75, 192

V
Valenti, J 67
Van Dam, C 131
Van der Kolk, B 74, 142, 151
Vanwesenbeeck, I 59
Venable Raine, N 1

W
Wade, A 190, 193
Wagoner, D 150
Walker, G 192
Walker, H x
Walker, M 70, 75
Walter, B 69, 75
Watson, A 103
Watson, J 2, 45, 85
Watts, J 85, 94
Weaver Francisco, P 1
Webb, L 70
Webster, S 131
Weinstein, H 1
Weiss, K 69
Westmarland, N 109
Wheeler, S 119
Whitaker, R 192, 196
White, C 196
White, M 188, 191, 196, 197–198

Whyte, D 150
Wilkins, P 108
Williams, J 42
Wilson, D 72
Winters, K 75
Wise, S 109
Wittgenstein, L 194
Wood, J 73
Woodger, K 184
Woods, D 56
Woodward, A 87
World Health Organization (WHO) 53
Worrall, M 145

Y
Young, M 42

Z
Zulcic, N 68

Subject index

#ChurchToo 2
#itsnotok week 102, 103
#JustThem 84,
#MeToo
    celebrity involvement 1–3, 39–40
    fear of 'going public' 1, 84–86, 170, 194
    origins of the movement 1, 97
    and social media xi, 1–3, 84, 86, 214
    and testimony 1–3, 26–28, 38–39, 59, 83, 105, 201
#MeTooPhD 2
#MeTooPsychotherapyTraining 106
#TherapistsToo 2, 90, 95
#TimesUp 53, 55
#WeToo 26–28, 188, 199–202

A

abandonment 21, 152
ableism 75, 219
abstinence 56–59, 67
abuse
    faith-based, 31
    online, 126, 128, 132, 134, 139
    opportunistic, 127, 131
    ritual, 31
addiction 50, 170
Adverse Childhood Experiences (ACE) 49, 191
affect regulation 208
aftermath 15, 218
    of sexual abuse and violence 23, 135, 212
aggressive sexuality
    in American culture 56

anonymity 28, 30–31, 33, 87, 205
anthropocentrism 219
anxiety 94, 135, 152, 206
apartheid 48
art therapy 73
attachment theory 206, 208
Auschwitz 182
authenticity 8, 83
autoethnography 9, 10, 103, 144, 158
authorities (see police) 6, 40, 183
autistic 76, 78
autobiography 158
avoidance 43, 136

B

Black, Asian and minority ethnic (BAME) 9
befriending (see grooming)
being believed
    importance of, 144, 198
beneficence 46
betrayal 127, 129, 178, 198
Bible 66
biocapitalism 143
biopower 143
biphobia 75
blame/self-blame 28, 36, 49, 77, 134
body psychotherapist 61
Borderlander 220
boundaries 130, 145, 149, 169, 170, 196, 207, 212
broken 37, 193
    feeling of being, 65, 135, 200, 217
Buddhism 208

C

capitalism 214, 219
categorising
    of people 91
Catholicism,
    and sex education 169
childlessness 216
choice
    its meaning for survivors 44, 93, 162–163, 177, 208, 217
chronic illness 225
class
    working-, 189
clinical perspectives,
    on sexual violence and abuse 2
coaching 200
coercion 55, 75, 160
cognitive behavioural therapy (CBT) 10, 76, 208
cognitive dissonance 97
collaboration 198, 200–201
colonialism 68
communal dissociation 43, 49, 50
communication 159, 165
    non-verbal, 145
community 1, 28, 34, 40, 93, 120, 188, 191, 200–201
compassion-focused therapy (CFT) 208
congruence 94, 105, 145
consent 7, 56, 58, 61, 128, 178
conversation partners 5
coping strategies 35, 77
counselling and psychotherapy
    as cause of harm 45–46, 64, 77
    experience of, 46, 84, 88, 98–121
countertransference 166, 168, 170
Court 92, 115, 186
creationism 66
creativity 169, 216, 217
criminal justice system 23, 41, 186

D

dance 149, 151, 153, 154
dance movement psychotherapy (DMP) 141–142, 144–146, 154
dating violence 56
defence mechanism 132
denial 135, 144, 175, 179
    of sexual abuse and violence 41, 87, 134
depression 135, 142, 144–145, 147–148
diagnosis/es (see also labelling)
    disproportionately given to women 85, 91, 191, 193
    and being 'disordered' 45, 191, 193
dialectical behaviour therapy (DBT) 73
discrimination 102
disclosure
    of sexual violence and abuse 35, 42, 170, 183–184
    responses to, 41
    self-, 104
    therapist, of personal experience 173, 196
    verbal, 137
disconnection
    from more-than-human and other-than-human life 12
dis-ease/disease 183
disembodiment 144
dissociation 23, 24, 77, 139
diversity 9
drama triangle (Karpman) 164
dreaming 225
Diagnostic and Statistical Manual of Mental Disorders (DSM-5) 71, 120
domestic violence 44, 132, 170
dyads
    in therapy 11, 158, 167

E

eating disorders 49
ecocide 214
ecology 151
ecopsychology 143, 219
embodied, embodiment 148, 151–152
    dilemma of, 147
    narrative of, 154
emotional wellbeing 50, 73, 77
empowerment 60, 135, 153, 173
enmeshment 158, 167–168
ethics/ethical principles 105
evolutionary psychology 208
externalisation 90

Subject index

extinction crisis, 6th 214, 220
eye movement desensitisation and reprocessing (EMDR) 73

F

false accusation 87
family 22
   abuser within the, 33, 39, 170
   responses of, 33–34, 40–41
family planning (see birth control) 57
family psychotherapy/ist 73, 195
family system/context 73, 196, 206
   internal, 73
feminism 73, 74, 143
   eco-feminism 219
   intersectional, 77
feminist new materialism 142, 143, 154
First Nation peoples 214
flashbacks 27, 34, 36, 37, 72, 73
focusing (Gendlin) 211
forgiveness 19, 20, 179, 186–187
freedom to and freedom from (Fahs) 55

G

gender 58, 195, 214, 237
   cis-, 75
   nonconformity 65–66, 70, 74–75
   norms 65–66, 68, 75, 78, 195
   nonbinary, 65–66
   socially constructed, 61, 65–66
genderfluid 65–66, 70, 75
genitals 61
God 7, 67, 69
GP (general practioner) 26, 44
grief 46, 135, 152, 218
grooming 127–129, 183, 223
groupwork 188, 191, 194, 196–199, 201–202
guilt 19, 31, 33, 54, 135, 163, 220
Gujarati 159, 162

H

harm 70, 75
   caused by therapy/ists 45–46, 64, 77
healing 73–75, 151–154, 221
   planetary, 214, 221
health and social care systems 188, 192

helping professions 65
heteronormative 58
heterosexual 58, 71
heuristic 101, 103, 104, 104, 108, 121
Holocaust 22
homophobia 70, 110
homosexuality 67, 70–71
'honour' killing (see also *izzat*) 19, 34
human rights legislation 66
human-centricity/human supremacy 142, 219
humiliation 67, 164
hyper-intellectualisation 91

I

Identification & Referral to Improve Safety (IRIS) 44
identity
   personal, 89
   professional, 89
   as survivor
      debates about, 215–216, 219
      and trainee 84, 90
   as victim 207
incest 127, 188
   pseudo-incestuous 163
injustice 55, 93, 119, 165, 190
insomnia 215
integrative counsellor/ing 6, 9, 10
intergenerational 75, 107
internet abuse 126–139
intersectionality 7, 10, 12, 219, 221
intimacy 6, 34, 59, 195, 199, 211, 220
invisibility
   of survivors 3
Irish 68–69, 77–78
   identity 5
   discrimination against, 69
I-thou 218
Izzat 34

K

kidnap 18, 20
kindertransport/ee 5, 22, 24

L

label/ling

with borderline personality disorder 91, 102, 120, 191, 192
with emotionally unstable personality disorder 91
psychiatric, of women 85
language
challenging pathologising, 71, 75, 86, 90, 193–194, 196
mother tongue 157, 159, 162, 167
LGBT 66–67
learning journal 108
lived experience 2, 8, 50, 83–98
Lolita 162,
loss 152, 182, 197

M

make-up (as disguise/protection) 31
male
rites of passage 7, 62
sexuality 57
manipulation 70, 129, 139
mansplaining 71
masturbatory object 21
meaningfreeness (Loy) 220
media reporting 38, 67, 88, 102, 186, 193, 198
medicalising, of distress 10, 43, 45, 188, 198, 207
meditation 208, 216
Metta Bhavana 208
mental health 30, 45, 49–50, 102, 188, 191–192, 196–198
mentors (see also supervisor/ision) 9, 88, 90, 176
MGTOW 87
military conflict
and women's bodies 68
mind-body connection 9, 145
misogyny 62
misuse
of medication 45
more-than-human (see also other-than-human) 9, 12, 142, 214, 219–220
MRA 87
music industry
sexual violence within, 56

N

naming, importance of 98, 192–193
narrative enquiry 10, 158
narrative exploration 157–158
narrative therapy 73, 191, 194
nature, connection with, 143–144, 152–153, 219–220
negative liberties 55
neuroscience 208
NHS Sexual Assault and Abuse Strategy 50
Neuro Linguistic Programming (NLP) 200
nonconformity 70, 71, 74
normalising
of sexual abuse and assault 119
norms 32, 68, 74, 75, 78, 162, 195
Northern Ireland 65–71, 75, 78
numb/numbing 77, 144, 151, 210

O

Omerta (Sicilian honour code) 40
One in Four charity 50, 170
online abuse 126, 128, 132, 134, 139
online survivor communities 137
Open Dialogue 45
Other than Mother: choosing childlessness with life in mind (Kamalamani) xi, 216
Our Encounters With... series x
orgasm 55, 59, 139
other
being othered xi, 96
other-than-human (see also more-than-human) 9, 10, 12, 142–143, 150–151, 154, 214, 219
overcomer
identifying as, 4, 152

P

pandemic
sexual violence and abuse as, 3
passivity 165
pathologising 2, 39, 44–45, 73, 75, 189, 192, 196
and non-pathologising 2
survivors 65, 84
patienthood 11, 188, 193, 196

Subject index

patriarchy 105, 171, 219
peer support 48, 85, 95
peer-led 42
perpetrators 20, 40, 45, 86–87, 92, 98, 173, 198
personal account 66, 144
person-centred counsellor/psychotherapist 7, 8, 19, 191, 231, 233
person-centred and experiential therapy 7, 8, 19, 36, 91, 109, 145
physical touch
 use in therapy 36
Pink Therapy 9
pleasure 55, 56, 59, 146, 207, 212
poetry 10, 12, 104, 144, 150, 152, 153, 236
police 38, 41, 68, 133, 139, 183, 189
polyvagal theory 44
positive liberties 55
posthumanism 9, 154
post-Reichian character structure 216
Power Threat Meaning Framework (PTMF) 45
powerlessness 23
prayer 146
pregnancy 56, 57, 58
process-oriented psychotherapists 12
processwork (process-oriented psychology) 231
procreation 67
prosecution (*see* Court) 20, 186
psychiatry
 critical, 191, 196
 post-, 196
psychoanalytic psychotherapy 19
psychology
 violent, abusive, coercive aspects of, 65
psychology
 critical, 74–76
 feminist, 74–76
Psychotherapy & Politics International x, 233
public health 6, 38, 44

Q

queer 7, 65–66, 70, 75, 78

R

racism 69, 75, 219

 institutional, 68, 214
rape
 accusations of, 1
 apologism 65, 76
 culture 56, 67, 119, 179, 192, 201
 debunking rape narratives 65
 emotional, 116
 myths 64, 86–87
rapport, importance of in therapy 200, 217
ReConnected Life Community 200, 201, 232
recovery 45, 134, 152, 181, 182, 186, 200
relationship therapy 73
religion 28, 34, 69
remembering, process of 27, 107
resilience 95, 164, 189, 190, 191
resistance 129, 188, 199–200
 acts of, 189–194, 196
 societal, 84
resourcefulness 191, 196, 202
responsibility 62, 94, 109, 161, 167, 180, 183, 192, 198
Resurrection After Rape (Atkinson) 135
retraumatise/ing 43, 45
retribution 15, 21, 23, 180, 186
revenge fantasies 18, 19, 21
revictimisation 129
risk-taking behaviours 65, 72, 77
rites of passage 7, 62

S

sadism 19
safe places/spaces 91
safeguarding 183, 187
same-sex marriage 66
sanism 74, 75
school, schooling 16, 56, 66, 69, 139
science fiction 8, 103–104, 107
script (abuser technique) 131
secrets 20, 144, 214
self-actualisation (Rogers) 85
self-care 74, 77, 153
self-esteem 7, 62
self-harm 26, 34–35, 49, 135, 144, 184, 207
self-worth 144
separation 158, 167
seven-stage process (Rogers) 8, 85

sex
  coercive, 68
  conversations about, 53–62, 86
  education 7, 53–54, 56–62, 67
  online, 9, 127–139
  painful, 56, 68
  positivity 6, 53–60
  research 53, 58
  safer-, 56
sexism 67, 75, 219
sexual abuse 1–4, 8, 31, 65–66
  childhood, 9, 10–11, 39, 44, 49–50, 141, 157, 169, 186
  definitions of, 128, 181
  pleasure/arousal during, 139, 173, 207
  trauma of, 49, 74–76, 141
sexual assault prevention programmes 56
sexual exploitation 21, 31, 33, 131, 138, 143, 174
sexual violence
  and abuse 1–4, 8, 75–76, 102, 141, 173, 182
  prevalence of, 38, 84, 193, 198
sexualisation
  of children 131, 165
sexuality
  bisexuality 65, 70
  harmful ideas about, 55–56, 59, 67, 70–71
  men's, 57, 62
  young women's, 55
sexually transmitted diseases (STD) 57
sharam (Gujarati) 162
shaming 1, 78, 190
  slut, 67, 70
Sicilian culture 6, 40–41
  immigrant community 6, 40–41
Sikh 5, 31, 34
silence
  being silenced 31, 34, 42, 67, 76, 161, 188, 201, 205
  breaking, 38, 48, 50, 76, 94, 157, 206
  maintaining, 163, 179, 190
slavery 48
sleep
  lack of, 30, 34, 135, 215, 218
social exclusion 67

socialisation
  around sexual abuse 132
socio-economic privilege 91
solidarity 1, 11, 28, 83, 120, 188–189, 193–201
somatic
  experiencing 12, 215, 221–222, 224
  psychotherapy 144–145, 151, 233
speaking out 48, 54, 70, 89, 94, 193, 211
spiritual/ity 61, 146, 149
statutory mental health services 44
stigma 96, 102, 152, 201
stories 158, 190–191
  ancient, of healing 220–221
  herstory 104
  importance of telling, 54, 59, 170, 188, 194–200
Story Aid 135
stranger danger 134, 139
suicidal ideation 135, 144
suicide 64, 73, 135, 175–176, 215
supervision/supervisors (see also mentor) 43, 46, 88, 90, 108, 110, 144, 164, 181, 220
survivor-led training 43
survivor
  identifying as, 4, 7, 12, 26–28, 146, 152, 158, 181–182, 195, 215, 221
  mission 48
Survivors' Voices project 6, 10, 42, 45, 46, 50, 170
survivor-therapists 120, 169
systemic psychotherapy/ist 11, 188, 190–191, 201, 235

T

terrorism 68
testimony 12, 50, 105
therapeutic alliance 143
'thriver', identifying as 4
torture 19, 182–183
trainee/training
  about sexual violence/abuse 3, 9, 84–85
  'coming out' in, 54, 84, 89, 94
transference 167–168
transformation 101, 164, 195, 198
transpersonal counsellor 5, 237–238

trauma
    complex, 44
    developmental, 216
    intergenerational, 75, 107
    war, 12
Trauma & Recovery (Herman) 45
trigger warning 4, 91
trigger/triggering 6, 33, 59, 72, 74, 76, 130, 147, 152, 165, 206
trust/trustworthiness 9, 120, 127, 129–130, 138, 144, 198, 217

U

UK All Party Parliamentary Group (APPG) on Adult Survivors of Child Sexual Abuse 44
UK government 44
unconditional positive self-regard 101

V

victim
    -blaming 1, 7, 9, 42, 71–72, 75–76, 78, 86, 96, 98, 103, 134, 197
    identifying as, 4, 7, 65, 152, 158, 182, 215

W

war/war trauma 12
white supremacy 219
Woman on the Edge of Time (Piercy) 107
women's rights 55
working safely (with clients) 132
wound/woundedness 26, 90, 101, 157–158, 163, 217, 221

Z

zeitgeist 84

Also by available from PCCS Books

Drop the Disorder!
Challenging the culture of psychiatric diagnosis

Edited by Jo Watson

ISBN 978 1 910919 46 0

In October 2016, the very first 'A Disorder for Everyone!' event took place in Birmingham and launched an ongoing, national campaign dedicated to exploring and exploding the culture of psychiatric diagnosis.

How and why does psychiatric diagnosis hold such power? What harms does it do? What are the alternatives to diagnosis, and how can it be challenged?

This book brings together psychologists, counsellors and psychotherapists, users and survivors of services to propose answers to these questions. The contributors represent a wide range of expertise built through experience, research, campaigning and activism. All seek to offer an alternative vision for how we respond to those in extreme emotional distress.

It is an essential book for every one of us who looks beyond the labels.

'Anyone who wants to deal with the epidemic of distress and despair in our society should engage deeply with Jo Watson's work and this massively important book.'
Johann Hari, journalist and writer; author of *Lost Connections: why you're depressed and how to find hope*

'Drop the Disorder! is a clarion call for change.'
Robert Whitaker, author of *Mad in America* and founder of madinamerica.com

'Challenging, insightful and often controversial... a truly innovative and valuable book that functions both as a learning resource and an ardent call to arms.'
Dr Eleanor Longden, Psychosis Research Unit, Greater Manchester Mental Health NHS Foundation Trust

---

Discounted prices and free UK postage at www.pccs-books.co.uk

Also by available from PCCS Books

*Inside Out, Outside In:
transforming mental health practices*

Edited by Harry Gijbels, Lydia Sapouna & Gary Sidley

ISBN 978 1 910919 49 1

Human distress has historically been understood and responded to almost exclusively either as a biological disorder or a psychological deficit. This has led to the development of powerful structures, 'mental health systems', that have dominated thinking and practice around mental health and been controlled by the psychiatric profession. Despite widespread recognition that such systems are often ineffective and can even be harmful, the bio-medical ethos, with its focus on 'mental illness' and primary use of drug treatments, continues to prevail in mental health practices.

This book showcases current projects that offer user-centred, context-informed, non-medical ways of helping people experiencing distress and overwhelm. The first section of the book includes projects located inside mainstream services that seek to influence change from within, including the education of future generations of practitioners. The second section describes projects that have established themselves as independent entities, outside mainstream structures and services, giving them the freedom to be truly radical in their approaches and influence by example. In a final section, the book looks at work aiming to challenge the wider societal influences that maintain the status quo and perpetuate factors that lead to mental distress and overwhelm.

'I would encourage anyone wanting to learn more about the limitations of current mental health care, and what to do about it, to read this book.'
Bob Diamond, clinical psychologist

'This book deserves to be read by all who have an interest in transforming and humanising care of people in distress.'
Liz Brosnan, survivor researcher

Discounted prices and free UK postage at www.pccs-books.co.uk